Special Education
for the Early
Childhood Years

JANET LERNER
Northeastern Illinois University

CAROL MARDELL-CZUDNOWSKI
Northern Illinois University

DOROTHEA GOLDENBERG
West Suburban Association for Special Education

Prentice-Hall, Inc., Englewood Cliffs, New Jersey 07632

i

Library of Congress Cataloging in Publication Data

LERNER, JANET W

Special education for the early childhood years.

Includes bibliographies and index.
1. Handicapped children—Education (Preschool)
2. Child development. I. Mardell-Czudnowski,
Carol, joint author. II. Goldenberg, Dorothea,
joint author. III. Title.
LC4019.2.L47   371.9   80-23279
ISBN   0-13-826461-9

*To our first teachers,
our parents,
and to the memory
of Jean Piaget
(1896–1980)*

Editorial/production supervision and interior design
by Dianne Poonarian
Cover design by Edsal Enterprises
Manufacturing buyer: Edmund W. Leone

Photos are courtesy of Anthony Buijnarowski;
Childcraft Educational Corporation; Alan Goldenberg;
and Ravenswood Hospital Medical Center

Prentice-Hall International, Inc., London
Prentice-Hall of Australia Pty. Limited, Sydney
Prentice-Hall of Canada, Ltd., Toronto
Prentice-Hall of India Private Limited, New Delhi
Prentice-Hall of Japan, Inc., Tokyo
Prentice-Hall of Southeast Asia Pte. Ltd., Singapore
Whitehall Books Limited, Wellington, New Zealand

ii

Contents

Part Two   **The Curriculum**

Part Three   **The Environment**

Appendixes

Foreword

Interest in the early education of handicapped children is not new, but the support of such programs is relatively new. The history of early intervention for handicapped children is a history of procrastination. It has been rationalized that early training of all children is the responsibility of the parents and not of a public agency. The recent activist parent movements in behalf of their handicapped children have challenged the rationalization and have rekindled the drive to organize early intervention programs for handicapped children.

In the late 1930s I attended a lecture by Harold Skeels who then told us that he was obtaining phenomenal results by initiating early stimulation for young mentally handicapped children. He informed us that as a psychologist for the Board of Control in Iowa he was responsible for orphanages and institutions for mentally deficient individuals. At one visit, the superintendent of the orphanage requested Dr. Skeels to find placement for two very young girls who appeared to be mentally defective at the age of 1½ to 2 years. These children were not talking or walking and, according to the superintendent, were developmentally delayed. The institution for the mentally deficient did not accept children below age 6, but upon the urging of Dr. Skeels, the superintendent accepted the two girls, placing each in a ward with older mentally deficient women. They became the babies of the ward and obtained a great deal of attention and stimulation from these women. Two years later Skeels was surprised to find these girls near normal in intelligence. They were tested, paroled, and placed in foster homes.

Dr. Skeels followed up this accidental experiment by bringing 12 young babies (ages 1 to 2), who tested below average on intelligence tests, from the orphanage to the state institution and leaving 13 similar children in the orphanage. Two years later he found that the children in the state institution for the mentally deficient placed in wards with older mentally retarded women increased in IQ by 26 points, while those in the orphanage dropped 25 points in IQ during the same period.

The publication of the article by Skeels and Dye in 1939 met with a cold reception by psychologists and social workers. Critics felt that the data was faked. How could anything change the IQ when it had been "proven" that the IQ was constant and unchangeable beyond the probable error of measurement?

Since the 1930s there have been a series of experiments in the United States and in England that have confirmed Skeels' results. My own study on *The Early Education of the Mentally Retarded,* published in 1958, showed that early intervention of 4 year old mentally handicapped children accelerated their social and mental growth. Similar results were obtained in England by Lyle, and by Heber in Milwaukee, Wisconsin. The results of these experiments lead to the conclusion that initiating preschool education at an early age tends to accelerate the social, mental, and physical development of handicapped children, and further, the greater the environmental change the more rapid the development of the child.

In addition to the evidence on the benefits of early intervention, there is now a greater need for preschool education of handicapped and disadvantaged children. We have gone through and are going through a series of societal changes that are making it necessary to establish preschools. These include major changes in family life, more mothers working, and more females assuming the responsibilities for the family. No longer can one depend on "grandma" taking care of the children while momma or papa works. These and other societal changes are increasing the need for preschools, and increasing the need for early intervention.

Today we have more preschools, and today we are concentrating, not on whether we are producing results, but on what to teach and how to teach what we want to teach. This book by Lerner, Mardell-Czudnowski, and Goldenberg is aimed to meet this latter need.

Samuel A. Kirk

Preface

Society has at last recognized that young children with special needs can be identified and helped. The new field of *early childhood special education* has emerged to meet this challenge. The field of special education historically focussed on older handicapped children. The field of early childhood education served nonhandicapped young children. By merging these two disciplines, the field of early childhood special education has been created. The development of this new field of concentration has been bolstered by a number of recent events: the federal legislation of Public Law 94–142 recognized the educational needs of three- to five-year-old children; a growing number of states mandated education for the young handicapped child; research (such as that of the Headstart programs) showed that intervention programs for young children are effective; cognitive psychology underscored the importance of the early childhood years for both handicapped and nonhandicapped children; and finally, model early childhood special education programs throughout the country demonstrated how such programs can work.

It is clear that the young handicapped child can be helped and later learning failure prevented or ameliorated. It is now the responsibility of educational institutions to prepare teachers for this new role. The purpose of this book is to present information for training teachers. The text is designed to blend the findings, and information and practices from the fields of special education and early childhood education.

An "expanding systems" model provides the framework for this book, with three major parts. Part one deals with the smallest system, the child; Part two deals with a larger system, the curriculum; and part three deals with the most comprehensive system, the environment.

In part 1, *The Child*, the nature of the field of early childhood special education is discussed in chapter 1; the characteristics of the young child with special needs is presented in chapter 2; and the problems of locating, identifying and diagnosing are analyzed in chapter 3.

In part 2, *The Curriculum*, an overview of curriculum design is presented in chapter 4. The balance of this part deals with each curriculum area: teaching motor and perceptual skills in chapter 5, teaching cognitive skills in chapter 6, teaching communication skills in chapter 7, and teaching social-affective skills in chapter 8.

In part 3, *The Environment*, the largest system is discussed: the parent-professional partnership in chapter 9, ways of providing educational services for young handicapped children and legislation in chapter 10, and two illustrative case studies are given in chapter 11.

The appendixes include information which should be helpful to teachers: testing instruments (appendix A), teaching materials (appendix B), model programs (appendix C), publishers addresses (appendix D), and a glossary.

As a field of study, early childhood special education is still in its infancy. While there is much yet to be learned, there are practical suggestions and information that teachers working in this area can use. This book has grown out of the author's experiences in teaching young handicapped children and in preparing teachers to work in this field.

We wish to thank the many colleagues, students, and parents with whom we have worked over the years. In particular, we wish to thank Dr. Rosemary Egan, Dr. Kenneth James, and Dr. Lynne Reynolds who worked with the authors in the development of the Early Childhood Special Education program at Northeastern Illinois University and the staff of the nursery at Ravenswood Hospital.

We also wish to thank Childcraft Corporation for the access to appropriate photographs; Anthony Buijnarowski and Alan Goldenberg for their assistance as photographers; West Suburban Association for Special Education Early Childhood Program and Project Childcheck for current IEP practices and procedures; Greg Romaneck for his assistance in compiling the appendixes and glossary; Renee Durand for her assistance in compiling the indexes; and Paula Propst for her patience while typing the manuscript. Finally, most authors give credit to their husbands, wives, and/or children for their encouragement, patience, and endurance; we simply must give thanks for our families putting up with us until the completion of this book.

Janet W. Lerner

Carol D. Mardell-Czudnowski

Dorothea S. Goldenberg

The Child

Part **One**

The Field of Early Childhood Special Education

Chapter **One**

There is a growing concern in our society for the young child who deviates from the norm. Parents, educators, psychologists, and governmental agencies recognize that the early childhood years are crucial for all children; but for the atypical child, they are especially critical. By the time the child reaches school age, precious learning time has passed and developmental delays may have led to academic failure. Early detection makes it possible to intervene with children and increase the likelihood that such intervention will reduce the numbers of children needing special education as well as increase the potentials for those severely involved children requiring longer programming.

Those who have been committed to early education of the handicapped strongly believe that all handicapped children can function at higher levels, if appropriate identification and treatment is provided in the early years. Some conditions can be alleviated, some can be overcome to a large extent, while others can be helped so that the child can live a better life.

This growing interest and concern for the exceptional child during the early years has created a new field of study referred to as *early childhood special education*. This rapidly expanding field integrates concepts from two established disciplines—early childhood education and special education.

The first discipline, *early childhood education*, is a field that studies the development and growth of young children, along with the child-rearing practices that can enhance that development. Starting with the work of Froebel (1896) in the nineteenth century, the field has seen an unprecedented expansion of interest in young children. This has been reflected in an explosive increase in the establishment and enrollment in nursery schools, kindergartens, daycare centers, and Head Start programs.

The second discipline, *special education*, deals with the identification, diagnosis, and treatment of exceptional or atypical individuals. The categories of exceptionalities include hearing impairments, visual handicaps, mental retardation, orthopedic impairments, emotional disturbances, learning disabilities, speech disorders, and other health impairments. Also special education is concerned with the needs of gifted and talented children. Over the past twenty-five years, the increase of special education programs and services for handicapped students at both the elementary and secondary school ages has been significant.

Each of the two fields, early childhood education and special education, developed quite separately. However, it is now apparent that knowledge, concepts, and practices from both disciplines are needed to study and help the young handicapped child. A framework that encompasses the contributions of both fields is needed. By integrating the strengths of the two fields, the young child who also happens to fit into the rubric of exceptional children can be helped and understood. This chapter concentrates on the nature of this new discipline, *early childhood special education*. The chapter discusses the following topics: (1) the need for early childhood special education; (2) the field of early childhood education; (3) the field of special education; and (4) the organization of this book.

Need for Early Childhood Special Education

The crucial importance of the early years to later success is becoming increasingly evident. Research has verified that the early formative years are the most important as the initial period of development in a child's life. Child development authorities, such as Freud (1938), Gesell (1940), Erikson (1950), Piaget (1952), Bloom (1964), and White (1975), have all emphasized that these first five or six years are periods of the highest potential growth in physical, perceptual, linguistic, cognitive, and affective areas. Moreover, recent research indicates that environmental experiences during these crucial years affect intelligence and mental growth (Bloom 1976).

The early periods of rapid development may be even more crucial for the handicapped child than for the normal child. The sooner handicapped and high-risk children are recognized, the greater are the chances that academic failure can be lessened and the child's handicaps ameliorated. Early treatment of the child with potential handicaps is viewed as one of the most promising methods of dealing with special learning needs. Authorities in all areas of exceptional education— mental retardation, behavioral disturbance, learning disabilities, hearing and visual handicaps, as well as the gifted, recognize the critical need for early identification and treatment.

The early childhood movement for the handicapped has received support from both state and national sources. On the federal level, the recently created Office for Special Education and Rehabilitative Services within the Department of Education has placed early childhood special education programs as a "top priority" item. Public Law 94–142 (the *Education for All Handicapped Children Act*), which is considered landmark federal special education legislation, mandates free appropriate public education for all handicapped children, ages 3 to 21. The federal mandate for children in the three to five-year-old age range is subject to the provisions in state law for this age group. The essential features of Public Law 94–142 and other legislation, particularly as these pertain to early childhood special education, are presented in Chapter 10.

Legislation in many states is designed to assure that schools develop programs for identifying potential failure in young children and providing preventive services. Certain states have passed even more far-reaching legislation, mandating special education for children as early as infancy. As of January 1977, 28 states had provisions for preschool education for handicapped children which were either mandatory or permissive (State Statutory Responsibilities for the Education of Handicapped Children 1978). A recent survey by Lessen and Rose (1980) indicates that seven states have even developed a specific definition for preschool handicapped.

Much of the education for young handicapped children prior to 1961 centered in private agencies or associations for specific disabilities. However, the current belief is that services should be provided by public agencies, and that handicapped preschoolers should be integrated with nonhandicapped children whenever possible. One example is the *Head Start* program which was established in 1965 as a massive fiscal and programmatic effort to offer services to deprived preschool children. Current Head Start legislation requires that at least 10 percent of the children enrolled in Head Start be identified as handicapped. The Head Start program and related research are completely detailed in Chapter 10.

One of the strongest arguments for early programming is that it can eliminate many problems that may become entrenched if they persist into later years. Preschool education can be a preventive program for many children who are likely to need special education support. For other children, preschool education can enable the handicapped to function at a higher level than would be possible without early intervention (Karnes 1973).

The goal of early intervention, then, is to prevent or reduce the severity of a handicapping condition so that the child is able to function adequately. It is imperative, therefore, that services be provided to meet the needs of the population of children who evidence handicaps or potential learning problems at the preschool level.

The Field of Early Childhood Education

The concerns of the field of early childhood education include the study of normal developmental growth of the young child and the study of how child-rearing practices within the home and teaching procedures in schools and child-care organizations affect that growth and development./The historical evolution of the field reflects changes in the beliefs and values of society, changes in attitudes toward children, and added knowledge through research in child development. The impact of several of these forces is discussed in this section.

Changes in Attitudes about Legal Responsibility

In the United States, young children occupy a unique and important place within each individual family, even though the child's role may be viewed somewhat differently among the various socioeconomic levels of American society. By law, children below compulsory school age are the complete responsibility of the family.

There are, however, several exceptions to the law. Parents may not physically abuse their children, and laws are emerging which protect children from such neglect and abuse. There are also a variety of state and federal laws which affect the young handicapped child. Because the range of services for the young handicapped child varies from state to state, each local school district abides by individual state guidelines. For children below school age with several exceptional needs, the law is now quite explicit (Weintraub and others 1976). Specialized early intervention programs can include home intervention, and most programs include parent participation for educational goals.

Changes in Family Structure

Some changes in the care of young children have resulted from changes in the lifestyles of society. One such change was the release of the parents' supervision of young children which came about with the outbreak of the Second World War. The political stress of the late thirties and early forties altered the pattern of family life in American communities. There was a heightened need for increased production of war materials, and the young men who would normally have filled such positions were joining the armed forces. Consequently, large factories sought women to fill the open assembly-line positions. The series of events which followed brought about a total family reorganization. Mothers who were caught up in the national effort found that overlapping work shifts forced them to seek alternative methods of providing competent care for their young children while they were working. The pressures of the times permitted little concern about the possible side effects of these childcare methods. National patriotism and fear of an enemy invasion overrode the philosophical questions of early forced separation of mothers as primary caregivers. Daycare for young children became an important part of the factories and shipyard employment fringe benefits. In a few exemplary programs, children of the employees were given attractive playrooms, fed meals, and often provided with sleeping arrangements as well (Weber 1971).

When the parents observed that their children not only survived, but even enjoyed the daycare program, similar enriching experiences were sought for their children after the war years. Interest in preschool education was also encouraged by numbers of academic studies in child development theory. Generally, early childhood education was seen as cultural enrichment, and many of the developing models of early childhood education seemed to be directed at stimulating young middle-class children.

Although the benefits of early education were discussed in the literature, there was little hard research data to substantiate the effects

of preschool programming. The extensive longitudinal studies of Shirley (1931), Gesell and Ames (1937), Bayley (1949, 1956, 1968), and Bergman and Escalona (1949) provided data for establishing the normative stages of child growth.

Today, the trend to leave young children in daycare homes, centers, or nursery schools is rapidly increasing with over 60 percent of all women part of the labor force. Many women no longer feel guilty about leaving their young children since most studies have emphasized that the quality of the time parents spend with their children is more significant than the quantity of time. With the spiraling cost of living, two incomes have become necessary to adequately support many households. Another factor is the number of children being reared in single parent households, which necessitates that the parent work. Recognizing that many employees have young children, many large business establishments are opening suitable facilities, so parents can see their preschool children at various times during the day.

Changes in Educational Theory

Other events in society were also affecting the development of early childhood education. In the broader realm of general education, the progressive movement, begun in the thirties, instituted changes in attitudes toward formal school curricula. Dewey (1962) had stressed the value of early experiences as well as environments which offered active learning, rather than static methods of rote learning and drill. In addition, Montessori (1967) had shown evidence of preschool program success with the use of her didactic materials. Private schools were the first to include these new practices in their general curriculum guides, and public schools also began to assimilate some of the new ideas.

Impact of Parent Education

Other events produced changes in the attitudes of parents and educators. Meetings, newspaper articles, and films focused attention on the significance of learning environments upon children's intellectual capacities. Books written by child psychologists and pediatricians, such as the widely used book of Dr. Benjamin Spock (1946), popularized new views of child rearing and provided parents with practical suggestions for solving the day-to-day problems which all families were likely to face. With birth rates skyrocketing during this period, masses of parents were interested consumers of such literature and found that they were able to make immediate applications of educational findings and medical suggestions.

The permissive child-rearing attitudes coming out of the thirties and the forties may have resulted from limited parental instruction about child-rearing practices. In viewing differences in patterns of child-rearing styles, one sees many changes over the past fifty years. In the early years, "mothering qualities" were assumed to be almost instinctive. A good mother was thought to possess natural traits which would provide a store of information, easily drawn from, which could only lead to positive results (White 1975). These tidbits of necessary information were handed down verbally from one generation of mothers to the next. Current research now supports some major revisions of that preconceived notion. Much monitoring of mothering styles confirms the importance of positive interaction and mother-child sensitivity. Negative styles of mother-child interactions can lead to emotional stress for both mother and child in later years (Thomas, Chess, and Birch 1968).

Approaches to Early Childhood Education

It is important to understand that there is not one single approach to early childhood education. Rather, there are many diverse and competing positions which differ in philosophy, pedagogy, and psychological foundations. The various bases of early childhood education are discussed in other contexts throughout this book. Yet, it seems worthwhile at this point to briefly review the major conceptual frameworks for studying the young child. These constitute six basic approaches to early childhood education.

Philosophical or moral approach. This framework views early childhood education as an extention of parental child rearing. Its purpose is to prepare children to fit into a socialized role in society. An early advocate of this concept was Froebel (1896), who pioneered the first kindergarten in Germany.

Developmental or normative approach. This is a psychological view of child development. Research within this framework focuses upon the description of sequential stages of growth for the average or normal child. The position emerging from this view suggests that educational instruction be provided only when the child is developmentally ready. Teachers and parents are advised to wait until the child reaches appropriate developmental stages before trying to teach certain tasks. The research of Gesell (1940) and his colleagues at Yale University in which extensive developmental data on large numbers of children were collected contributes much to this perspective. The research also provides the basis for much of our knowledge about young children. One of the most apparent applications of this position concerns the teaching of reading to preschool children. The proponents of the normative perspective of early childhood education argue that most preschoolers are not developmentally ready for formal reading instruction (Ames 1968).

Psychoanalytic approach.   This perspective of the young child focuses on the development of the child's personality or psychodynamic structure. The position is based on the theories of Sigmund Freud (1938) and his followers and disciples. Current early childhood programs within this perspective are likely to follow the teachings of Erikson (1950). The approach postulates that human personality unfolds through the development and satisfaction of stages of psychosocial behavior. Fixations, or arrested development at an early stage, can thwart or distort development in the child and create problems for both the child or adults. The emphasis in child rearing is to help the child go through the various psychodynamic stages in as healthy a fashion as possible to prevent a fixation at any developmental psychodynamic stage and to encourage and permit the child to follow natural responses.

Compensatory education approach.   This approach suggests that there are crucial inadequacies in the culture, family, or environment in which certain children live. Formal training is needed to help such children compensate for these deficits in their background. An early advocate of compensatory education in the field of early childhood education was Margaret Macmillan (1919), who began the first nursery school in England. In the United States, the early *Head Start* program was based upon the compensatory education approach to early childhood education.

Behavioral approach.   Behavioral psychology has contributed another view of early childhood education. According to the concepts underlying reinforcement learning theory, the child's environment can be planned and arranged to bring about the desired behavior within the child. B. F. Skinner (1953) is often considered a pioneer of the behavioral approach to learning. Reinforcements, rewards, careful counting of observable behavior, and the baseline measurement of skills to be learned are all important to this approach. The early childhood program developed by Bereiter and Engelmann (1966) is based upon this method of education.

Cognitive psychology approach.   One of the most recent approaches to child development concentrates on the child's maturing thinking abilities and the changing ways children view and understand the world about them. An in-depth analysis of the growth of the child's intellectual structures was accomplished by Jean Piaget (1952). His research into the cognitive development of young children is currently being enlarged by present-day scholars (Elkind 1974; Kamii 1973; Lavatelli 1971; Weikart 1970), who are applying Piaget's theories and ideas of the intellectual development of children to early childhood curriculum and instruction.

These approaches are discussed in more depth as they are incorporated in the teaching of various skills to young handicapped children. The types of experiences young children encounter depend upon many factors, such as the family size, financial conditions, and educational background of the primary caregivers (Almy 1975). There is a growing belief that all children benefit from a generalized early educational program, and there seems to be a trend toward providing more equal opportunities for positive early childhood experiences. A basic assumption of early education is that environment and instruction can greatly influence a child's ability and enhance prognosis of school success. Early childhood education is still a comparatively young but growing field of study. As interest in the young child expands, and as our knowledge increases, we can expect many educational advances in early childhood education.

The Field of Special Education

The field of special education evolved, historically, as a collection of categories of atypical children; that is, children who deviated from the norm to such a marked degree that special kinds of educational services were needed. The categories that make up the field called special education include exceptionalities that are physical, sensory, emotional, and intellectual deviations from the norm. Each specific category of education was established when there was sufficient interest in that type of exceptionality. The field called special education, then, is comprised of the total collection of all the categories of exceptionality.

Special education began with programs and services to assist children with severe sensory and intellectual deficits, such as blindness, deafness, and mental retardation. However, other areas of special need were soon recognized. As the field developed, additional categories of exceptionality were established. Each category became a field within itself with its own research, professional personnel, and literature to study the specific symptoms as well as design instructional procedures for that category.

What areas of exceptionality make up the field of special education? Kirk and Gallagher (1979) define the exceptional child as the child who deviates from the average or normal child in (1) mental characteristics, (2) sensory abilities, (3) neuromuscular or physical characteristics, (4) social or emotional behavior, (5) communication abilities, or (6) multiple handicaps to such an extent that he or she requires a modification of school practices or special education services in order to develop to maximum capacity.

Federal legislation known as Public Law 94-142 defines "Handicapped Children" as children evaluated as being deaf, deaf-blind, hard-of-hearing, mentally retarded, multihandicapped, orthopedically handicapped, other health impaired, seriously emotionally disturbed, with specific learning disabilities, speech impaired, or visually handicapped who because of those impairments need special education and related services (*Federal Register* 1977). The term *exceptional children* is a little broader and includes the category of gifted and talented children as well. P.L. 94-142 defines the categories of handicapped children as follows:

Deaf means a hearing impairment which is so severe that the child is impaired in processing linguistic information through hearing, with or without amplification, which adversely affects educational performance;

Deaf-blind means a concomitant hearing and visual impairment, the combination of which causes such severe communication and other developmental and educational problems that such children cannot be accommodated in special education programs solely for deaf or blind children;

Hard-of-hearing means a hearing impairment, whether permanent or fluctuating, which adversely affects a child's educational performance but is not included under the definiton of "deaf" in this section;

Mentally retarded means significantly subaverage general intellectual function existing concurrently with deficits in adaptive behavior and manifested during the developmental period, which adversely affects a child's educational performance;

Multihandicapped means concomitant impairments (such as mentally retarded-blind, mentally retarded-orthopedically impaired, and so on), the combination of which causes such severe educational problems that these children cannot be accommodated in special education programs solely for one of the impairments. The term does not include deaf-blind children.

Orthopedically impaired means a severe orthopedic impairment which adversely affects a child's educational performance. The term includes impairments caused by congenital anomaly (for example, clubfoot, absence of some member, and so on), impairments caused by disease (for example, poliomyelitis, bone tuberculosis, and so on), and impairments from other causes (for example, cerebral palsy, amputations and fractures, or burns which cause contractures).

Other health impaired means limited strength, vitality, or alertness, due to chronic or acute health problems, such as a heart condition, tuberculosis, rhumatic fever, nephritis, asthma, sickle cell anemia, hemophilia, epilepsy, lead poisoning, leukemia, or diabetes, which adversely affects a child's educational performance.

Seriously emotionally disturbed means a condition which exhibits one or more of the following characteristics over a long period of time and to a marked degree which adversely affects educational performance: (a) an inability to learn which cannot be explained by intellectual, sensory, or health factors, (b) an inability to build or maintain satisfactory interpersonal relationships with peers and teachers, (c) inappropriate types of behavior or feelings under normal circumstances, (d) a general pervasive mood of unhappiness or depression, or (e) a tendency to develop physical symptoms or fears associated with personal or school problems. The term includes children who are schizophrenic or autistic. The term does not include children who are socially maladjusted, unless it is determined that they are seriously emotionally disturbed.

Specific learning disability means a disorder in one or more of the basic psychological processes involved in understanding or using language, spoken or written, which may manifest itself in an imperfect ability to listen, think, speak, read, write, spell, or do mathematical calculations. The term includes such conditions as perceptual handicaps, brain injury, minimal brain dysfunction, dyslexia, and developmental aphasia. The term does not include children who have learning problems which are primarily the result of visual, hearing, or motor handicaps; or mental retardation; or of environmental, culture, or economic disadvantage.

There are additional criteria for determining the existence of a specific learning disability (*Federal Register* December 29, 1977). (A) The child does not achieve commensurate with his or her own age and ability levels in one or more of seven learning areas when provided with learning experiences appropriate for the child's age and ability areas; (B) The child has a severe discrepancy between achievement and intellectual ability in one or more of the following areas: (1) oral expression, (2) listening comprehension, (3) written expression, (4) basic reading skill, (5) reading comprehension, (6) mathematics calculation, or (7) mathematics reasoning.

Speech impaired means a communication disorder, such as stuttering, impaired articulation, language impairment, or a voice impairment, which adversely affects a child's educational performance.

Visually handicapped means a visual impairment which, even with correction, adversely affects a child's educational performance. The term includes both partially seeing and blind children.

In addition, *gifted and talented* means performance in any valuable line of human activity which is consistently or repeatedly remarkable. It includes unusual performance in any of the following: general intellectual ability, specific academic aptitude, creative and productive thinking, leadership ability, visual and performing arts, or psychomotor ability.

Historical Roots in Special Education

Tremendous changes have taken place over the years in society's attitude toward the exceptional individual. Three stages in the development of attitudes toward the handicapped child and adult have been recognized. The first was one of persecution, neglect, and mistreatment; the second stage was one of pity and protection; the third and current stage is marked by acceptance of the handicapped person and integration into society to the fullest extent possible (Kirk and Gallagher 1979). Current legislation for the handicapped in the United States accepts this latter position and recognizes the "civil rights" of the handicapped.

The public school movement in special education began quite slowly in the early 1900s, but in the past 25 years there has been rapid growth. Today, special education programs of almost all types and degrees of exceptionality can be found in public and private school programs. As noted earlier, current federal and state legislation supports the notion that handicapped children have the right to a free appropriate public education. Funded federal projects provide exceptional children with programs designed to meet the specialized needs of atypical children. After many years of relative administrative indifference, school budgets have been updated to include increases in special services and pupil personnel staff for added testing and guidance components. The legislative branches of the federal and state governments found it imperative to specify guidelines, certification procedures for teaching positions, and preservice and in-service teacher training programs. Special education has an important role in the new Department of Education which was established by Congress on May 4, 1980. The Office of Special Education and Rehabilitative Services was created within the new department to assure that the needs of exceptional children will not be neglected.

How many children in the general population are considered exceptional? Giving specific prevalance figures has been difficult because various studies use different criteria to specify an area of exceptionality, thereby coming up with different estimates. Nevertheless, the U.S. Office of Education has issued percentages of handicapped children as shown in Table 1–1.

Public Law 94–142 specifies that a state may not count more than 12 percent of the number of children between ages five through seventeen as handicapped. This count or identification becomes the criterion for reimbursement purposes from the federal government. However, the federal law also specifies that services must be provided for handicapped children ages 3 to 21. The three- to five-year-old age group must be served unless state guidelines limit such services.

How many preschool children are in need of special education services? Table 1–2 indicates the number of preschool handicapped children receiving special education and related services as reported by state under P.L. 94–142. These figures account for far less than the actual number of preschool handicapped children.

Recent Trends in Special Education

In a field developing as rapidly as special education has in the past few years, changes, modifications, and new directions are inevitable. Some of the trends have occurred as a natural extension of ongoing programs;

TABLE 1–1 Percentage of School-aged Children Served by Handicapping Condition School Year 1977–78

Exceptionality	Percentage
Speech Impaired	2.39
Learning Disabled	1.89
Mentally Retarded	1.84
Emotionally Disturbed	0.56
Other Health Impaired	0.27
Orthopedically Impaired	0.17
Deaf and Hard-of-Hearing	0.17
Visually Handicapped	0.07
Total	7.36

Adapted from U. S. Office of Education, *Progress Toward a Free Appropriate Education, A Report to Congress on the Implementation of P.L. 94–142: The Education for All Handicapped Children Act.* Washington, D. C.: U. S. Department of Health, Education, and Welfare, January, 1979 p. 162.

TABLE 1–2   Number of Preschool Handicapped Children Receiving Special Education and Related Services as Reported by State Under P.L. 94–142 School Year 1977–78

State	Ages 0–2	Ages 3–5	Total
Alabama	0	443	443
Alaska	11	378	389
Arizona	225	745	970
Arkansas	11	447	458
California	908	24,370	25,278
Colorado	266	1,936	2,202
Connecticut	17	1,244	1,261
Delaware	8	474	482
Florida	87	5,274	5,361
Georgia	124	3,719	3,843
Hawaii	162	190	352
Idaho	149	658	807
Illinois	523	20,891	21,414
Indiana	23	1,214	1,237
Iowa	297	3,845	4,142
Kansas	38	2,575	2,613
Kentucky	10	1,471	1,481
Louisiana	539	4,759	5,298
Maine	9	679	688
Maryland	213	1,145	1,358
Massachusetts	2,016	4,751	6,767
Michigan	456	13,725	14,181
Minnesota	88	4,221	4,309
Mississippi	20	1,195	1,215
Missouri	40	5,846	5,886
Montana	0	449	449
Nebraska	129	2,493	2,622
Nevada	220	764	984
New Hampshire	47	289	336
New Jersey	365	4,755	5,120
New Mexico	85	667	752
New York	269	6,114	6,383
North Carolina	62	4,110	4,172
North Dakota	26	403	429
Ohio	81	4,069	4,150
Oklahoma	36	2,762	2,798
Oregon	835	2,280	3,115
Pennsylvania	653	11,007	11,660
Rhode Island	9	1,069	1,078
South Carolina	102	3,778	3,880
South Dakota	18	452	470
Tennessee	6	7,316	7,322
Texas	1,781	23,066	24,847
Utah	88	1,478	1,566
Vermont	1	535	536
Virginia	495	4,231	4,726

TABLE 1-2 *(Continued)*

State	Ages 0–2	Ages 3–5	Total
Washington	23	1,582	1,605
West Virginia	18	835	853
Wisconsin	97	4,032	4,129
Wyoming	37	337	374
Dist. of Col.	71	790	861
Puerto Rico	3	241	244
Other*	3	188	191
TOTAL	11,800	196,287	208,087

Adapted From U. S. Office of Education, *Progress Toward a Free Appropriate Education, A Report to Congress on the Implementation of P.L. 94–142: The Education for All Handicapped Children Act.* Washington, D. C.: U.S. Department of Health, Education, and Welfare, January, 1979 pp. 132–134.

* American Samoa, Guam, Trust Territories, Virgin Islands

others result from shortcomings experienced in earlier programs; and still others have come about because of outside pressures. The passage of P.L. 94–142 has revolutionized the field in terms of identification, evaluation, and the provision of services. Teachers working with handicapped young children should be familiar with the features of the federal law and state compliance to implement the law. Public Law 94–142 is discussed in Chapter 10. Many of the following trends in special education have particular impact on programs for young handicapped children.

The noncategorical movement. The noncategorical movement reverses the direction in special education to classify children into specific areas of exceptionality, that is, mental retardation, learning disabilities, emotional disturbance, and so on. Rather than perceiving each category of special education as clearly differentiated from the others, the emphasis is placed on the common characteristics across the categories. There are, unquestionably, common techniques and methods for diagnosing and treating children no matter what specific label they are given. Moreover, it is often difficult to determine one specific category of exceptionality into which the child fits. Young children's performance during a diagnostic assessment may be erratic, and testing, in many cases, is tenuous at an early age. The problem of categorizing or of making a differential diagnosis based on assessment tools and observation with young children is particularly difficult.

There is a move toward noncategorical programming to meet the multiple needs of young handicapped children. Since early symptomatic conditions are not easily identified and classified into deficits and categories by labels, it appears better to develop programs designed to meet functional needs rather than to perpetuate discrete and separate categories for young children. Labeling often causes irrepairable damage, inappropriate placement, and negative feedback. The issue of noncategorical programming is discussed further in Chapter 2.

Expanded age range in special education.   While the first programs in special education concentrated on the children in the elementary grades, the field is now expanding the ages at both ends of the continuum. Programs for the secondary school student and the adolescent are growing at the same time that better programs for the preschool handicapped child are being provided. As noted earlier, federal and state legislation mandates services beginning with three year olds in many states. Some states and some private programs offer diagnostic and treatment services from birth to three years of age for those suspected of having problems identifiable at birth, as well as counseling and training for the parents of these babies.

Degree or intensity of exceptionality.   Children differ in their degree of exceptionality as well as in their type of exceptionality. In mental retardation, for example, the degrees of retardation are specified as four levels: mild, moderate, severe, and profound. Similar levels can be determined for the other areas of handicapping conditions. The literature and programs differentiate between programs for the mildly handicapped and programs for the severely handicapped. Prevalence rates are also related to the degree or intensity of the handicap. Thus, mild handicaps are often termed *high incidence handicaps* because they occur more frequently than severe handicaps known as *low incidence handicaps*. The Department of Education has set a priority on the severely handicapped because these are the children who have often been most neglected in the past. The preschool population, of course, will have youngsters who are mildly handicapped as well as those who must be considered within the realm of the severely handicapped.

Other new directions.   Several other new directions in special education that affect the preschool child should be mentioned. They include language disorders, mainstreaming, legislation and litigation, medication, and biochemical treatment. All of these topics are discussed in other contexts throughout this book.

Organization of This Book

The organization plan for this book can be thought of as an "expanding systems" model. Part 1 deals with the central component of these systems—*The Child.* Part 2 deals with *The Curriculum,* a larger system that incorporates the child-system. Part 3 deals with the most comprehensive system—*The Environment.* It contains both the Curriculum and the Child systems. The three systems, as shown in Figure 1–1 can be viewed as three concentric circles, with each larger system or circle containing the smaller system or circle.

In Part 1, *The Child,* several aspects of the child are discussed: Chapter 1 deals with the nature of the field of early childhood special education; Chapter 2 discusses the characteristics of the child with special needs at the preschool level; and Chapter 3 discusses the problems of evaluation and assessment in identifying and diagnosing the preschool handicapped child.

Part 2, *The Curriculum,* deals with the subject of teaching. An overview of Curriculum Design is presented in Chapter 4; Chapter 5 discusses the teaching of motor and perceptual skills; Chapter 6 describes the teaching of cognitive skills; Chapter 7 presents the teaching of language and speech skills; and Chapter 8 discusses the teaching of social-affective skills.

Part 3 discusses the largest system—*The Environment.* Chapter 9 discusses the parent-professional partnership; Chapter 10 looks as ways of delivering educational services to young handicapped children and legislation affecting them; and Chapter 11 presents illustrative case studies of young exceptional children.

The Appendixes include testing instruments for screening and diagnosing young children (Appendix A), materials for teaching (Appendix B), model programs for early childhood special education

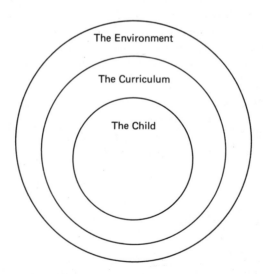

Figure 1–1   Three Expanding Systems: The Child, The Curriculum, The Environment

(Appendix C), and publishers' addresses (Appendix D). A glossary follows the Appendixes.

Summary

There is growing concern for the young handicapped child on the part of many: parents, educators, psychologists, governmental agencies. To best serve the young handicapped child, two fields of study must be merged—special education and early childhood education.

There is much evidence for need of programs in early childhood special education: the work of cognitive psychologists, state and federal legislation, special programs such as Head Start. The goal of early childhood special education study is to prevent or ameliorate future failure through early identification and treatment.

There are many changes occurring in the field of early childhood education. There are changes in attitude about responsibility, a drastic change in family structure, changes in educational theory about learning, and changes about the parenting role.

Six basic approaches to early childhood education include (1) the philosophical or moral approach, (2) the developmental or normative approach, (3) the psychoanalytic approach, (4) the compensatory educational approach, (5) the behavioral approach, and (6) the cognitive psychology approach.

The field of special education consists of a collection of categories of atypical children. In the federal legislation, P.L. 94–142, these categories of exceptionality are deaf, deaf-blind, hard-of-hearing, mentally retarded, multihandicapped, orthopedically impaired, other health impaired, seriously emotionally disturbed, specific learning disability, speech impaired, and visually handicapped. The gifted-talented are also considered exceptional. The young handicapped child could evidence characteristics from several of these categories.

The historical roots of special education derive from collections of categories of atypical children. The prevalence of the various handicapping conditions is difficult to determine with certainty, but data are available on numbers of children in various categories served.

Recent trends in special education affecting young handicapped children include the noncategorical movement, the expanding age range in special education, and the categorization of children according to degree or intensity of exceptionality.

This book has a systems approach organization. Part I deals with the central component—the child; Part II deals with a larger system, the curriculum, and Part III deals with the largest—the environment.

Review Questions

TERMS TO KNOW

a. *exceptional children*

b. *prevalence*

c. *early childhood education*

d. *special education*

e. *noncategorical movement*

f. *behavioral approach*

g. *Public Law 94–142*

h. *categorical placement of handi-capped children*

i. *characteristics of exceptionality*

j. *cognitive approach*

k. *compensatory approach*

l. *developmental approach*

m. *philosophical approach*

n. *psychoanalytic approach*

1. What is the historical evolution of the field of early childhood special education?

2. Define each of the twelve categories of Exceptional Children in your own terms.

3. Six approaches to early childhood education are discussed in this chapter. Describe the differences among them.

4. The field of early childhood education and the field of special education have been integrated into early childhood special education. List three major concepts from each of the two disciplines. How are they similar and how are they different?

5. What is the behavioral approach? Give an example of its use in a special education setting for three year olds who are not toilet trained.

6. The noncategorical movement is gaining importance in early childhood special education placement. What is it, and how does it differ from a self-contained categorical placement?

7. Check your own state law regarding mandatory legislation for three to five year olds. Does your state law require special education for three to five year olds?

References

ALMY, MILLIE. *The Early Childhood Educator at Work.* New York: McGraw Hill, 1975.

AMES, L. B. Learning Disabilities: The Development Point of View, in *Progress in Learning Disabilities*, Vol. I., ed. H. Myklebust. New York: Grune & Stratton, 1968, pp. 39–76.

BAYLEY, NANCY. Consistency and Variability in the Growth and Intelligence from Birth to Eighteen Years. *Journal of Genetic Psychology*, 1949, 75, 165–196.

BAYLEY, NANCY. Individual Patterns of Development. *Child Development,* 1956, 27, 45–74.

BAYLEY, NANCY. Behavioral Correlates of Mental Growth: Birth to Thirty-Six Years. *American Psychologist,* 1968, 23, 1–17.

BEREITER, C. and S. ENGELMANN. *Teaching Disadvantaged Children in the Preschool.* Englewood Cliffs, N.J.: Prentice-Hall, Inc., 1966.

BERGMAN, P. and S. K. ESCALONA. Unusual Sensitivities in Young Children. *Psychoanalytic Studies of Children,* 1949, 332–352.

BLOOM, B. S. *Stability and Change in Human Characteristics.* New York: John Wiley, 1964.

BLOOM, B. S. *Human Characteristics and School Learning.* New York: McGraw-Hill, 1976.

DEWEY, J., and E. DEWEY. *Schools of Tomorrow.* New York: Dutton, 1962.

ELKIND, D. *A Sympathetic Understanding of the Child: Birth to Sixteen.* Engelwood Cliffs, N.J.: Prentice-Hall, Inc., 1974.

ERIKSON, ERIK H. *Childhood and Society.* New York: W. W. Norton, 1950.

Federal Register, Department of Health, Education, and Welfare, Office of Education, Education of Handicapped Children, August 23, 1977.

Federal Register, Procedures for Evaluating Specific Learning Disabilities, Office of Education, December 29, 1977.

FREUD, S. *The Basic Writings of Sigmund Freud.* New York: Modern Library, 1938.

FROEBEL, FRIEDRICH. *The Education of Man.* New York: Appleton and Co., 1896.

GESELL, A., and others. *The First Five Years of Life: A Guide to the Study of the Preschool Child.* New York: Harper & Row, 1940.

GESELL, A. and L. AMES. Early Evidences of Individuality in the Human Infant. *Scientific Monthly,* 1937, 45, 217–225.

KAMII, CONSTANCE. A Sketch of a Piagetian Derived Preschool Curriculum Developed by the Ypsilanti Early Education Program, in *Early Childhood Education,* ed. B. Spodek. Englewood Cliffs, N.J.: Prentice-Hall, Inc., 1973, pp. 216–218.

KARNES, MERLE. *Not All Little Wagons Are Red,* eds. J. Jordon and R. F. Dailey. Arlington, Va.: Council for Exceptional Children, 1973, pp. xi–xv.

KIRK, SAMUEL and JAMES GALLAGHER. *Educating Exceptional Children.* Boston: Houghton Mifflin, 1979.

LAVATELLI, C. *Piaget's Theory Applied to an Early Childhood Curriculum.* Boston: American Science and Engineering, 1971.

LESSEN, E. and T. ROSE. State definitions of preschool handicapped population, *Exceptional Children,* 1980, 46, 467–469.

MACMILLAN, M. *The Nursery School.* London: J. M. Dent & Sons, 1919.

MONTESSORI, MARIA. *The Absorbent Mind.* New York: Holt, Rinehart & Winston, 1967.

PIAGET, JEAN. *The Origins of Intelligence in Children.* New York: International University Press, 1952.

SHIRLEY, M. M. The First Two Years: A Study of 25 Babies. *Institute for Child Welfare Monographs.* Minneapolis: University of Minnesota Press, 1931, I, 6.

SKINNER, B. F. *Science and Human Behavior.* New York: MacMillan, 1953.

SPOCK, B. *Baby and Child Care.* New York: Pocket Books, 1946.

State Statutory Responsibilities for the Education of Handicapped Children, 1977, *DEC Communicator,* 1978, 4, 12–15.

THOMAS, A. S., S. CHESS, and H. G. BIRCH. *Temperament and Behavior Disorders in Children.* New York: New York University Press, 1968.

U. S. Office of Education, *Progress Toward a Free Appropriate Public Education: A Report to Congress on the Implementation of Public Law 94–142: The Education for All Handicapped Children Act.* Washington, D. C.: U. S. Department of Health, Education, and Welfare, January, 1979.

WEBER, L. *The English Infant School and Informal Education.* Engelwood Cliffs, N.J.: Prentice-Hall, Inc., 1971.

WEIKART, D., and others. *Longitudinal Results of the Ypsilanti Perry Preschool Project.* Ypsilanti, Mich.: High-Scope Educational Research Foundation, 1970.

WEINTRAUB, F. J., and others, eds. *Public Policy and the Education of Exceptional Children.* Reston, Va.: Council for Exceptional Children, 1976.

WHITE, B. *The First Three Years of Life.* Engelwood Cliffs, N.J.: Prentice-Hall, Inc., 1975.

Characteristics of Exceptional Preschool Children

Chapter **Two**

The universe of children contains an assortment of individuals. Each child has a variety of unique and distinguishing characteristics, but within the larger majority of average children, there resides a smaller number of children so special in learning needs that ordinary teaching measures cannot produce a successful achievement rate. These children's exceptional needs require specialized services and alternative programs (Mayer 1974).

Categories and Labels

A specific area of exceptionality is often referred to as a *category* in special education. As discussed in Chapter 1, Public Law 94–142 designates specific categories of handicapped children which are recognized under the law by the Department of Education. The concept of categories in special education serves several useful purposes. First, it mobilizes an advocacy force to recognize and help a certain type of handicapped child. Further, it provides a clearcut set of characteristics to classify the needs and specific problems of each category of exceptionality. It also encourages highly specific research on causes, diagnosis, and treatment of a particular condition. Finally, it provides a convenient way to communicate.

While the use of categories of exceptionality has definite advantages, there are, at the same time, certain problems related to the concept. A child may exhibit characteristics that fall within several of the categories of exceptionality, making a differential diagnosis difficult. These children are frequently classified as multihandicapped. For example, a particular child could exhibit characteristics of visual impairment, mental retardation, and speech disorders simultaneously. Children who have characteristics representative of several of the categories can be thought of as *cross-categorical, noncategorical,* or *trans-categorical* youngsters. The cross-categorical concept is particularly useful in dealing with preschool handicapped children. When working with a three- or four-year-old child, it is often difficult to determine the specific type of handicapping by categorical definition. Early symptoms of developmental problems may have characteristics which span the categories.

Another problem with the categories is that the effect of labeling a child can be detrimental for all children, but especially harmful for the young child. Premature categorization of the child's problem can result in a destructive, self-fulfilling prophecy. By placing a label on the child, teachers and parents set up expectations based on that label, and the child often fulfills that prophecy by becoming like the child with that label.

There are other difficulties in the process of categorization. It is difficult to know if a problem is due to a specific handicap or if it is due to a lag in maturation, one which the child will outgrow in time. The noncategorical approach offers an alternative to making a premature judgment. Such an approach encourages early identification and educational services but not categorical placement (Anastasi 1976; Caldwell 1970; Keogh 1972; Kirk and Lord 1974).

Because of these difficulties with the traditional categories, many authorities in special education suggest thinking about functional areas of learning rather than traditional categories of handicap. Figure 2–1 is a matrix that illustrates the relationship between the traditional categories of handicapping conditions and functional categories of

Traditional Categories of Handicapping Conditions	*Functional Categories of Handicapping Conditions*	Motor Development	Cognitive Development	Language Development	Social-Affective Development
Visual Impairment					
Auditory Impairment					
Mental Retardation					
Physical Handicaps					
Speech-Language Disorders					
Learning Disabilities					
Behavior Disorders					

Figure 2–1   Matrix of traditional categories and functional categories of handicapping conditions for young children   *Adapted from J. Lerner, Children with Learning Disabilities, 3rd ed. Boston: Houghton-Mifflin, 1981.*

learning and development. Each of the functional categories represents an area of instruction. Part 2 of this book is organized according to these functional categories, with one chapter discussing each of the functional areas.

Early childhood special education programs are usually noncategorical programs, geared to the child's functional behaviors. Even though this chapter is organized according to categories of disability for ease of discussion, young children are often not placed within one of these groups initially.

Visual Impairment

The term *visually impaired* describes an extensive range of visual problems. Measurement of vision can extend from normal vision to a total lack of sight. A visual impairment indicates a limitation somewhere along that continuum. In addition to reduced visual acuity, there may be difficulty in recognizing colors. Each type of impairment can seriously limit the amount of visual information a child receives from the environment.

Blindness and the Partially Sighted

Visual impairment can be separated into two groups in terms of severity: *blind* and *partially sighted*.

Blind.   Legal blindness has been defined as including central visual acuity of 20/200, or less, in the best eye or with corrective lenses, as well as visual acuity of 20/200 if there are visual field limitations of 20 degrees or less (Dunn 1973). The notation of 20/200 refers to the distance at which the subject can see objects. A normal seeing person can see, with clarity, the same image or object at 200 feet which the blind person sees at 20 feet.

The blind child's lack of sight necessitates the need for reading instruction in Braille. Braille is a method by which persons lacking sight can use the sense of touch to identify letter symbols impressed or raised on a paper surface instead of the traditional printed letter symbols.

Partially sighted.   The partially sighted are those whose lack of vision restricts them to the use of magnification and large print, but who do have some usable vision. Partially sighted children usually have visual acuity between 20/200 and 20/70 in the best eye with possible correction.

To be eligible for programs for the blind or visually impaired, an opthalmic measurement of acuity is needed. The usual practice is for the child to be examined by an opthalmologist, a medically licensed expert in the study of eye disease and disorders, by an optometrist, or by a general practice physician. The optometrist is limited to acuity measurement only and cannot prescribe medicine or perform medical procedures.

Types of Visual Impairment

The most common visual difficulty affects central vision and results in nearsightedness or farsightedness. Farsightedness, called *hyperopia,* results in an inability to see objects which are close. Nearsightedness, called *myopia,* is a result of light which is focused in front of the retina rather than directly on the retina. Objects and images that are in the distance are blurred.

Strabismus, often referred to as "cross eyes," is a muscle coordination problem whereby the eye muscles do not move in unison. One or both eyes may move outward or inward.

Early detection of strabismus is of great concern for young children since it affects about 3 percent of the population and is critical for correction prior to the age of seven. If treated before the age of seven, the prognosis for correction is good. If left uncorrected, amblyopia results (Illinois Society for the Prevention of Blindness no date). This is the direct repression of images received by an eye (that is, the child loses vision in that eye) and may result in the loss of function for that eye.

While central vision and acuity problems are the most common visual impairments, total visual ability is affected by diseases or damage to the retina or optic nerve. Such conditions of disease as *optic atrophy, retinal detachment, retinis pigmentosa,* or *retrolental fibroplasia* can cause an interruption in the generalized visual process.

Causes of Visual Impairment

General causes of visual impairment include infection and disease, accidental injury, poisoning, tumors, muscle deficits, and perinatal conditions. Premature birth has produced large numbers of infants suffering from a condition known as *retrolental fibroplasis.* This abnormal eye condition found in premature infants can result in complete blindness. Fibrous scar tissue forms a film or curtain behind the lens of the eye, cutting off light. During the 1950s, research scientists discovered that excess oxygen, in the incubators which held premature infants, was causing this condition. Since then, a more careful monitoring of the oxygen supply has dramatically reduced the number of such cases.

Another common cause of visual impairment is when the mother contracts *rubella* (German measles) during her pregnancy. The 1964 rubella epidemic added substantially to the number of visually impaired and multiply involved children. It is estimated that approximately 25,000 miscarriages occurred and 25,000 to 30,000 children were born with developmental disorders following that 1964 epidemic (Cooper and Krugman 1966). Congenital rubella creates general abnormalities throughout the child's body, including cataracts, glaucoma, hearing loss, and heart defects (Johnston and Magrab 1976).

Symptoms of Visual Problems

Early vision screening for preschool children is one of the measures by which identification and remediation can be employed. Symptoms of general visual difficulty could include frequent rubbing of eyes; sensitivity to light; tears produced by close work; difficulty playing games with judgment of distance; headache, nausea, or dizziness; squinting; crusty, watery, or red eyes; eyes turning inward or outward; difficulty keeping a place when reading; covering of one eye to see an object; double vision.

The Society for the Prevention of Blindness endorses the visual screening of all children between the ages of three and five. The recommendation is that children with identified visual disorders be placed under a physician's care as soon as possible.

Early Identification of Visual Problems

Interest is being directed toward the visual intactness of the newborn child. Research shows that the newborn *does* attend to visual stimuli and even scans in a totally dark room (Mendelson and Haith 1976). However, there are many questions that as yet are unanswered regarding the full acquisition of visual capacity (Bronson 1974). The effects of visual damage to young children are not easily followed in longitudinal study since the total number of cases has been small and the range of damage so wide. Large epidemics can offer sizable numbers for such study, but the attrition rate is a great drawback; thus there is little opportunity for a rigorous research design.

New improvements in the mechanical measurement of infant responses through physiological recordings for pulse, heart, and breath rate should provide increases in those studies which will strive to more clearly define sequences in increments of visual growth rather than the effects of deficits.

Impact of Visual Impairment on the Young Child

One out of every four children has some type of visual problem (Illinois Society for the Prevention of Blindness no date). It is vital to identify any visual problem as early as possible since a young child's environment is constantly filled with all kinds of visual stimulations which color and shape the ability to relate to objects and people. Moving a toy car, grasping a block, watching a fish swim in a bowl of water, each of these activities involves seeing and integrating those sights with future concepts. Lesser visual capacity can narrow the range of experiences; lost glimpses of facial expressions, the indistinct shades of color and configurations are not easily replaced. But, if visual problems are found, all efforts must be made to offer sensory stimulation through other sensing systems.

It is important to be aware of the fact that children experiencing visual impairment are first of all children. As children, they need continuous and consistent interactions with both their parents and their peers (Donlon 1976). The severity of handicap will result in greater dependence upon a caretaker. The more limited a child is visually, the more there is a need to use tactual and auditory sensitivities to make sense out of the world.

Blindness in young children does not alter many aspects of the general patterns of growth and development. However, blind children are delayed in body posture movements and self-awareness (Millar 1976). The visually handicapped child learns to move towards sounds rather than objects. Contrary to popular belief, the blind do not sing or play musical instruments any better than the average person. However, young children who find themselves limited in the early stages of development may practice using other senses with more frequency and success.

The impairment should not be the central focus of remediation without including the importance of peer and adult interactions. Sometimes parental concerns can lead to overprotection. It is important for visually impaired children to be encouraged to explore the world around them. Falling down or getting a small bump here and there are all a part of that learning experience. Once the environment is made safe for experimentation, there is usually less reason for a parent to fear for that child's safety. Soon that child will learn to *trail*. This is a way in which blind children explore and touch things around them to determine pathways and general directions for safe movement.

Children who are visually impaired often display self-stimulating behaviors which are referred to as *blindisms*. These including rocking, finger poking, spinning about, and the initiation of strange noises. These behaviors can be reduced and eliminated if replaced with more positive activities; a genuine attempt should be made to distract the child when such behavior occurs, and a careful observation and documentation should be kept of the time of day and previous activity which may have stimulated the action.

Young children with visual handicaps need and gain from peer experiences (Wilson 1976). Educational intervention which integrates these children into their own communities increases the probability for more normalized social interactions. Early identification of such problems can offer wider educational alternatives once a determination is made that a visual problem exists.

Auditory Impairment

The ability to hear is crucial to learning. Yet, a hearing impairment is often overlooked as a possible cause of slow development.

Deafness and the Hard-of-Hearing

Children with hearing impairment are usually categorized into one of two groups for educational purposes: *hard-of-hearing* or the *deaf*. *Hard-of-hearing* is a term used to identify children who have functional hearing even though they have a deficit in auditory acuity. The acuity level may or may not be improved through the use of hearing aids.

The term *deafness* refers to children with the most severe auditory impairment. Children who are deaf usually have that disability at birth. In addition, however, loss of hearing by accident may result in deafness. Wooden (1963) suggests thinking of two groups: *prelanguage deaf* which includes those whose deafness came before language developed and *postlanguage deaf*, those who lost their hearing after the development of language.

Types of Hearing Loss

Three principle types of hearing loss are, (a) conductive impairment, (b) a sensorineural impairment, and (c) central impairment based upon a strict threshold acuity. *Conductive impairment* is a loss of ability to hear loudness due to an outer or middle ear problem. *Sensorineural* impairment is a nerve or nerve pathway disorder resulting in a lack of tonal clarity. *Central impairment* is a term which describes the interference of sound perception due to pathway, brain system, and cerebral cortex involvement (Myklebust 1964).

Measurement of Severity of Hearing Loss

Degrees of hearing impairment are determined through the use of pure tone and language assessment. Since the general term, hearing impairment, describes both pure and speech tone difficulties as well as disease conditions, the hearing specialist must also judge if the condition is a temporary one due to injury or disease.

The severity of the hearing loss is measured by assessing hearing thresholds in decibel levels (dB) at varying frequencies. *Decibel levels* refer to the loudness of the sound. The *frequency* refers to the highness or lowness of the pitch of the sound. Table 2–1 classifies different degrees of hearing loss in terms of ability to understand speech (Davis and Silverman 1970, p. 255).

With each successive level of decibel loss, there is a range of

TABLE 2–1   Classes of Hearing Handicap

CLASS	DEGREE OF HANDICAP	Average Hearing Threshold Level for 500, 1000 and 2000 Hz in the Better Ear		ABILITY TO UNDERSTAND SPEECH
		MORE THAN	NOT MORE THAN	
A	Not significant		25 dB (ISO)	No significant difficulty with faint speech
B	Slight handicap	25 dB (ISO)	40 dB	Difficulty only with faint speech
C	Mild handicap	40 dB	53 dB	Frequent difficulty with normal speech
D	Marked handicap	55 dB	70 dB	Frequent difficulty with loud speech
E	Severe handicap	70 dB	90 dB	Can understand only shouted or amplified speech
F	Extreme handicap	90 dB		Usually cannot understand even amplified speech

From H. Davis and S. R. Silverman, eds. *Hearing and Deafness*, 3rd ed. Copyright © 1947, 1960, 1970 by Holt, Rinehart and Winston, Inc. Reprinted by permission of Holt, Rinehart and Winston.

limitation which correlates with the age of onset of the condition as a critical factor. The loss of hearing prior to the development of speech and language *can significantly delay and distort a young child's ability to verbally express ideas.*

Symptoms of Auditory Impairment

Caregivers to young children should be alert to the symptoms of auditory deficits. They should be aware of the following signals:

1. A child who does not appear to respond to sound.
2. A child who is unusually attentive to facial expressions and lip movements.
3. A child who is unduly sensitive to movement and other visual clues.
4. A child who has a perpetual cold or runny nose, frequent earaches, or is a mouth breather.
5. A child who has recently recovered from scarlet fever, measles, meningitus, or from a severe head injury.
6. A child who needs much repetition before demonstrating understanding.
7. A child who is unusually active, running about and touching things.
8. A child who does not respond to being called in a normal voice when out of sight.
9. A child who needs many activities and visual cues before responding.
10. A child who does not talk or even attempt to talk.
11. A child who uses indistinct speech.
12. A child whose voice has a nonmelodious quality.
13. A child who does not moderate his or her own voice and either talks too loudly or too softly.

Early Identification of Auditory Problems

Ways of screening early for hearing disorders continue to develop. Newborn babies' hearing acuity can be measured; however, it is not uncommon for a definitive diagnosis to be delayed until the infant is older and more receptive for evaluation. Parents need to be informed about the importance of an infant's responses to sounds as they are the most reliable early screeners of potential hearing impairments.

New developmental models of auditory competence are now investigating the value of internalized coding and organizing of acoustic information. Eisenberg (1976) has developed a model which incorporates both direct and indirect pathways involved in the decoding of acoustic information at the earliest ages. Through laboratory testing, audiologists have progressed to now ask *how* infants hear rather than *if* they hear. Infant cardiac patterns and overt behaviors are being measured to differentiate changes in arousal and orienting behavior for both constant and patterned signals. As can be seen in Table 2–2, level and states differ even at the neonatal ages.

Impact of Auditory Impairment on the Young Child

Children suffering from auditory impairment are handicapped in many ways. The most obvious delay is seen in speech and language. The isolation experienced by deaf children often causes behavior problems due to excessive frustration.

Cognition as an entity separate from language is not impaired in the young deaf child. However, when measured with standard intelligence tests, deaf children may perform poorly.

Children with auditory impairments have differing amounts of hearing. Sometimes this is referred to as residual hearing. Residual hearing can be assisted with a sound amplifier or a hearing aid. Most audiologists will agree that the earlier a child is fitted with an aid, the better. The hearing aid helps the child to make use of the greatest amount of residual hearing at the time that language is developing.

If a hearing aid is recommended for a young child, it is important

TABLE 2–2 Stimulus Variables as a Determinant of Neonatal Responses to Sound

INPUT	PROCESSING LEVEL	Most Frequently Observed Outputs	
		OVERT BEHAVIOR	CARDIAC PATTERN
High frequency tones and noisebands	I	Freezing; startle	Very shortlasting; accelerative
Low frequency tones and noisebands	II	Undifferentiated movements	Relatively shortlasting; accelerative
Tonal sequences and other nonspeech ensembles	III	Differentiated movements; utterance	Somewhat prolong; diphasic
Speech and speech-like sounds	IV	Differentiated movements; utterance	Very prolonged; decelerative

From R. B. Eisenberg, *Auditory Competence in Early Life*. Baltimore, Md.: University Park Press, 1976, p. 140.

to check to determine that there is a proper fit, to see that the batteries are operable, that the cords are not worn out or broken, that the child can easily operate the aid, and that if the ear is sore or infected, an appointment be made to see the personal physician.

Means of communication for the deaf and hard-of-hearing include lip-reading, fingerspelling, and the use of sign language. Total communication is the system in which speech, fingerspelling, signing, and lipreading are combined.

The more severe the impairment, the less intelligible is the speech. Deaf children *do* learn to speak. However, the *quality* of their speech is *different* and requires patience and attentiveness on the part of the listener. The earlier the child can benefit from amplification, the more likely the clarity of speech.

Mental Retardation

Definition of Mental Retardation

The problem of defining and describing mental retardation has plagued special educators for many years. No *one* set of criteria seems inclusive enough to meet the many diverse behaviors seen in children with varying levels of retardation. The American Association on Mental Deficiency (AAMD) presented the following definition in 1973:

Mental retardation refers to significantly subaverage general intellectual functioning existing concurrently with deficits in adaptive behavior and manifested during the developmental period. There is a definite lack of reason and personal management which implies a general inability to survive. (President's Committee on Mental Retardation 1977, p. 143)

Crucial to the AAMD definition is the inclusion of *both* low intellectual functioning (an IQ of less than 70) and deficits in adaptive behavior measures. Adaptive behavior means the degree to which the child can meet age level standards of self-sufficiency and social responsibility. The AAMD definition categorizes the functional levels of mental retardation as mild, moderate, severe, and profound retardation. Table 2–3 designates IQ scores on both the Stanford-Binet and the Wechsler Intelligence Scale for Children for each level of function.

Prior to the AAMD classification of retardation as shown in Table 2–3, mentally retarded children were categorized as *educable mentally handicapped* (EMH) or *trainable mentally handicapped* (TMH). Hobbs (1975) suggests that this older classification be continued because it can be helpful in educational planning.

TABLE 2–3

Level of Function	Stanford-Binet IQ (S.D. 16)	Wechsler IQ (S.D. 15)
Mild	68–52	69–55
Moderate	51–36	54–40
Severe	35–20	39–25 (extrap.)
Profound	19 and below	24 and below (extrap.)

Note that the borderline category (-1.0 to -2.0 s.d.*) is not included under the definition.

Adapted from H. J. Grossman, ed., *Manual on Terminology and Classification in Mental Retardation.* Washington, D.C.: American Association on Mental Deficiency, 1973, p. 18.

* Standard Deviation

Causes of Mental Retardation

There is a continuing debate about the causes of mental retardation and the factors that are key to intellectual functioning (Grossman 1973; Tarjian and others 1973). There are three opposing theoretical positions: One says that it is the environment in which the child lives that causes retarded behavior; the second theory claims that mental retardation is caused by genetic factors (Haring 1978). The third is an interactive relationship between the environmental and genetic factors.

Environmental causes. Environmental causes of mental retardation are numerous. The environmental point of view suggests that factors in intelligence are at least partly the product of home and school training. Children need stimulation and nurturance if they are to develop intellectually. The fact that so many mentally retarded children come from poor and disadvantaged environments lends support to this position. The experiments of Skeels and Dye, Kirk, and Heber, discussed in Chapter 6, suggest that IQ scores can be dramatically improved when children are provided with a stimulating environment (Kirk, Kliebhan, and Lerner 1978).

Genetic causes. *Genetic causes of mental retardation* may be related to a variety of factors. This genetic viewpoint suggests that causes of mental retardation are largely inherited. Jensen's controversial studies (1969, 1979) argued for the inheritability of intelligence. In addition, mental retardation may also be caused by various genetic deviations or conditions that occur during prenatal development. Examples include endocrinal dysfunctions, birth trauma, maternal nutritional deficits, and prenatal infection or diseases. Other genetic conditions that can lead to mental retardation are discussed in the next section under physical, genetic, and birth defects.

Interactive Relationships.   Interactive relationships between environmental and genetic factors are seen by most authorities as the cause of mental retardation. Heredity may set the limit that one may reach in intellectual capacity, but the environment can determine how close one comes to achieving this potential. While heredity may account for a large portion of intelligence, the environment and educational interventions can raise or lower the IQ as much as 30 points (Heber 1974). It is in the early years that educational intervention is most effective in providing for the stimulation of mental development.

Symptoms of Mental Retardation

Mentally retarded children have generalized delayed development. They do not develop perceptually in the normal fashion, resulting in slow development in body control and hand-eye integration skills. Speech and language abilities are acquired at a slower rate which affects the ability to communicate with others at expected age levels. Social and emotional behaviors also show slow development. The characteristics of severe and profound mentally retarded children are fairly obvious, and those children can be readily identified in the preschool years. The more subtle symptoms of the mild and moderate retarded are not as obvious, and identification may take place later on in time.

Impact of Mental Retardation on the Young Child

Teachers working with mentally retarded preschool children should be aware of the impact of their characteristics in a learning situation. Parents should be given reliable information concerning the educational limitations and reasonable expectations for their child's future.

Mentally retarded children need a structured environment and directed teaching. They need many repetitions of a single task in order to learn it. The teacher cannot conclude that the child knows the task until the child can perform it consistently over a long period of time. Instructional experiences should be concrete rather than abstract. For example, in learning to count, it is easier if the child uses concrete objects that can be held and manipulated rather than abstract symbols on a page.

The child is more likely to learn if the instruction is close to the child's daily experience. For example, to teach the subtle concept of "inside" and "outside," the teacher could peel a piece of fruit the child likes to eat.

Physical, Genetic, and Birth Defects

The developmental stages through which an infant progresses while housed within the protective environment of the mother normally advance without a major crisis. However, there are situations in which genetic, neurological, and physical insult create limiting physical and mental capacity.

A number of handicapping conditions in young children are due to physical factors, genetic conditions, and birth defects. These conditions are related to physical abnormalities, mental retardation, learning disabilities, sensory deficits, or personality disorders, several of which are discussed in this section.

Premature Birth

Premature birth may reduce the effectiveness of the infant's life support systems. Low birth weight infants often have great difficulty in performing independent survival tasks, since an immature physiological structure cannot operate independently. If the respiratory system is not functioning adequately, then oxygen does not flow to meet the needs of the organs and the brain cells. Any reduction of oxygen supply can have irreversible results. Oxygen imbalance also results in further metabolic and chemical imbalances which lead to more generalized cell damage. Babies born prematurely are usually smaller in weight and have less competent physiological systems.

Developmental Disabilities (DD)

The term *developmental disabilities* is one which has caused much concern in the field of special education. Legislative definitions have been revised to clarify the disorder, and yet there still seems to be an overlap with the other categories of exceptionality. Meier (1976) is most emphatic that there can be no separation of learning disabilities and developmental disabilities. He uses a term *developmental learning disabilities* to describe the kinds of behaviors and interventions useful for young children with learning problems.

The intent of the new definition was (a) to be less arbitrary for inclusion or exclusion, (b) more clearly focused on the most handicapped population, and (c) more consistent with trends toward functional approaches. It was not intended to (a) exclude individuals from services, (b) greatly expand the total developmentally disabled population, (c) result in establishment of segregated services, and (d) determine eligibility.

For funding purposes, the federal legislation has specified particular conditions for *developmental disabilities*. These are contained in Public Laws 95–602 and 94–103. Evidence of the disability must be apparent before the child is 22 years of age. The disability must be likely to continue indefinitely, resulting in substantial functional limitation in three or more of the following: (a) self-care, (b) receptive-expressive language, (c) learning, (d) mobility, (e) self-direction, (f) capacity for independent living, or (g) economic self-sufficiency. A combination and sequence of specialized treatment or generic care is expected to be required to meet the continued needs of these children as they grow and experience new handicapping difficulties, and the disability is attributable to a mental or physical impairment or a combination of impairments (Gollay 1979, p. 2).

Labels should not be the central focus for young delayed children. However, no matter how we try to avoid this problem, official terminology always demands that there be a description of a problem in order to plan the treatment. This procedure should be applied to guarantee more appropriate services for young children and avoid mere tagging for eligibility into federally funded programs.

Chromosomal Defects

Down's Syndrome, also referred to as mongolism, is the most common chromosomal cause of retardation affecting one in 660 births. This condition is caused by an aberration of genes for the twenty-first chromosome (Trisomy 21). The risk factor for this condition increases with the mother's age. A mother over forty has a thirty times greater chance to have a child with Down's Syndrome than a mother under twenty years of age. Of all Down's Syndrome children, 65 percent are born to women over thirty (Johnston and Magrab 1976). Children with this syndrome have abnormally small skulls, and there is a slow rate of learning with a relative decline during the first year or two. While not eradicating the handicap, home and infant stimulation have reduced, as well as slowed, the rate of decline once seen in institutionalized young children (Zausmer, Pueschel and Shea 1972; Hayden and Dmitriev 1974).

Turner's Syndrome and *Klinefelter's Syndrome* are the result of aberrations of sex chromosomes. In Turner's Syndrome, affecting females, there is only one X chromosome and no Y chromosome. Of XO fetuses, 95 to 98 percent fail to survive the birth process with abnormal spontaneous abortion being the mechanism which interrupts the process. Children with Turner's Syndrome are not mentally retarded on a generalized scale, but they do experience space and form perception difficulties.

Klinefelter's Syndrome, affecting males, is a form of male hypogonadism with the addition of an extra X chromosome (XXY). Sexual development and delayed onset of secondary sex characteristics require the application of hormonal therapy.

Muscular Disorders

A hereditary neuromuscular disability, *spinal atrophy* is a progressive condition which terminates in death before school age is reached.

A hereditary, sex-linked disease which is progressive and terminal, *muscular dystrophy,* affects the skeletal muscles. Mobility decreases with increased muscle weakness and the final result is death. Females are rarely afflicted with this condition, but they can pass it on to their male children.

Central Nervous System Disorders

Cerebral Palsy is a permanent movement disorder caused by injury or disease to the central nervous system. Causes may include birth process injury, trauma to the head, brain or spinal cord infection, lead poisoning, jaundice, and reduction of oxygen during delivery. The severity of the condition may range from barely noticable clumsiness to crippling muscle spasms which require the use of a wheelchair.

The largest numbers of children in physically disabled special education programs have problems which are due to cerebral palsy. The definition itself implies damage within the brain and developmental deficits. The general category describes motor disorders resulting in muscle action, posture, and balance problems (Bobath and Bobath 1975). The amount of incoordination may vary with the severity of the condition and the number of extremities affected. Muscles of the oral cavity may also be involved. Characteristics of cerebral palsy include spasticity—tight muscles, athetosis—uncontrolled irregular movements, ataxia—coordination and balance difficulties, mixtures—combinations of other types (Bigge and Sirvis 1978).

Convulsive disorders are conditions which involve seizures. Often called epilepsy, convulsive disorders can be severe or mild. They may be generalized, partial, or miscellaneous seizures. Partial and miscellaneous seizures affect both motor and behavior.

Children's incidence rate for epilepsy is approximately 2 to 3 percent of the population. The generalized seizures (major motor and grand mal) are the most frequent types of convulsive disorders in infancy and childhood. The onset of a seizure may be a cry and then a pale face, with pupils dilated and rolling, body tension, and rigidity followed by a loss of consciousness. If ambulatory, the infant or young child will fall, and the body will exhibit short jerking motions for a brief period of time. Since the grand mal seizure creates uncontrolled movements, there is possible bladder and bowel release, excessive salivation, and possible choking. Petit mal seizures are not as noticable as grand mal because behavior states may not change drastically. Children may have a mild lack of attention, disorientation, or five to ten second attention interruptions which are seen as staring, blinking, and an overall disorientation. The true petit mal seizure rarely occurs below four years of age and over 13 years of age.

Phenobarbital and Dilantin are anticonvulsant medications commonly prescribed to control seizures. Differences in the size and ages of children necessitate a careful monitoring of dosage reactions to the medication. Dosage requirements should be regulated under the direct supervision of the child's personal physician.

Spina Bifida, curvature of the spine, can occur through injury, trauma, or as the result of a congenital disorder in which one in every 1,000 births result in a myelomeningocele. Myelomeningocele, a congenital birth defect, interferes with nerve cord functions. Interuterine, the fetus or the developing embryo fails to accomplish the normal fusion process in portions of the neural tube. The malformations of the neural tube and vertebrae, which complete this fusion, can result in the cystlike formation of a translucent sac on the spinal column. The disruption of nerve function caused by this situation limits the child's use of the lower extremities and can even result in paralysis (Lansky 1975).

Currently, this condition is treated through various surgical procedures which provide a shunting. This is an insertion of tubing and plastic surgery to connect otherwise open spinal cord contents. Completing this closure requires a draining procedure which reduces the pressure from the cerebral ventricular system. The introduction of the shunting procedures has helped reduce fatalities. Many untreated cases died of infection before the shunting process was employed. Now the techniques are applied earlier, and the central nervous system complications are lessened.

There is no known cause of myelomeningocele at this time. It is regarded as a central nervous system malformation. There is a 5 percent likelihood for siblings to also have some spinal defect. Genetically, there is a significant risk factor for other children of the same union, and genetic counseling is advised. More abnormal infants are born to mothers beyond the age of thirty, but monitoring of such late age pregnancies has helped to identify the compounding factors contributing to birth defects.

Hydrocephalus, the retention of intracranial fluid within the brain structures, is another outcome of the incomplete spinal cord. Lack of proper drainage creates cranial pressure and possible infection. Selections for those cases to benefit from corrective surgery are made by the attending surgeon. The procedures instituted include connection by shunting and reconstruction to preserve the remaining tissues that are functioning.

Traumatic injuries are also quite common with young children. Some of the more serious accidents result in spinal damage and possible paralysis. Bicycle and automobile accidents provide the largest numbers of paralysis cases. Terms used to describe the residual effects of the damage include references to the number of extremities affected and the resultant loss of mobility. A child with paraplegia would have paralysis of both lower extremities. As the mobility decreases, the potential side effects of urinary and respiratory problems increases. Slower circulation and pressure sores are problems. The more debilitating the damage, the more adaptive aids are necessary to assist the child toward personal independence.

Other Defects

Hemophilia, often called "bleeder's disease," is a blood condition that is rare in females. Usually found in males, it is demonstrated by a poor blood-clotting ability. Bumps and bruises generally acquired by young active children can create mortal danger. Possible hemorrhage and internal bleeding are serious effects of even a minor jolt. Medical treatment includes the use of the missing clotting factor, cryoprecipitate, and a reduction of the activity brought about by the bleeding.

Cystic Fibrosis is another disorder. Here pancreatic deficiency gives rise to a chronic pulmonary condition.

Phenylketonuria (PKU) is an inborn metabolic disorder. The incidence rate for PKU is one in 10,000 to 20,000 children. It is identified by the Guthrie test. Newborn infants are routinely checked to determine the condition within the first few days of life. Correction is accomplished through a special diet begun almost immediately. Without such treatment, the child will become severely mentally retarded. The retardation is the result of a liver enzyme imbalance and elevated phenylalanine levels which affects brain cell development.

Asthma is a disorder which is difficult to categorize. Many leading medical experts consider it an allergic condition of the lungs. The symptoms include labored breathing, wheezing, and coughing. Medication relieves the constriction of the bronchial tubes and provides relief for the shortness of breath. There are those experts who believe that asthma can also be tied to emotional stress variables. In those cases, the asthmatic attack is considered an emotionally induced condition.

Prenatal Diagnosis

There are several techniques by which prenatal diagnosis of atypical development can be determined with a fair degree of accuracy.

Amniocentesis, removal of amniotic fluid from the uterus, is one of the methods to identify an abnormal condition. This procedure, done within the fifteenth to twentieth week of pregnancy, will detect elevated levels of chemical imbalance within 99 percent accuracy. Also, using the amniotic fluid for cultures allows determination of chromosomal abnormalities. Enzyme analyses identify specific metabolic problems since the fluid contains cells from the fetus.

Amniography or X-ray studies are of limited value since skeletal views of the fetus do not offer a stable diagnostic foundation. At twenty weeks, many disorders are not visibly apparent. Amniography is accomplished by injecting a radio-opaque fluid into the uterus of the mother to outline the fetus and identify physically visible malformations.

Sonography, or ultra sound, is a procedure used to measure size and location of the fetus. Sound waves are bounced into the pregnant uterus and the recording echos outline the configuration of the fetus.

Fetoscopy is the most direct method of determining birth defects. The medical team inserts a fetoscope, much like a small telescope, which allows the doctor to look inside the actual uterine cavity. There is danger of abortion from this method, since those fetoscopes which allow the best visualization are large and can possibly induce spontaneous abortion.

Smaller and more compact instruments need to developed before this technique can be used more extensively. Since there is such a high abortion risk using this method, it is reserved for the most serious of cases. Usually, the identification of a couple previously parenting a child with a specific birth defect or the older mother are cases which may require drastic diagnostic measures. These prenatal diagnoses are not without error, and there are many disorders not detectable through prenatal screens. For those couples who find themselves likely candidates for such procedures, family planning and counseling are a vital concern.

Speech and Language Disorders

Speech and language abilities are an essential aspect of human development. Other animal forms are able to communicate, but human beings are unique in their ability to use speech as a means of transferring information (Lennenberg 1967).

Speech, or speaking, involves the utterance of sounds in some organized fashion which conveys meaning to the individual listening to the sounds. *Language,* on the other hand, denotes an understanding of the structure by which the speech components are assembled.

Language acquisition is accomplished in a patterned, predictable way (Carroll 1961; McCarthy 1954). The procedure has a definite beginning and end; however, there may be varying degrees of performance along the way.

Causes of Speech and Language Disorders

There are many causes for children to have disorders in speech and language. Children in many of the exceptionalities are likely to evidence some form of speech or language problem.

Physical and neurological insults early in a child's life are one cause of late acquisition of speech and language. Neurological damaging conditions which retard general growth may also slow the onset of language. The mentally retarded child, usually slow in general development, is likely to have speech problems due to motor difficulties and language problems related to memory deficits.

Due to their hearing deficits, deaf children invariably have speech and language problems while hearing impaired children are also likely to have them.

Neurologically impaired children may exhibit greater or lesser degrees of speech damage directly proportional to the extent and areas of the brain in which the damage occurred. The earlier within the child's lifespan that the damage occurs, the greater the overall effect upon the entire communication system.

Emotional problems can inhibit the quality of language production, and traumatic events have been known to interrupt language.

Symptoms of Speech Disorders

When children's speaking patterns deviate conspicuously so that there is an interference with communication and attention is called to the deviation, a speech impairment is said to exist. Young children learning to talk often make many types of speech errors such as the consonant substitution errors of "wabbit" for rabbit or "widdle" for little. The continuation of those production errors long beyond the formative years of early childhood are considered to be speech impairments.

Articulation errors are additions of speech sounds, distortions, substitutions, and sound omissions. *Voice defects* include pitch, quality, and intensity deviation. The child may speak in a voice that is pitched too high, low, or even in a dull monotone. Hypernasal children sound as if they are talking through their noses. Children with cleft palates or a child who has suffered a type of paralysis may have hypernasal speech patterns. Growths or polyps on the vocal cords may cause hoarseness due to the strain or improper use of the voice.

Rhythm defects, another type of speech difficulty, includes stuttering, blocking, cluttering, or repetition of sounds, words, and phrases. The frustration of dysfluency may create emotional problems. On the other hand, it is also thought that emotional problems may be the cause of the dysfluency.

Symptoms of Language Disorders

Marked inability to use language or to verbally communicate can be called a language disorder. Delayed language is seen in limited vocabulary and skeletal construction of sentences. Some more severely delayed children will show little or no use of verbal communication; they will use nonverbal gestures to communicate their needs.

Impact of Speech and Language Disorders on the Young Child

Being unable to communicate to express one's wants becomes a very frustrating experience. Remembering Helen Keller, who was transformed from animal-like behavior to human behavior when she learned the mystery of language, those of us working with language disorders often wonder at the power that language wields. Without verbal communication skills, children must rely upon gestures, pointing, and temper tantrums. The teacher and parent, working with children who have speech and language problems, must be sensitive to the nature of the problem, the way in which language develops in atypical children, and instructional methods for speech and language skills. Methods for teaching speech and language skills to the young child are presented in Chapter 7.

Specific Learning Disabilities

The handicap of specific learning disabilities is the most recent category of exceptional children to be recognized. This category of exceptional education developed when parents, educators, and other professionals became concerned with certain children who were having extreme difficulties in learning yet were ineligible for existing special education services. These children encountered failure in learning specific skills such as speaking, reading, arithmetic, or writing despite the fact that they were not sensory impaired (blind or deaf). These children were not mentally retarded, nor were their difficulties due to emotional problems.

In the early attempts to understand this group of children, a variety of terms were used to identify them. Strauss and Lehtinen (1947), in their pioneering work, called these children *brain-injured*. A later term was *minimal brain dysfunction* (MBD), which is still often used by the medical profession (Wiederholt 1974). Kirk (1963) spoke of children with *learning disabilities*, a term which won general acceptance and is now part of federal and state legislation.

Symptoms of Learning Disabilities

The definition of specific learning disabilities as used in PL 94–142 is presented in Chapter 1. However, a brief discussion of the symptoms of learning disabilities can highlight the type of child who is learning disabled. The symptoms to be discussed are (a) neurological dysfunction, (b) uneven growth pattern, (c) difficulty in academic and learning tasks, (d) a discrepancy between achievement and potential, and (e) attentional deficit disorders (Lerner 1981; Torgeson 1979).

Neurological dysfunction, one symptom of learning disabilities, is descriptive of problems related to the central nervous system. At present, the neurological aspect of the problem is not emphasized by many educators for a number of reasons. First, it is often very difficult to ascertain the existence of a neurological abnormality from a medical examination. Often, the diagnosis is only presumed through observation of behavior (Gaddes 1976). Moreover, successful educational intervention is not dependent upon the diagnosis of the neurological dysfunction. A neurological dysfunction remains a presumption even though the condition cannot always be confirmed by examination or a laboratory study.

Uneven growth pattern, another symptom of learning disabilities, is displayed as uneven development in various mental functions. What is meant by this concept is that learning disabled children are not developing in an even or "normal" fashion. While some factors are maturing in an anticipated sequence and rate, other components are lagging in their development. This symptom of uneven growth pattern has been called *developmental imbalances* (Gallagher 1966), *the principle of disparity* (Meyers & Hammill 1976), and *intraindividual differences* (Kirk & Kirk 1971). It is based on the assumption that children without learning disabilities develop evenly. This is an assumption and not a fact.

Difficulty in academic and learning tasks are the obvious symptoms of the learning disabled child. The definition in PL 94–142 as reported in Chapter 1 mentions seven areas in which a child may have difficulty. The areas that are most likely to affect the preschool child are only the first two, the communication skills of listening and speaking.

Discrepancy between achievement and potential is still another symptom of learning disabilities. Here a gap exists between what the child is potentially capable of learning and what the child, in fact, has learned or achieved.

There are several serious problems inherent in this concept for the preschool child. First, it is very difficult to categorize the young child's potential learning capacity, particularly if the child manifests a problem, such as speaking. IQ tests that are used to make this judgment have undergone severe criticism in recent years. Secondly, there is a problem in measuring achievement. Finally, how much of a discrepancy is needed for it to be *a significant* discrepancy?

Achievement measures that are used to identify the learning disabled school-age child are frequently reading and arithmetic scores. Since preschool children should not be given such narrow evaluations, they must be identified as *potential* learning failures or high-risk children.

In short, valid criteria by which preschool children can be accurately identified as learning disabled do not exist at this time. However, preschool children with *potential learning disorders* are identifiable (Adkins 1971; Davidson and others, 1977; de Hirsch 1966; Jansky and de Hirsch 1972; Mardell and Goldenberg 1972, 1975; Matusiak 1976; Sarff 1974). Most authorities suggest that rather than describing preschool children as learning disabled, terms such as developmental delay or potential learning disorder be used. Children grow and mature with spurts and lags; evaluation at one point in time may appear to be slow only to rapidly advance and become average at yet another point in time.

Attentional deficit disorders, a particularly pertinent symptom of the learning disabled preschool child, are highly visible to even the untrained observer. This refers to the inability to focus and attend to the task at hand for a sufficient length of time to learn it. Children with attentional deficit disorders are often seen as hyperactive and distractable (Ross 1974).

Impact of Learning Disabilities on the Young Child

Most children with learning disabilities have school related problems; that is, difficulty with reading, arithmetic, or writing. Since the preschool child has not yet encountered these subjects, it can only be predicted that he or she will do poorly once involved in a regular school program. For this reason, it is very difficult to diagnose learning disabilities in the preschool child.

The more positive approach is to avoid labeling. The preschool child is viewed as high risk, as having a delay in maturation or a potential for a handicap and needing intervention. Early identification and individualized program for remediation of learning deficits is one way to prevent or reduce the all-inclusive effects of such problems.

Behavior and Emotional Disorders

Behavior disorders is a term that refers to youngsters who are in conflict with themselves or with others. Their difficulties may be either social, emotional, or both. The term is, in many respects, noncategorical in that it may occur in youngsters who are retarded, learning disabled, blind, or physically impaired (Kauffman 1977). Behavior disorders for some children appear during the preschool years; for others, the problem becomes evident in later years.

The terms *behavior disorders, emotional disorders, emotional disturbance,* and *social maladjustment* are all terms commonly used to describe inappropriate behaviors and socialization tactics. Young children may manifest symptoms of severe social and emotional disorders, such as *psychosis, childhood schizophrenia,* or *autism.* Symptoms may include hostility, unhappiness, and a general unsuccessful pattern of development or academic progress. Usually, these children *do not* and sometimes *cannot* comply with the controls and expectations applied by their parents, teachers, or peers. The behavior can range from withdrawal to uncontrolled, disruptive, or bizarre behavior.

Disruption and confusion identify the atmosphere in which most young children with behavior disorders reside. The quality of the social interactions identifies a particular pattern. When social behaviors become inappropriate, extreme, and offensive, the actions are deviant; they call attention to their unusualness and require direct actions.

Of course, there is a great variance of acceptability of a young child's social behavior. Some parents encourage their children to "do your own thing." To some degree, then, the range of tolerance rests with the demands of the supervising adult. Moreover, it is important that teachers, parents, and others not perceive a child as emotionally disturbed merely because of some arbitrary standard that has been set.

Symptoms of Behavior Disorders

What clear performances must take place to confirm a suspicion that a child is behaviorally disturbed? The child with emotional or behavior disorders *deviates significantly with aberrant behaviors persisting over a substantial period of time.* Coping skills are poor or nonexistent. Bower (1969) lists five symptoms as follows:

1. There is an absence of some knowledge or skill in acquiring academic and social behaviors. This absence is not attributed to intellectual capability, hearing, and visual status or physical health factors.
2. There is a lack of positive, satisfying, interpersonal relationships with adults and peers.
3. There are frequent instances of inappropriate behavior episodes which are unexpected and inappropriate for the conditions in which they occur.
4. The child goes through observable periods of diminished verbal and other motor activities; that is, moods of depression or unhappiness.
5. There are frequent complaints of a physical nature, such as stomach aches, headaches, pain in the arm or leg, or general tiredness and fatigue.

Thomas and Chess (1977) stress temperament as an important variable in understanding behavioral disorders. They view temperament as explaining the *how* of a young child's behavior without etiological complications. In their investigations of the effects of stress within a longitudinal model, they state, "The issue involved in disturbed behavioral functioning is rather one of excessive stress resulting from poorness of fit and dissonance between environmental expectation and demands and the capacities of the child at a particular level of development" (Thomas and Chess 1977, p. 12). The degree of emotional stability seems to be related to a fit between the environment and basic temperament.

Three kinds of atypical social symptoms that are found among preschool children are (a) *aggressive, acting out behavior,* (b) *immature, withdrawn behavior,* and (c) *autistic-like behavior.*

Aggressive behavior is demonstrated by children acting out because of a lack of inner controls. Often their energy patterns are spasmatic with activity spurts. They need and demand great amounts of physical contact. They will initiate situations which will guarantee that attention be drawn to them.

Withdrawn children are unusually quiet, having few emotional highs and lows. Preferring to be alone, they will avoid group activities. Their body posture is usually tight and strained. These children will not spontaneously initiate conversation and often avoid verbal contacts.

Autistic-like behaviors are the most severe of all behavior disorders seen in young children. Often referred to as *infantile autism,* this disorder is almost void of human interactions. The child exhibiting these behaviors is unable to establish relationships with other people. Physical contact is resisted, and even gentle handling will cause stiffening of the body and withdrawal. Infantile autism occurs rarely, and while suspected and noted in infancy, it is rarely confirmed until two to four years of age.

Children with behavior disorders are usually inflexible and difficult to manage. They are easily disturbed by changes and interruptions in prearranged routines.

Impact of Behavior Disorders on the Young Child

All young children, in the natural course of growth and development, may experience limited emotional upheavals or even minor socialization problems. Each child within that frame of reference acquires a tolerance for coping with emotions and handling involvements in nonself-directed activities. Accepting the authority of others and a willingness to follow another's lead are but a few of the many social graces that most children learn to accept. There are those children, however, who may swing erratically from one side of a flexibility scale to the other. Personality differences can influence a child's movement from one extreme to the other.

It is quite appropriate for a young child to be agreeable at one stage of development and negative at another. However, it is the recognition of serious interruptions in the expected pattern of coping mechanisms that is important. Inappropriate responses can be one of the first clues to a series of deeper emotional problems.

Early identification of emotional difficulties can provide assistance to both the family and the child if support is necessary, but early identification does not guarantee services. Identification will suggest that there is a need for some assistance. There is, then, the need for an acceptance of the problem and a generalized plan to work toward a solution.

Young children's involvement with peers of their own age in play exploration and groups offer an excellent resource for the development of good socialization skills. Opportunities for children with problems to participate in structured play activities is one of many treatment models. These models will be discussed in greater depth in Chapter 8.

Gifted and Talented

Children referred to as *gifted and talented* are another category of exceptional children. These children are considered exceptional because they deviate markedly from the normal population and require special educational procedures. Of course, it is obvious that these children are not handicapped in the same sense as the other children described in this book. The category of giftedness, however, is recognized by the Department of Education and many state and local school districts. The Office of Gifted and Talented is part of the Office of Special Education and Rehabilitative Services. Teachers who work with young children should be aware of the characteristics of this type of child.

Symptoms of Giftedness and Talent

By contrast with the other categories of exceptionality previously mentioned, gifted children demonstrate talents that are above, rather than below, the average. These talents take many forms. Giftedness can involve creativity as well as above-average intellectual capacity as defined in Chapter 1.

The inclusion of many kinds of talent to the definition of giftedness gives a greater breadth to the category. Outstanding talent may come in a variety of forms, requiring very specialized assistance from those accomplished professionals capable of recognizing such talent and making further recommendations.

Methods used in the identification of the gifted include standard-ized measures of mental ability and teacher nomination through check-lists or direct observation. However, the early identification of giftedness is not a simple task.

Several summaries of creativity traits have been compiled by Lucito (1974) to provide a variety of means for identifying the gifted and talented child. Renzulli (1973) attempted to identify gifted children in a minority population by requiring them to evaluate everyday reactions to ordinary situations. The results were mappings of student-structured learning styles which demonstrated creativity and inventiveness as a measure of outstanding problem solving.

Impact of Gifted and Talented Abilities on the Young Child

One of the major questions in working with gifted children is whether to accelerate their education or to provide enriched experiences without speeding up the educational process. In many research reports, accel-eration was found to result in good achievement, adjustment, and vocational success. In spite of the reported success of acceleration, it has not been accepted as a general practice. There is still concern for the mixing of chronological ages and the unique differences that each age exhibits. One way to accelerate giftedness is with early formal education. Some gifted children do apply for early entrance to school and begin their formal education prior to the age of five.

Whether to place gifted children in separate ability-ranked groups has been debated for years. Those who support ability grouping do so because they say it gives the bright children an opportunity to stimulate each other. This also allows a new set of leaders to rise in the less competent groups. Often, within a mixed ability class, the verbally competent child will monopolize class discussions and inhibit the others from participating. The opponents of ability grouping cite the need for all students to develop democratic principles usually gained from working within all levels of academic ability.

Current curricular innovations with more flexible grouping plans and individualized instructional objectives offer less emphasis on group participation and more on independent activities. Now groups of children may meet for limited specific instructional activities which are vital for the academic subjects while other groups are gathered for general socialization purposes. In this way, students can begin to set their own pace for work and attain a performance level which they can accept or change. More and more independent activity is in progress earlier in the child's school experience; these opportunities stimulate a child to produce in a self-directed fashion.

There has been attention given to the demonstrated success of the gifted child in regular educational settings. The argument is made that the gifted will seek out and learn in any environment. That might be true for the middle-class child; however, less motivated children may never reach their potential due to a lack of awareness. *No one knows to what levels of attainment a child would have risen when no attempt to assist the child was ever made.* Predictions are extremely difficult to make without some investment and monitoring of the outcome. The undiscovered will remain the unknown.

The academically bright child is usually taken for granted; some are even given greater pressures to perform within more meticulously outlined parameters. For example, the bright child may be given increased quantities of work to complete which may be dull and drill-like.

Special programs for the gifted have been called elitist, and the trend to train the more competent has received minimal support from state and federal funding sources. In many instances, the gifted programs have grown within schools due to teachers' interest and have called attention to themselves by word of mouth. Parents have been known to be the best public relations experts, and a brief hint that a gifted program is to be instituted can almost guarantee a full registry.

Within any specialized programs for the gifted, the continued use of explorative environments is important. It is necessary for all young children to have opportunities for creative experiences. The freedom to explore and test with alternative media and materials is a significant facet of a good gifted curriculum. Creativity will surface when the child's environment supports that growth. Young gifted children must be allowed to practice and experiment in environments which are open and stimulating.

Summary

Exceptional preschool children represent all areas of exceptional children. The term used to designate each area of special education is "categories." Because of a variety of problems with categorizing and labeling, most preschool programs are organized along noncategorical lines.

Children with visual impairment can be classified as either blind or partially sighted. The auditory impaired include the deaf and the hard-of-hearing. The impact on learning will depend upon many factors including degree of severity and the age of onset.

The concept of mental retardation has changed much in the past few years. The new definition includes both low performance on intelligence measures and poor adaptive behavior.

Some young children suffer from physical, genetic, and birth defects. There are a variety of conditions that can cause these defects. Prenatal diagnosis has been successful in identifying defects.

Speech and language disorders characterize a large number of children in early childhood special education programs. Speech refers to the production of language (articulation and voice). Language is the cognitive foundation underlying the speech. Disorders can be found in one or both areas.

Many exceptional young children have specific learning disabilities. This handicap is defined as a severe discrepancy between potential and achievement. It affects a variety of learning areas in the young child, especially oral expression and listening comprehension. Another characteristic of these children is an attention deficit.

Behavior disorders describe children who do not react in an appropriate social manner. They can be aggressive or withdrawn. Severe behavior disorders in infancy or at the preschool age may be identified as infantile autism.

Gifted and talented children are also found among preschoolers. These children need special educational planning so that they, too, can reach their potential. The gifted and talented child usually performs above rather than below the average child. Giftedness may include creative talents as well as above-average intellectual capacity.

Review Questions

TERMS TO KNOW

a. *visual impairment*

b. *auditory impairment*

c. *mental retardation*

d. *physical, genetic, and birth defects*

e. *speech and language disorders*

f. *specific learning disabilities*

g. *behavior disorders*

h. *gifted and talented*

i. *strabismus*

j. *infantile autism*

k. *convulsive disorder*

l. *decibel*

m. *conductive hearing loss*

n. *Spina Bifida*

1. List two purposes served by the use of categories of special education. Explain one disadvantage.
2. What is a self-fulfilling prophecy? How is that term applied in this chapter?
3. Describe the differences between the blind child and one with partial sight. List five of the symptoms of visual problems.

4. Prelanguage and postlanguage deafness are terms used to describe functional hearing loss. Explain each.
5. What are three of the more significant symptoms by which a parent could detect a hearing loss in a small child? Make them applicable to the parent-child interaction within the home.
6. How is the 1973 definition of mental retardation different from the traditional EMH and TMH classifications?
7. Are a developmental disability and a learning disability different? Explain.
8. There are several methods to diagnose atypical development prenatally. List three methods and explain each.

References

ADKINS, P., and others. Factor Analyses of the de Hirsch Predictive Index. *Perceptual and Motor Skills,* Part 2, 1971, 33(2), 1319–1325.

ANASTASI, A. *Psychological Testing,* 4th ed. New York: Macmillan, 1976.

BIGGE, J., and B. SIRVIS. Children with Physical and Multiple Disabilities, in *Behavior of Exceptional Children,* 2nd ed., ed. N. G. Haring. Columbus, Ohio: Chas. E. Merrill, 1978.

BOBATH, K., and B. Bobath. Cerebral Palsy, in *Physical Therapy Services in the Developmental Disabilities,* eds. P. Pearson and C. E. Williams. Springfield, Ill.: Chas. C. Thomas, 1975.

BOWER, E. M. *Early Identification of Emotionally Handicapped Children in School,* 2nd ed. Springfield, Ill.: Chas. C. Thomas, 1969.

BRONSON, G. W. The Postnatal Growth of Visual Capacity. *Child Development,* 1974, 45, 873–890.

CALDWELL, B. M. The Rationale for Early Intervention. *Exceptional Children,* 1970, 36, 717–726.

CARROLL, J. B. Language Development in Children, in *Psycholinguistics,* ed. S. Saporta. New York: Holt, Rinehart & Winston, 1961.

COOPER, L. Z. Rubella: A Preventable Cause of Birth Defects, in Birth Defects: Original article series, *Intrauterine Infections,* Vol. 4, New York: National Foundation March of Dimes, 1964, pp. 23–25.

COOPER, L. Z., and S. KRUGMAN. Diagnosis and Management: Congenital Rubella. *Pediatrics,* 1966, 37, 335.

DAVIDSON, J. B., and others. *Directory of Developmental Screening Instruments.* Minneapolis: Minneapolis Public Schools, 1977.

DAVIS, H, and S. R. SILVERMAN, eds. *Hearing and Deafness.* New York: Holt, Rinehart & Winston, 1970.

DE HIRSCH, K. *Predicting Reading Failure.* New York: Harper & Row, 1966.

DONLON, E. T., and L. F. BURTON. *The Severely and Profoundly Handicapped: A Practical Approach to Teaching.* New York: Grune & Stratton, 1976.

DUNN, L. M., ed. *Exceptional Children in the Schools: Special Education in Transition.* New York: Holt, Rinehart & Winston, 1973.

EISENBERG, R. B. *Auditory Competence in Early Life*. Baltimore, Md.: University Park Press, 1976.

GADDES, W. H. Prevalence Estimates and the Need for Definition of Learning Disabilities, in *The Neuropsychology of Learning Disorders*, eds. M. Knights and J. Bakker. Baltimore, Md.: University Park Press, 1976.

GALLAGHER, J. J. Children with Developmental Imbalances: A Psychoeducational Definition, in *The Teacher of Brain-Injured Children*, ed. W. Cruickshank. Syracuse, N.Y.: Syracuse University Press, 1966.

GOLLAY, E. The Modified Definition of Developmental Disabilities: An Initial Exploration. HEW Contract #105–78–5003, Rehabilitation Services Administration, March, 1979.

GROSSMAN, H. J., ed. *Manual on Terminology and Classification in Mental Retardation* (1973 revision). Washington, D.C.: American Association on Mental Deficiency, 1973.

HALLAHAN, D., and J. KAUFFMAN. *Exceptional Children*. Englewood Cliffs, N.J.: Prentice-Hall, Inc., 1978.

HARING, N. G. Perspectives in Special Education. In *Behavior of Exceptional Children: An Introduction to Special Education*, ed. N. G. Haring. Columbus, Ohio: Chas. E. Merrill, 1974, 1978.

HAYDEN, A., and V. DMITRIEV. *New Perspectives on Children With Down's Syndrome*. Paper presented at Down's Syndrome Congress, Milwaukee, Wisconsin, September, 1974.

HEBER, R., and others. *Rehabilitation of Families at Risk of Mental Retardation, A Progress Report*. Madison, Wisconsin: University of Wisconsin, 1974.

HOBBS, N., ed. *Issues in the Classification of Children*. 2 Vols. San Francisco: Jossey-Bass, 1975.

ILLINOIS SOCIETY FOR THE PREVENTION OF BLINDNESS. *Amblyopia*. Chicago, Ill.: Illinois Society for the Prevention of Blindness, no date.

JANSKY, J., and K. DE HIRSCH. *Preventing Reading Failure*. New York: Harper & Row, 1972.

JENSEN, A. R. How Can We Boost IQ and Scholastic Achievement? *Harvard Educational Review*, 1969, 39, 1–11.

JENSEN, A. *Bias in Mental Testing*. New York: MacMillan, 1979.

JOHNSTON, R. B., and P. R. MAGRAB. *Developmental Disorders: Assessment, Treatment, Education*. Baltimore, Md.: University Park Press, 1976.

KAUFFMAN, J. M. *Characteristics of Children's Behavior Disorders*. Columbus, Ohio: Chas. E. Merrill, 1977.

KEOGH, B. K. Psychological evaluation of exceptional children; old hangups and new directions. *Journal of School Psychology*, 1972, 10, 141–146.

KEOGH, B. K., and L. D. BECKER. Early Detection of Learning Problems: Questions, Cautions and Guidelines. *Exceptional Children*, 1973, 40, 5–11.

KIRK, S. A. *Behavioral Diagnosis and Remediation of Learning Disabilities*. Conference on Exploration into the Problems of the Perceptually Handicapped Child. Evanston, Ill.: Fund for the Perceptually Handicapped Child, 1963.

KIRK, S. A. *Educating Exceptional Children*. Boston: Houghton Mifflin, 1972.

KIRK, S. A., and F. E. LORD, eds. *Exceptional Children: Educational Resources and Perspectives*. Boston: Houghton Mifflin, 1974.

KIRK, S., and KIRK, W. *Psycholinguistic Learning Disabilities.* New York: John Wiley, 1971.

KIRK, S., J. KLIEBHAN, and J. LERNER. *Teaching Reading to Slow and Disabled Learners.* Boston: Houghton Mifflin, 1978.

LANSKY, L. L. *Pediatric Neurology.* New York: Medical Examination Publishing Co., 1975.

LENNENBERG, E. *Biological Foundations of Language.* New York: John Wiley, 1967.

LERNER, J. *Learning Disabilities: Theories, Diagnosis and Teaching Strategies.* 3rd ed. Boston: Houghton Mifflin, 1981.

LUCITO, L. The Creative, in *Identification of the Gifted and Talented,* ed. R. Martinson. Ventura, Calif., June 21–23, 1974.

MARDELL, C., and D. GOLDENBERG. *Learning Disabilities Early Childhood Research Project.* Office of the Superintendent of Public Instruction, State of Illinois, Springfield, Illinois, August, 1972.

MARDELL, C., and D. GOLDENBERG. *The Predictive Validation of a Prekindergarten Screening Test.* Paper presented at International Conference of IFLD, Montreal, Canada, 1976.

MATUSIAK, I. *Preschool Screening for Exceptional Education Needs in a Large Urban Setting.* Doctoral Dissertation, Milwaukee, Wisconsin, June 1976.

MAYER, C. L. State Master Planning for Special Education: A National Survey of Current Status. *Journal of Learning Disabilities,* 1974, 9, 633–637.

MCCARTHY, D. Language Development in Children, in *Manual of Child Psychology,* ed. L. Carmichael. New York: John Wiley, 1954.

MEIER, J. *Developmental and Learning Disabilities.* Baltimore, Md.: University Park Press, 1976.

MENDELSON, M. J., and M. M. HAITH. *The Relationship Between Audition and Vision in the Human Newborn.* Monograph for the Society for Research in Child Development, 1976, 41 (4) (167).

MEYERS, P., and D. HAMMILL. *Methods for Learning Disorders.* New York: John Wiley, 1976.

MILLAR, S. Spatial Representation of Blind-Sighted Children. *Journal of Experimental Child Psychology,* 1976, 21, 460–479.

MYKLEBUST, H. *The Psychology of Deafness.* New York: Grune and Stratton, 1964.

PRESIDENT'S COMMITTEE ON MENTAL RETARDATION. *Mental Retardation, Past and Present.* Washington, D.C.: DHEW Pub. (OHD) 176–43579, 1977.

RENZULLI, J. Talent Potential in Minority Group Students. *Exceptional Children,* 1973, 39, 437–444.

ROSS, A. O. *Psychological Disorders of Children: A Behavioral Approach to Theory, Research and Therapy.* New York: McGraw-Hill, 1974.

SARFF, L. W. *A Comparison of the DIAL Variables and the PPVT Variables.* Doctoral Dissertation, Walden University, July 1974.

STRAUSS, A. A., and L. E. LEHTINEN. *Psychopathology and Education of the Brain-Injured Child.* New York: Grune & Stratton, 1947.

TARJIAN, G., and others. Natural History of Mental Retardation: Some Aspects of Epidemiology. *American Journal of Mental Deficiency,* 1973, 77(4), 367–379.

THOMAS, A., and S. CHESS. *Temperament and Development.* New York: Brunner-Mazel, 1977.

TORGESON, J. What Shall We Do With Psychological Processes? *Journal of Learning Disabilities,* 1979, 514–521.

WIEDERHOLT, J. L. Historical Perspectives on the Education of the Learning Disabled, in *The Second Review of Special Education,* eds. L. Mann and D. Sabatino. Philadelphia: Journal of Special Education Press, 1974.

WILSON, J. D. and others. Early Intervention: The Right to Sight. *Education for the Visually Handicapped,* 1976, 8, 83–90.

WOODEN, H. Deaf and Hard-of-Hearing Children, in *Exceptional Children in the Schools,* ed. L. Dunn. New York: Holt, Rinehart & Winston, 1963, pp. 339–412.

ZAUSMER, E., S. PUESCHEL and A. SHEA. *A Sensori-Motor Stimulation Program for the Young Child with Down's Syndrome: Preliminary Report.* MCH Exchange, 1972, 2(4), 1–4.

Assessment: Locating, Screening, and Diagnosing the Child

Chapter **Three**

Our society is increasingly seeking to prevent the occurrence of diseases rather than placing total emphasis on curing a disease once it has occurred. As a result, the process of assessment or evaluation of young children takes on new importance. There is an increased emphasis in promoting health and there are increased funds for preventive health care. However, one should always keep in mind that young children are more difficult to assess than older children or adults. One can even assume that the younger the child, the less valid and reliable are predictions across all measurable dimensions. Despite the measurement problems, the movement towards early assessment continues, for there is general agreement that early identification may eliminate or ameliorate problems, minimize formation of undesirable habit patterns, while reducing frustration and emotional reactions. The ultimate goal of assessment is to improve the child's general welfare.

Overview of Assessment

Assessment is the total system of selecting those children who should receive special services required by their unique characteristics and needs in specific areas of behavior. This is a complex task, particularly due to the more subtle types of handicapping conditions which cannot be readily observed. Obvious or severe handicaps are often recognized at birth (that is, physical abnormalities. Down's Syndrome) or shortly thereafter. One widely used measurement of infants is the *Apgar Rating*. Five easily observed signs—heart rate, respiratory effort, muscle tone, reflex response, and color are rated both one minute and five minutes after delivery. The rating scale goes from 0 (poor) to 2 (good); thus the best possible score is 10 (Apgar 1965). Another tool gaining popularity, the *Brazelton Neonatal Scale,* is a more detailed examination which identifies abnormalities in the sensory abilities and the central nervous system (Brazelton 1973).

Once the infant leaves the hospital, recognition of problems becomes dependent upon parents, relatives, and friends who may have no means

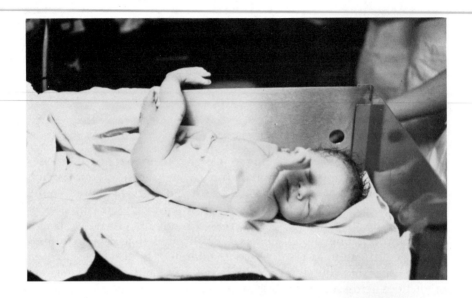

of comparison or background in normal child development. The *Guide to Normal Milestones of Development* (Haynes 1966) lists signs of development at intervals from one month through thirty-six months to assist primary caregivers. Too often pediatricians have little time for developmental assessment and limit their concerns to physical health and growth. Thus, problems are not recognized during a critical time when appropriate services can have the greatest impact.

Children should receive a comprehensive health examination at

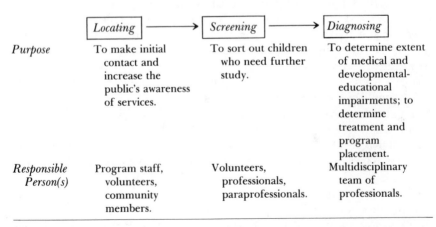

	Locating ⟶	Screening ⟶	Diagnosing
Purpose	To make initial contact and increase the public's awareness of services.	To sort out children who need further study.	To determine extent of medical and developmental-educational impairments; to determine treatment and program placement.
Responsible Person(s)	Program staff, volunteers, community members.	Volunteers, professionals, paraprofessionals.	Multidisciplinary team of professionals.

Figure 3–1 An Overview of Assessment *Adapted from L. Cross and K. Goin, eds.* Identifying Handicapped Children. *New York: Walker & Co., 1977, p. 5.*

regular intervals during the preschool years. The purpose of such a systematic assessment is treatment of problems as early as possible. According to Friedlander (1975), less than half of American children receive regular systematic health care before they go to school. In addition, that part of the population which has the least contact with health services is the most likely to have developmental problems. These facts led to the establishment of *Early, Periodic Screening, Diagnosis, and Treatment* (EPSDT) in 1967, a federal program for approximately 12 million individuals from birth to twenty-one years of age in Medicaid eligible families. More recent legislation, the *Child Health Assessment Act,* enables children from other than low-income families to take advantage of these preventive health care services.

Assessment can be divided into three processes which will be defined and described in depth: (1) locating; (2) screening; and (3) diagnosing. Figure 3–1 outlines the total procedure (Cross and Goin 1977).

Nature of the Locating Process

Locating handicapped or potentially handicapped children who will profit from early intervention services can be accomplished through a systematic process (Cross 1976). The locating process is the first stage in total assessment. It includes any or all of the following activities:

- Defining the target population
- Increasing the public's awareness of services
- Encouraging referrals
- Canvassing the community for children in need of services

This is the basis of *Child Find,* a federal program which mandates states to actively seek out those handicapped children who are currently unserved, underserved, or inappropriately served. This process of locating handicapped children is also called *casefinding* (Cross and Goin 1977).

Defining the Target Population

The definition of the target population (both *age limits,* that is, zero to five, three to five, and so on and *types of handicapping conditions,* that is, physical handicaps, mental handicaps, emotional problems, and so on) will affect every aspect of the total assessment procedure, particularly prevalence rate. For purposes of this chapter, the discussion is limited to the location of all preschool children (zero to five years of age) who will profit from early intervention services because they have a disability or delay of some type. Children who for physical, social, intellectual, emotional, or communicative problems will need additional or special assistance in order to succeed in school and/or society are those being sought. The goal is to locate every eligible, handicapped child in this target population. This group of children would be those referred to in P.L. 94–142 as handicapped children entitled to a free appropriate public education. Thus, defining the population is a systematic "needs assessment."

Increasing the Public's Awareness of Services

The success of the location process is dependent upon informing the community of the importance of early identification. This can take the form of press releases, bulletins, brochures, radio and television spot announcements, posters, and flyers sent home with school children. Referral postcards can be distributed in utility bills, welfare checks, bank statements, school mailings, and payroll checks to name but a few means of spreading the message. Many federal and state agencies have made tremendous strides since 1974 to develop effective "child find" systems which include public awareness. An admirable attempt to put these data together was sponsored by Project SEARCH and the National Association of State Directors of Special Education (Cronin and Schipper 1976).

The responsibility of recognizing developmental problems cannot be left to parents alone. Free vision, hearing, and developmental check-ups should be encouraged for all children, not just those children whose parents may suspect a problem.

The strategies for increasing the public's awareness vary throughout the country. A specific technique that may work in one locale, with a certain population, and for a certain problem, might not be effective in a similar area across town. Variables which affect the selection of strategies include local customs, size of the target population, literacy and economic levels of the community, and availability and type of transportation.

Zehrbach (1975) experimented with various means of informing the public of available services. He found that a mass mailing, an open house, radio and television spots, and press releases were less effective than flyers sent home with school-age children and a telephone survey. His community was basically a rural, midwestern population.

Certain principles seem important to address regardless of the particular population. These should be used in planning a public awareness campaign:

1. *Understand the nature and intricacies of the community.* Any community, regardless of size, is a series of small groups that need to be treated separately in terms of locating potentially handicapped children.

2. *Emphasize the nature of normal child development,* the nature of exceptional developmental patterns and their early signs, the need for early intervention, the available services, and the right to a free and appropriate education.

3. *Develop a broad-based, multidimensional system.* This will insure overlapping contact and will increase chances of finding all handicapped children. This effort need not be more expensive if planned well.

4. *Determine prior to the effort what "success" will be and how it will be measured.* Variables to consider are cost, time, percentage of children found in the effort, creation of public atmosphere (either positive or negative), and general spin-off effect to other agencies in the community. Evaluation need not be complex, just consistent and thorough.

The most important aspect of the public awareness effort is to make sure the parents view the activity positively. Schools need to create the feeling of *helping* in a cooperative way if this portion of identification is to succeed.

Encouraging Referrals

Agencies which serve both handicapped and nonhandicapped children, daycare centers, nursery schools, and pediatricians are all excellent contacts to establish awareness of services and also as referral sources. Other private practitioners, such as psychiatrists, psychologists, dentists, orthopedists, optometrists, neurologists, and therapists, should be informed of the population sought and the range of services offered. In addition, coordination is necessary with the public health department, the welfare department, mental health clinics, family services, the state department of education, local colleges and universities with training programs in early childhood and/or special education, hospitals, medical schools, civic organizations, and religious groups. Parents are also an important potential referral source. Project Child in New Jersey (Winkler 1975) reported that one of every two parents who suspected a potential learning problem was found to be correct by actual clinical follow-up. However, this does not mean that parents can *always* recognize that their child needs special services.

A door-to-door census designed to locate and register all children below school age in a particular community has been found to be one of the most effective child-find procedures (Cross 1976; Zehrbach 1975). Macy (1976), however, reports varying success in a large metropolitan area with door knocking. Generally, this procedure was least productive in low socioeconomic areas due to the small number of people at home during the daytime hours. As more mothers join the labor force, this will be an increasing barrier. A telephone survey can also be part of this canvassing process, provided most families in the community own telephones. Both techniques are time consuming and costly. Thus, they require the use of volunteers and ample funding for complete effectiveness.

Nature of the Screening Process

Screening is an efficient sorting out process by which individuals who may have certain characteristics are separated from the general population. In the area of screening for potential high-risk learners, that is children with handicaps or potential handicaps, a screening process sorts out children who *may* need special attention (about 10 to 12 percent of the total population) from those who do not. Through specific diagnosis and evaluation, this suspicion is confirmed or denied. The purpose of screening is to move up the time of identification in order to implement treatment earlier. The method "must be appropriate and reasonable with regard to the economics of time, money and resources for dealing with large numbers of persons" (Lessler 1974, p. 609). North (1974) urges medical and educational screening be combined in the interests of cost, convenience, and effectiveness. Figure 3–2 lists many of the conditions which have been recommended for pediatric screening programs (Frankenburg and Camp 1975).

The screening process is the second stage in total assessment. It should be viewed as a continuous spiraling process, beginning at preconception and repeated periodically throughout life. Screening includes any or all of the following activities:

- Selecting conditions to be screened
- Selecting test(s)
- Training staff
- Screening children
- Reporting results

Anemia	Language
Bacteriuria	Lead Poisoning
Color Blindness	Learning Disorders
Congenital Dislocation of Hip	Maple Syrup Urine Disease
Congenital Heart Disease	Mellituria
Cretinism	Phenylketonuria
Dental Problems	Rheumatic Heart Disease
Development	School Readiness
Gargoylism	Sex Chromosome Abnormalities
Galactosemia	Speech
Glucose-6-Phosphate Dehydrogenase	Succinylcholinesterase Deficiency
Deficiency	Tay-Sachs Disease
Hearing	Tuberculosis
Hereditary Angioneurotic Edema	Venereal Disease
Hypercholesterolemia	Vision
Hyperlipoproteinemia	Wilson's Disease
Inguinal Hernia	

Figure 3–2 Conditions Currently Recommended for Screening Programs *Adapted from W. Frankenburg and B. Camp, eds.* Pediatric Screening Tests. *Springfield, Ill.: Chas. C. Thomas, 1975, p. 9.*

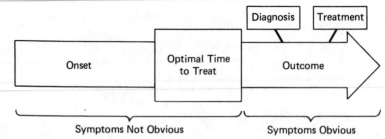

Figure 3–3 **Progression of a Handicapping Condition** *From E. Kazuk and others.* Introduction to Pediatric Screening. *Denver: University of Colorado Medical School, 1974.*

Selecting Conditions to Be Screened

Kazuk, Cohrs, and Frankenburg (1974) list six criteria for selecting conditions which necessitate screening procedures:

1. The conditions are treatable or controllable.
2. The prognosis is improved by early detection and treatment.
3. The screening time is adequate. Figures 3–3 and 3–4 illustrate the progression of a handicapping condition and the effect of screening.
4. Firm diagnosis is possible. The conditions can be recognized as present or absent.
5. The prevalence rate is high enough to warrant screening but not high enough to warrant diagnosing every child.
6. The conditions are serious or potentially serious if left untreated.

It is generally unnecessary to screen for severe handicaps. Such children are usually identified during the locating process, and they would proceed directly to the diagnostic process.

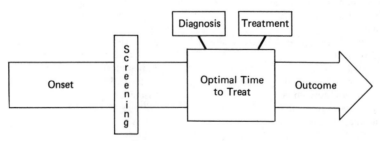

Figure 3–4 **Effects of Screening** *From E. Kazuk and others.* Introduction to Pediatric Screening. *Denver: University of Colorado Medical School, 1974.*

A good example of a screening instrument or test is the clinical thermometer. It sorts out those who have a fever from those who do not. It does not give the cause of the fever (etiology) nor does it give the treatment.

Thus, a screening test for identifying children who may be in need of further services is one that can be routinely administered by a technician or examiner with special limited training to large numbers of children in a relatively short period of time at a modest cost during the asymptomatic stages. The interpretations of such a test by a qualified examiner would also require little professional time. A screening test cannot stand alone and may not be used for purposes of intervention, placement, or treatment because it does not provide specific information which will pinpoint atypical development or deficiencies. Its function is to identify those in need of full assessment or diagnostic evaluation.

Screening tests are currently available which look at all areas of development in young children. Tests should be selected according to predetermined criteria established by the person or committee in charge of the screening process. Parent input is also crucial.

Some possible questions that should be considered in the test selection process are:

1. *Is the screening test valid or accurate?* Supporting data in the manual should report on content, concurrent, and predictive validity studies. Predictive validity is the most important factor for a screening test.

2. *Can the test be administered in a short length of time?* Procedures must be short due to young children's short attention span and the cost factor of screening large numbers of children. The length of the test is also affected by the test's efficiency. The test should have a well-organized scoresheet, clear, specific directions, and explicit scoring standards.

3. *What problems are being screened for?* Where there are services and referral agencies available, handicaps should be considered as primary problems. As a secondary consideration, other problems can be screened for planning purposes.

4. *Are the costs of screening reasonable?* This is dependent on the budget, the initial cost of the test, and purchase of consumable items (that is, forms), maintenance, depreciation, and the utilization of volunteers and paraprofessionals. The cost of screening should be compared to the cost of treatment after the usual time of diagnosis and to the human grief spared by early intervention. This is illustrated in Figure 3–5 (Kazuk, Cohrs, and Frankenburg 1974).

5. *Is the test scored objectively so results are reliable?* Objective scoring is of particular importance when using people other than professionals in

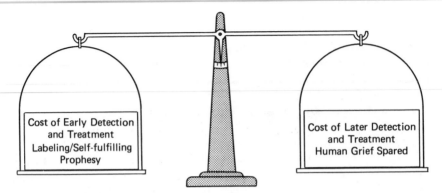

Figure 3–5   Cost of Screening vs. Cost of Treatment Later *Adapted from E. Kazuk and others.* Introduction to Pediatric Screening. *Denver: University of Colorado Medical School, 1974.*

the administration so that results are reproducible regardless of the tester. There should also be test-retest reliability.

6. *Is the test physically and psychologically harmless and nonthreatening to both child and parent?* A good round-up screening procedure, whether at a well-baby clinic, a local church, school, or park district building, can establish goodwill and strong positive public relations if it is seen as a good use of funds and time by the general public. Gamelike procedures and materials and a relaxed atmosphere where coffee is available and socializing can take place aid in establishing such a feeling. Parents and children should not be separated from each other for this only produces unnecessary anxiety.

7. *Is the test accepted by the specialists who will do the diagnosis?* The easiest way to accomplish this acceptance is to involve these specialists in the selection of the screening test(s) whenever possible.

8. *Who will administer the screening test?* It is important to determine that trained paraprofessionals, volunteers, and parents can administer the test, saving the professional staff for the diagnostic process. Service organizations, such as Kiwanis, Junior Women's League, parent-teacher associations, and retired-citizen groups, can all play important roles in this process. Students in testing courses are another source of people who can help. One cautionary note regards confidentiality. All screening staff should be reminded that parent and child rights of privacy must be respected as a matter of human ethics and law.

9. *Was the test normed on children similar to those in the population to be screened?* The test manual should state the age range, sex, race, socioeconomic status, and other demographic characteristics of the population on which the test was standardized. This may avoid the use of standards derived from the performances of white, middle-class children as the comparison basis for the performance of minority children. However,

even when using a test on a population with similar characteristics, substantially different results may be obtained (Krakow, Kelfer, and Reinherg 1978).

10. *Is the test both sensitive and specific?* That is, does it identify most of the children who should be identified (inclusion index) without identifying too many children who should not go through the diagnostic procedures (exclusion index)? Frankenburg and Camp (1975) have devised formulae for determining these two factors of sensitivity and specificity.

11. *After the process is completed, does the screening test(s) selected continue to meet these criteria?* The screening test can be a powerful and effective technique when it is used carefully and realistically.

Many lists of available screening instruments appear in the literature (Cross and Goin 1977; Davidson, and others 1977; Fallen and McGovern 1978; Frankenburg and Camp 1975; Hare and Hare 1977; Hoepfner, and others 1971; Johnson 1979; Jordan, and others 1977; Mardell and Goldenberg 1973; Matusiak 1976, Meier 1976; Safford 1978; Zeitlin 1976). They deal with age range of test, time of administration, training level of person administering the test, developmental skills or domains covered by the test, and whether the test screens or diagnoses. The Test Collection Bulletin, published quarterly by Educational Testing Service, is a current source of this information. Appendix A presents a listing of widely used screening tests for young children.

Caution in test selection must be stressed. According to a recent study of forty-four preschool assessment tests available nationally, only five met the American Psychological Association (APA) guidelines for educational and psychological tests, as reported by Berman (1977).

Examples of Comprehensive Screening Tests

Screening and diagnostic instruments which address themselves to one particular developmental domain will be discussed later in this chapter. The trend, however, has been to develop comprehensive screening or diagnostic systems which test many different areas of development. Three examples of such screening tests are the *Denver Developmental Screening Test* (Frankenburg, Dodds, and Fandal 1970), *Developmental Indicators for the Assessment of Learning* (Mardell and Goldenberg 1972, 1975), and the *Developmental Screening Inventory* (Knobloch and Pasamanick 1974).

The *Denver Developmental Screening Test* (DDST) was designed according to a medical model for use in identifying young children who may have developmental problems. It is administered individually and

DENVER DEVELOPMENTAL SCREENING TEST

Date

Name

Birthdate

Hosp. No.

STO. = STOMACH
SIT = SITTING

PERCENT OF CHILDREN PASSING
25   50   75   90

May pass by report →

Footnote No. - →
see back of form

Test Item

PERSONAL-SOCIAL

FINE MOTOR-ADAPTIVE

MONTHS

YEARS

* 100% pass at birth

PERSONAL-SOCIAL items:

REGARDS FACE

SMILES RESPONSIVELY

SMILES SPONTANEOUSLY

INITIALLY SHY WITH STRANGERS

PLAYS PAT-A-CAKE

FEEDS SELF CRACKERS

RESISTS TOY PULL

50%

PLAYS PEEK-A-BOO

WORKS FOR TOY OUT OF REACH

IMITATES HOUSEWORK

PUTS ON CLOTHING

USES SPOON, SPILLING LITTLE

PLAYS BALL WITH EXAMINER

WASHES & DRIES HANDS

BUTTONS UP

INDICATES WANTS (NOT CRY)

HELPS IN HOUSE – SIMPLE TASKS

DRESSES WITH SUPERVISION

DRINKS FROM CUP

PLAYS INTERACTIVE GAMES e.g., TAG

SEPARATES FROM MOTHER EASILY

REMOVES GARMENT

DRESSES WITHOUT SUPERVISION

FINE MOTOR-ADAPTIVE items:

FOLLOWS TO MIDLINE

EQUAL MOVEMENTS

*

FOLLOWS PAST MIDLINE

GRASPS RATTLE

REGARDS RAISIN

REACHES FOR OBJECT

FOLLOWS 180°

HANDS TOGETHER

SIT, LOOKS FOR YARN

SIT, TAKES 2 CUBES

RAKES RAISIN ATTAINS

PASSES CUBE HAND TO HAND

BANGS 2 CUBES HELD IN HANDS

THUMB-FINGER GRASP

NEAT PINCER GRASP OF RAISIN

SCRIBBLES SPONTANEOUSLY

TOWER OF 2 CUBES

TOWER OF 4 CUBES

DUMPS RAISIN FROM BOTTLE SPONT.

DUMPS RAISIN FROM BOTTLE-DEMONSTR

IMITATES VERTICAL LINE WITHIN 30°

TOWER OF 8 CUBES

IMITATES BRIDGE

COPIES O

COPIES +

DRAWS MAN 3 PARTS

PICKS LONGER LINE 3 OF 3

IMITATES DEMONSTR.

COPIES □

DRAWS MAN 6 PARTS

PERSONAL-SOCIAL

FINE MOTOR-ADAPTIVE

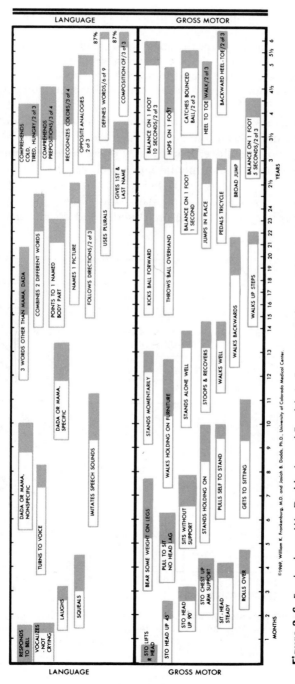

Figure 3-6 Frankenburg, W., Dodds, J., and Fandal, A. Denver Developmental Screening Test. Denver: Ladoca Publishing, 1970.

73

can be used with children aged two weeks to six years. The test consists
of 105 tasks which are grouped into four sectors:

    1. personal-social: the ability to get along with others and to care for
oneself;
    2. fine motor-adaptive: the ability to see and to use one's hands for
various purposes; ability to solve nonverbal problems;
    3. language: abilities related to hearing and speaking;
    4. gross motor: abilities such as sitting, walking, and jumping.

    A child of any given age will usually be tested on about twenty
items. Task norms indicate the age at which 25, 50, 75, and 90 percent
of boys, girls, and all children successfully complete each item. Cut-off
points for suspected developmental lags which require further testing
are given. Figure 3–6 shows the DDST scoresheet (see pp. 72–73).
    Developmental Indicators for the Assessment of Learning (DIAL) was
designed according to an educational model and covers the develop-

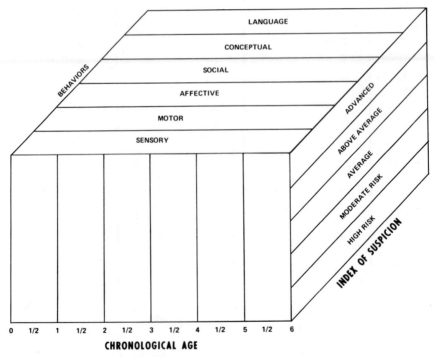

Figure 3–7   Dial Conceptual Model *From C. Mardell and D. Goldenberg.* Developmental Indicators for the Assessment of Learning Manual. *Edison, N.J.: Childcraft, 1972,
p. 26.*

mental areas of gross motor, fine motor, concepts, and language skills. Social and emotional factors are also considered but are used as an addition to the objective scores obtained in the screening process. These behaviors can be seen in the conceptual model (Figure 3–7). DIAL assesses all areas except sensory behaviors. The screening of vision and hearing is crucial and should be done in conjunction with developmental screening. Sensory screening scores can be recorded on the DIAL scoresheet (Figure 3–8).

The screening is accomplished by a team providing for individual assessment within a setting which simulates a typical early childhood setting, such as a nursery school or daycare center.

Another way to look at the skills tapped by DIAL can be found in Figure 3–9. Each DIAL item was analyzed to determine whether it tapped perceptual, memory, previous learning associations, kinesthetic awareness and coordination, and/or language skills. In addition, each DIAL item was analyzed in terms of input (visual, auditory, haptic) and output (verbal, motor) to identify strong and weak modalities (Figure 3–10).

One of the most comprehensive tests for children up to three years of age is the *Developmental Screening Inventory* (DSI) which consists of selected items from the *Gesell Developmental Schedule*. It covers the

Name _____

Address _____

Street _____ City _____ State _____

Phone No. _____

Parents' Names _____ Mother _____ Father _____

1 2 3 4

School _____

Child # _____

Hearing + −

Vision + −

Date Today _____

Birth Date _____

C. A. _____

Boy _____ Girl _____

yr. mo. day

DECISION		
OK	REDIAL	FOLLOW-UP

GROSS MOTOR

	SCALED SCORE			
	0	1	2	3
1. Throwing Right Left Both	0	1	2	3
2. Catching	0	1	2	3
3. Jumping	0	−	2	3
4. Hopping 1 2 3 4 5 R / 1 2 3 4 5 L	0	1-4	5-8	9-10
5. Skipping	0	1	2	3
6. Standing Still	0-9	10-19'	20-29'	30'
7. Balancing	0	1-2	3-4	5-6

TOTAL (Max.= 21) _____

TIME ___ Min. ___ Sec.

OBSERVATIONS 1 2 3 4 5 6 7 8 9 10 11 12

Age (Yrs.-Mos.)	Boy	Girl
3-3 - 3-5	5	5
3-6 - 3-8	6	6
3-9 - 3-11	7	7

Cut-off Points

Age (Yrs.-Mos.)	Boy	Girl
2-6 - 2-8	4	5
2-9 - 2-11	5	6
3-0 - 3-2	6	7

FINE MOTOR

	SCALED SCORE			
	0	1	2	3
1. Matching	0	1-3	4-7	8-10
2. Building	0	1	2	3
3. Cutting Right Left	0	1	2	3
4. Copying Shapes	0	1-5	6-9	10-12
5. Copying Letters	0	1-5	6-9	10-12
6. Touching Fingers Right Left	0	1	2	3
7. Clapping Hands	0	1	2	3

TOTAL (Max.= 21) _____

TIME ___ Min. ___ Sec.

OBSERVATIONS 1 2 3 4 5 6 7 8 9 10 11 12

Age (Yrs.-Mos.)	Boy	Girl
4-0 - 4-2	12	13
4-3 - 4-5	13	14
4-6 - 4-8	14	15

CONCEPTS

	SCALED SCORE			
	0	1	2	3
1. Sorting Blocks	0	1-5	6-8	9-12
2. Naming Colors R Y B G O P	0	1-5	6-10	11-12
3. Counting 1 2 3 4 5 6 7 8 1 3 5	0	1-4	5-12	13
4. Positioning on under next back front	0	1-2	3-4	5
5. Following Directions	0	1	2	3
6. Identifying Concepts □ big □ little / □ fast □ slow / □ hot □ cold / □ long □ short / □ empty □ full / □ day □ night / □ more □ less	0	1-5	6-11	12-14
7. Identifying Body Parts □ Mouth □ Chin / □ Eye □ Elbow / □ Nose □ Shoulder / □ Ear □ Ankle / □ Neck □ Hip / □ Knee □ Wrist	0	1-4	5-8	9-12

TOTAL (Max.= 21) _____

TIME ___ Min. ___ Sec.

OBSERVATIONS 1 2 3 4 5 6 7 8 9 10 11 12

Age (Yrs.-Mos.)	Boy	Girl
4-9 - 4-11	15	16
5-0 - 5-2	16	17
5-3 - 5-5	17	18

COMMUNICATIONS

	SCALED SCORE			
	0	1	2	3
1. Articulating bed hammer fork tail / knife wagon dog fish / match king lamp dress / pin garbage rat chair	0-16	17-21	22-26	27-32
2. Remembering [2] [5-3] [7-1-4] I am a big boy (girl). Grass is green in the summer. Alligators always brush their teeth.	0	1-3	4-5	6
3. Naming Nouns, Verbs dog car eating / fish TV swimming / horse train walking / bird phone flying / cat sleeping / girl washing	0-16	17-24	25-30	31-32
4. Coping hungry 0 1 2 / sleepy 0 1 2 / cold 0 1 2 / toy 0 1 2	0-4	5-6	7-8	—
5. Naming Self, Age & Sex	0-1	2	3	4
6. Classifying Foods	0	1-3	4-5	6
7. Telling a Story noun pron. adj. verb adv. conj. prep. interj.	0-1	2-4	5-8	—
Sentence Length	0-2	3-4	5-6	—

TOTAL (Max.= 21) _____

TIME ___ Min. ___ Sec.

OBSERVATIONS 1 2 3 4 5 6 7 8 9 10 11 12

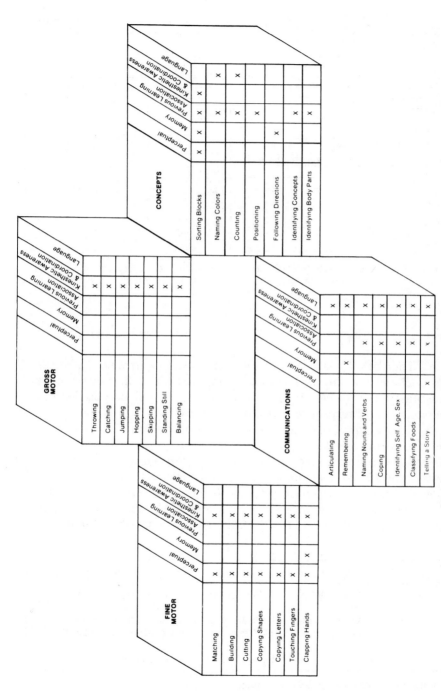

Figure 3–9 Dial Area Codes *From C. Mardell and D. Goldenberg. Developmental Indicators for the Assessment of Learning Manual. Edison, N.J.: Childcraft, 1972, p. 31.*

GROSS MOTOR					
	INPUT			OUTPUT	
Items	Visual	Auditory	Haptic	Verbal	Motor
Throwing	x	x			x
Catching	x	x	x		x
Jumping	x	x			x
Hopping	x	x	x		x
Skipping	x	x			x
Standing Still	x	x			x
Balancing	x	x	x		x

FINE MOTOR					
	INPUT			OUTPUT	
Items	Visual	Auditory	Haptic	Verbal	Motor
Matching	x	x	x		x
Building	x	x			x
Cutting	x	x			x
Copying Shapes	x	x			x
Copying Letters	x	x			x
Touching Fingers	x	x			x
Clapping Hands	x	x			x

CONCEPTS					
	INPUT			OUTPUT	
Items	Visual	Auditory	Haptic	Verbal	Motor
Sorting Blocks	x	x			x
Naming Colors	x	x		x	x
Counting a		x		x	x
Counting b		x			x
Positioning		x			x
Following Directions		x			x
Identifying Concepts	x	x			x
Identifying Body Parts	x	x	x		x

COMMUNICATIONS					
	INPUT			OUTPUT	
Items	Visual	Auditory	Haptic	Verbal	Motor
Articulating	x	x		x	
Remembering		x		x	
Naming Nouns and Verbs	x	x		x	x
Coping		x		x	x
Identifying Self Age Sex	x	x		x	x
Classifying Foods		x		x	
Telling a Story	x	x		x	

Figure 3–10 **DIAL SWITCHBOARD** *From C. Mardell and D. Goldenberg. Developmental Indicators for the Assessment of Learning Manual. Edison, N.J.: Childcraft, 1972, p. 32.*

five areas of adaptive, gross motor, fine motor, language, and personal-social behavior.

The DDST, DIAL, and DSI are all *norm-referenced* screening tests. Children taking such tests are compared with others on whom the test was standardized. Thus, such a test uses a specific population of persons as its interpretive frame of reference.

A *criterion-referenced* screening test, in contrast, measures performance relative to precise developmentally based objectives. Scores are interpreted in terms of a specific standard of performance. Such a test thus uses a specific content domain as its interpretive frame of reference. Good examples of criterion-referenced screening tests for young children are the *Learning Accomplishment Profile* (LAP), (Sanford 1974) and the *Carolina Developmental Profile* (Lillie 1976). Generally, these tests are

Name	Age Range	Measures
1. Child Research Council Growth Charts	birth–25 years	length and weight; head circumference
2. Harvard Growth Charts	birth–18 years	length and weight; stature
3. Infant Growth Chart of Kaiser-permanence	1–24 months	head circumference; length
4. Iowa Growth Charts	birth–18 years	length and weight

Figure 3–11 **Physical Growth Screening**

most useful when applied to curriculum planning and ongoing evaluation of achievement (pretest and post-test measures) than as screening tests for identifying total handicapped populations (Davidson, and others 1977; Safford 1978). Detailed use of criterion-referenced tests will be covered in Chapter 4.

Screening Tests for Specific Areas

There are other screening tests which assess one particular area of development. We will look at the following areas of development—physical, perceptual motor, cognition, speech and language, and social-emotional.

Physical. The parent interview is an important aspect of screening in this area. Through the use of a questionnaire (Meier 1976), suspicions regarding general health and physical intactness can be noted and followed further.

For the screening of physical growth, there are the following charts (Figure 3–11).

Children should also be screened for immunization status since there are seven diseases (diphtheria, tetanus, whooping cough, poliomyelitis, measles, rubella, and mumps) against which all children should be protected. This screening is done through parent interview and record review.

Visual screening can be readily conducted by trained paraprofessionals in the community. This procedure is generally well accepted by the public. Visual tests should screen for amblyopia (lazy eye), refractive error, strabismus, and other eye diseases. The following chart (Figure 3–12), adapted from Frankenburg and Camp (1975), lists visual screening tests appropriate for preschool children.

Auditory screening is often conducted in conjunction with visual screening for children between three and five years of age. Even with younger children, a skilled technician may assess both modalities. The most commonly used tests are listed in Table 3–1, which was adapted from Frankenburg and Camp (1975).

Another screening test which looks primarily at physical aspects of development is the *Learning Problem Indication Index* (LPII). Developed by Hoffman (1971), this short list of perinatal and developmental factors appears to have good predictive validity for determining which children warrant further study.

Perceptual motor. Screening tests in this area include the *Developmental Test of Visual Motor Integration* (VMI), the *Bender-Gestalt with Koppitz* scoring, and the *Winterhaven Perceptual Forms Test*. Most screening tests in

Test	Age Range	Amblyopia	Refractive Error	Strabismus	Other Disease
Vision Tests					
1. Allen Picture Cards	2½ years and above	X	X		X
2. Fixation Test	2 months and above	X			X
3. Illiterate E	3 years and above	X	X		X
4. Optokinetic Response	Any age	X			X
5. Sjogren Hand Test	3 years and above	X	X		X
6. STYCAR	6 months - 7 years	X	X		X
7. White Vision Chart	3 years and above	X	X		X
Muscular Balance Tests					
1. Cover Test	Any age	X		X	
2. Hirschberg	Any age			X	
Combination of Vision and Muscle/Machines					
1. Altantic City Vision Screener	3 years and above	X	X	X	X
2. Michigan Screener	3 years and above	X	X	X	X
3. Screening Insta-line	3 years and above	X	X	X	X

Figure 3–12 Screening Tests of Eye Function *Adapted from W. Frankenburg and B. Camp, eds.* Pediatric Screening Tests. *Springfield, Ill.: Chas. C. Thomas, 1975, p. 299.*

TABLE 3–1   Auditory Screening

Name of Test	Time	Equipment Required	Age Range
1. Ewing Procedure	2 minutes or less	Voice and noisemaker	6–30 months
2. Neonate Screening	1 minute	Infant Screening Audiometer	24 hours–1 year
3. Verbal-Auditory Screening of Children (VASC)	5 minutes	Tape cartridge and Tape Recorder	3–5 years
4. Preschool Screening Audiometer	5 minutes	Audiometer and toys	3–5 years

Adapted from W. Frankenburg and B. Camp, eds. *Pediatric Screening Tests.* Springfield, Ill.: Chas. C. Thomas, 1975, p. 352.

Appendix A assess some aspects of perceptual motor development. These aspects include basic fundamental movements which emerge without training (gross and fine motor) and perceptual abilities (visual and auditory discrimination, body image, and visual-motor coordination).

Cognition.   There are few screening tests which are confined to this area of development, because it is difficult to define and limit the elements of cognition independent of the other areas of development and to do so in a short period of time. One widely used group test, *Boehm Test of Basic Concepts,* assesses the child's understanding of space (location, direction, orientation, and dimension), time, and quantity (number). This test is designed for children between the ages of 4–0 and 8–0 but is most useful in kindergarten and first grade screening. Many of the screening tests in Appendix A assess cognition or some aspect of intelligence, concept formation, memory, thinking processes, sequencing, and classifying, but not in isolation.

Speech and language.   There are several speech and language screening tests, among them the *Arizona Articulation Proficiency Scale,* the *Houston Test for Language Development,* the *Northwestern Syntax Screening Test,* the *Peabody Picture Vocabulary Test,* and the *Templin-Darley Screening Test of Articulation.* The purpose of screening in this area is to locate and refer for further evaluation children who have any of the following symptoms:

- Frequent misunderstanding of speech
- Difficulty in expressing needs and wants
- Irrelevant responses to speech directed to the child
- Decreased sensitivity to sound stimuli
- Difficulty in articulating speech sounds (Preston, 1973)

Social-emotional.   Walker (1973) states that screening should not be done in this area because there is no quick and simple way to evaluate socioemotional growth. After examining 143 socioemotional measures for preschool and kindergarten children, she recommends the use of observational strategies in naturalistic settings due to their objectivity, complete nonverbalness, and their ability to become a source for theory generation regarding socioemotional development.

Appendix A lists over eighty screening tests in detail for use in all areas of development with preschool children.

Training Staff

It is crucial that the people who administer the screening tests are properly trained. Thorpe and Werner (1974, p. 369) state that "a tool is only as good as its user. Reliable performance is directly related to the preparation, training and supervision of the examiners. Not until these aspects are standardized can it be accepted that a developmental appraisal is made adequately."

Frankenburg and his associates (1970) suggest a tutorial approach for training one or two nonprofessionals. When the group to be trained consists of ten or more people, a uniformly prepared format including written material, films or videotapes for consistent presentation, role playing, and supervised practice experience is advised. In the revised *Denver Developmental Screening Test Manual* (Frankenburg, Dodds, and Fandal 1970), the authors caution that proficiency of test administration or observation is decreased when the aides no longer think their work is being monitored. It is important to make periodic checks of screening results to assure a high level of screening accuracy. The person in charge of such periodic checks should be a professional, preferably one trained in testing procedures, and certainly one properly trained in the administration of the screening tools used in the program.

Screening Children

The smooth administration of the screening procedure is dependent upon careful planning and coordination of many groups: community leaders, volunteers, school administrators, professionals, paraprofessionals, parents, and the press. Kucienski (1976) fully describes the screening program used in his school district, along with the forms and timeline he uses for communicating with all of the previously mentioned groups. He begins the process at least ten weeks before the actual screening takes place, orienting volunteers and alerting the community about the upcoming screening of all preschool children. The children are registered in advance and assigned appointments for both sensory and developmental screening. Some communities do both screenings on the same day. Included in the plan are follow-up contacts to parents, telling them that either their child passed the screening, needs to be rescreened, or needs a diagnostic evaluation.

Reporting Results

Parents should be adequately prepared and involved in the screening process. They should be informed in advance about the purposes, strengths, and weaknesses regarding this process. At the conclusion of the screening procedure, information should be coordinated on multiple functions, such as vision, hearing, and development (Lessler 1974). At this point, decisions must be made whether there is a need for rescreening of any function or whether diagnosis is warranted. Results of the screening should be shared with parents and other caregivers (that is, pediatrician, teacher, and so on) as soon as possible to allay any unfounded concerns and to reassure those parents whose children were identified that further diagnosis is necessary before any conclusive decisions can be made.

Screening results to parents should not be overly detailed or definitive. When telling parents the results, professionals should strive to avoid conveying misinformation. Interpretation should be in terms of the child's present functioning rather than through the use of labels.

Parents should not be underestimated in terms of what they know about their own child, or how this information can help in the assessment of their child. For instance, parents can be taught to observe and complete developmental checklists, measure and chart their child's growth, and assist in vision and hearing screening.

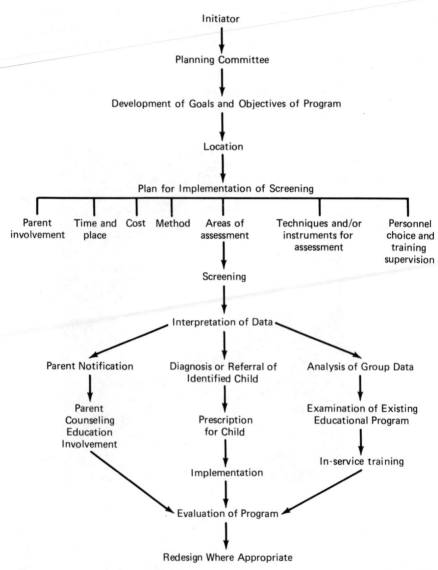

Figure 3–13 Screening Program *Adapted from S. Zeitlin.* Kindergarten Screening. *Springfield, Ill.: Chas. C. Thomas, 1976, p. 17.*

Screening activities have many potential benefits, but also some real dangers such as

1. Screening leading to nowhere—screening is only as good as the service that follows.

2. Screening leading to inaccurate labeling—some techniques are unreliable enough that certain percentages of children screened and diagnosed will be inaccurately labeled or placed.

3. Screening only for the purpose of labeling (hardening of the categories)—too often the only result of screening and diagnosis is a label with a negative connotation; it is imperative to train staff to utilize labels in a positive manner.

4. Screening as a one-shot program—it should be part of ongoing periodic evaluations.

5. Screening as research, not service—it should end in better services for more people in need and if it provides data for research, that should be a side product.

6. Screening programs as a delaying tactic—"We must know how many there are before we can build programs" is the logic of delay and a danger.

7. Screening leading to false security—it is never 100 percent accurate. How does one differentiate between the child who has reached a temporary plateau but will go on again, the slow starter who will "outgrow it," and the child who will never catch up if not assisted? Keogh and Becker (1973, p. 7) caution that the ". . . relation between single, specific preschool test findings and later school achievement are too low to allow definitive prediction about individual children."

8. Screening leading to a self-fulfilling prophesy (Rosenthal and Jacobson 1968)—teachers and/or parents expecting less from a child who has been identified as having a problem may alter the child's self-concept and status among peers as well.

The dangers can be overcome if screening is developed as part of a comprehensive program which includes location, screening, diagnosis, service delivery or intervention, and evaluation. It is important to plan the entire screening program, not just the administration of the test alone. Zeitlin (1976) has developed a flowchart which illustrates the screening process in relationship to diagnosis, intervention, and evaluation (Figure 3–13).

Nature of the Diagnostic Process

Diagnosis is an in-depth process which confirms or rejects the existence of a problem, serious enough to require intervention, which has been detected in the locating or screening process. The two processes of screening and diagnosing are related in the following manner:

problem exists   *diagnosis*

yes   no

		yes	no
	yes	high-risk	false +
screening	no	false −	normal

Most of the total population (88–90 percent) will fall into the "normal" category. The number or percentage of under-referrals (missing children who should be identified *false-negatives*) and over-referrals (identifying children who do not have problems *false-positives*) is a function of the cut-off points. For example, when screening and diagnosing a population of 50 children, if one establishes a low cut-off point, the four categories may look like this:

5	5
0	40

With a high cut-off point, the four categories may look like this:

5	0
5	40

The cut-off point decision affects (a) the number of children going through the diagnostic process which is costly and (b) the number of children who are missed or "fall through the cracks" which ultimately is more costly.

Diagnosis serves the following functions:

1. determines the severity of the problem
2. determines the possible causes (etiology)
3. determines the treatment needs
4. determines the most appropriate service

Courtesy United Feature Syndicate, Inc.

Once the *kind* of treatment has been designated, individualized curriculum design (discussed in Chapter 4) determines the *content* of the treatment. In essence, diagnosticians must decide on the types and amount of data necessary to perform these functions adequately. This is accomplished through *analysis*—collecting data in various ways regarding the concerns about a particular child and *synthesis*—examining the data collected and developing a comprehensive interpretation. These two processes are usually performed by a multidisciplinary team, also referred to as a cross-disciplinary or transdisciplinary team. Cross and Goin (1977) list typical areas of investigation in diagnosis (Table 3–2).

Meier (1976) illustrates another way of looking at the multidisciplinary team (Figure 3–14). The middle circle designates the diagnostic process while the outer circle indicates the intervention possibilities. Note the location of the child and family in the center. It is important to emphasize that it is usually not necessary to utilize all of these

Figure 3–14 The Multidisciplinary Team *From J. Meier.* Developmental and Learning Disabilities. *Baltimore, Md.: University Park Press, 1976, p. 94.*

TABLE 3–2   Typical Areas of Investigation in Diagnosis

Area of Investigation	Personnel Involved	Type of Information Obtained
1. Social History	Social Worker	Information relative to the functioning of the total family unit, note what the child's problem means to the family
2. Physical Examination	Pediatrician	Child's general health at present; review the child's medical history; note any physical defects that may be present.
3. Neurological Examination	Neurologist	Specific information of any central nervous system impairment if brain damage is suspected; run an EEG to detect possibility of seizures or other malfunctioning.
4. Psychological Examination	Psychologist	Data from the administration of psychometric techniques; use diagnostic tests to measure child's performance against normative standards and projective tests to determine nature of child's emotional responses.
5. Hearing Examination	Audiologist or Public Health Worker	Data from the application of audiometric procedures to determine any type of hearing impairment.
6. Vision Examination	Ophthamologist or Public Health Worker	Detection of any visual impairment.
7. Speech Examination	Speech Pathologist	Child's ability to understand and/or use words, phrases, concepts.
8. Educational Examination	Special Education/Early Childhood	Diagnostic instruction to determine child's learning style and abilities (general here; more specific within the area of assessment).

From L. Cross and K. Goin, eds. *Identifying Handicapped Children*. New York: Walker & Co., 1977, p. 28.

specialists. Information from the screening process is used in designing the construction of the diagnostic team and its activities.

The diagnostic process is the third stage in total assessment. It includes any or all of the following activities:

- Obtaining data from all sources
- Interviewing the parent(s)

- Testing
- Observing the child
- Determining the treatment needs and most appropriate services

The rationale for a combination of these activities rests on an eclectic approach to diagnosis which is based on four models. Each of these models is a conceptual framework that can contribute to the total picture of young children within their environment.

Interaction model.   One must look at child and environmental variables together. Known as the interaction or transactional model (Sameroff and Chandler 1975), it can be illustrated as follows:

$$\text{Child} \qquad C_0 \underset{E_0}{\overset{}{\times}} C_1 \underset{E_1}{\overset{}{\times}} C_2 \underset{E_2}{\overset{}{\times}} C_3$$
$$\text{Environment} \qquad E_0 \quad E_1 \quad E_2 \quad E_3$$

Thus, information about the people and the environment that influence the child's learning must be obtained.

Developmental model.   A child's development may be categorized into interdependent and interrelated areas. These areas have many components which affect the child's total functioning. Figure 3–15 lists the major areas of development related to learning (Zeitlin 1976).

Information processing model.   The manner in which a child receives, interprets, and transmits information is very significant. Analysis of testing and teaching tasks can indicate the child's preferred modes of functioning and where deficits occur.

Behavioral model.   Observation of children can lead to understanding patterns or typical responses which may be changed, modified, or conditioned by types and schedules of reinforcement.

The activities of diagnosis should overlap to the extent that they analyze different aspects of data according to these four models.

Obtaining Data From All Sources

An adequate developmental history includes information about the family, the specific pregnancy, the delivery and neonatal stage, illnesses, developmental milestones, history of seizures, and pertinent environmental and social variables (Knobloch and Pasamanick 1974). No history is ever totally accurate or complete, but the goal remains to strive towards both accuracy and completeness. Requesting parents to fill out a developmental questionnaire before the interview enables parents to

Figure 3–15 **Major Areas of Development Related to Learning** *From S. Zeitlin.* Kindergarten Screening. *Springfield, Ill.: Chas. C. Thomas, 1976, p. 28.*

I. *Physical*
   a. physical intactness
   b. general health
   c. activity level
   d. vision
   e. hearing
   f. nutrition—eating patterns
   g. neurological structure
   h. endocrine balance

II. *Perceptual Motor*
   a. gross motor—large muscle coordination
   b. fine motor—small muscle coordination
   c. body image—identification of body parts
   d. laterality
   e. directionality
   f. perception of space relations
   g. figure-ground perception
   h. visual motor coordination
   i. auditory discrimination
   j. visual discrimination
   k. perceptual constancy
   l. dominance or sideness

III. *Cognition*
   a. IQ
   b. thinking processes
   c. concept formation
   d. memory—auditory, visual
   e. sequencing
   f. classifying
   g. creativity

IV. *Speech and Language*
   a. communication—receptive and expressive language
   b. rhythm
   c. syntax (grammar)
   d. vocabulary

V. *Social Emotional*
   a. self-concept
   b. motivation
   c. adaptive behavior—coping style
   d. social skills—interaction patterns
   e. level of maturity (psychosexual development)
   f. dependence—independence
   g. aspiration level (self-expectation)
   h. nervous tendencies

think about the pertinent areas, check baby books and memories, and form their own hypotheses about where the problem(s) lie.

Depending upon the age of the child and the severity of the problem, the child may have been seen by other professionals who can supply data upon the consent of the parent(s). If the child has been in some kind of school setting, teachers may be able to offer many insights into the child's behavior. The child may have been seen by a pediatrician, dentist, or therapist who may be able to contribute significant data. These should be requested whenever possible.

Cross and Goin (1977) outline the areas which are most often covered on general case history forms (Figure 3–16).

Interviewing the Parent(s)

The purpose of the interview is to obtain a detailed account of the child's current behavior. Although an unstructured format generally lends itself to obtaining the parent(s)' feelings, concerns, attitudes, interactions, and expectations, a structured procedure generally produces more specific information. Two important questions to ask parents are "Has your child ever lost any behavior once acquired?" and "Has your child ever failed to make progress?" (Knobloch and Pasamanick 1974).

Some principles should be kept in mind during the interview.

1. *Be flexible.* Let the parent(s) lead the way as long as the conversation is relevant.
2. *Provide adequate time.* This helps the parent(s) feel more relaxed.
3. *Gather all pertinent information.* Details about the child can add to the complete picture.
4. *Accept and interact with the parent(s) as equal(s).* Parents should feel their participation and contribution are essential to the process.
5. *Ask open-ended questions.* Try to avoid questions which lead to limited responses such as "yes" and "no."
6. *Minimize distracting behaviors.* Unconscious behavior on the part of the interviewer, such as twiddling a pencil, might be distracting.

Interviewing is a skill that requires constant evaluation of what is heard in order to proceed in a meaningful way. It is not routine questioning and therefore the interviewer must keep in mind a global outline but be prepared to go off on tangents when desirable.

Testing

Testing is a technique or tool for obtaining information in an organized form that is deemed to be valid and reliable. The younger the child is, the greater the assumption that testing can be relied upon and the less

Figure 3–16 Areas Often Covered on General Case History Forms *From L. Cross and K. Goin, eds.* Identifying Handicapped Children. *New York: Walker & Co., 1977, p. 30.*

1. **BIRTH HISTORY**
   Previous pregnancies
   Miscarriages
   Mother's health/attitude
   Labor
   Delivery
   Birth Weight
   Trouble breathing, sucking
   Jaundice, cyanosis
   Oxygen

2. **MOTOR DEVELOPMENT**
   Sat alone
   Crawled
   Fine and gross motor coordination
   Feeding, sucking, chewing
   Drooling
   Toilet training
   Enuresis
   Self-help

3. **LANGUAGE**
   Comprehension
   Gestures
   Echolalia
   Perseveration
   Onset of words
   Current number of words
   Onset of sentences
   Examples of sentences
   % understood by parents
   % understood by other adults
   % understood by siblings
   % understood by peers
   Child's awareness of problem
   Previous assessment
   Previous training

4. **FAMILY**
   Parent's age, health
   Parent's occupation
   Parent's education
   Parent's income
   Marital status
   Is child adopted
   Siblings, age, health
   Others in home; age, health
   History of learning problems in family
   Other problems
   Language spoken in home
   Transportation

5. **INTERPERSONAL RELATIONSHIPS**
   General disposition
   Playmates and play habits
   Parent-child relationships
   Other adult relationships
   In contact with environment
   Discipline
   Affectionate
   Aggressive
   Compulsive
   Cries easily
   Daydreamer
   Fears
   Hyperactive
   Jealousy
   Leader or follower
   Perseveration
   Sleep habits
   Social perception
   Tantrums
   Psychological assessment(s)
   Psychological treatment(s)
   Psychiatric assessment(s)
   Psychiatric treatment(s)

6. **MEDICAL HISTORY**
   Convulsions
   Fever
   Childhood diseases
   Cerebral problem(s)
   Glandular disturbance
   Excessive sweating
   Allergies
   Drug therapy
   Auditory problems
   Vision problems
   Operation
   Accidents
   Congenital defects
   Name of doctor

7. **ADDITIONAL COMMENTS**

assurance that it reflects the child's true abilities. Preschool children are a particular challenge to test for several reasons. They are not in the least interested in their performance, they generally follow their own impulses, and they are difficult to coerce (Sattler 1974). Therefore, it is important to have all testing materials arranged systematically but out of sight until needed, provide consistent limits, stay attuned to the child's pace, and provide adequate praise to the extent the child needs and wants it.

However, as assessment skills improve, clinicians are more able to obtain useful information from standardized tests. In all instances, good testing is marked by respect for the individual child, respect for the individual test so it is used as it was intended, and respect for the setting so that diagnoses do not occur without existence of intervention options.

In addition to the criteria for screening tests, diagnostic tests should also be relevant, credible, timely, and efficient (Stufflebeam, and others 1971). Appendix A lists many of the diagnostic tests currently in use.

By using standardized, diagnostic tests, diagnosticians obtain another measure of current status. Tests merely provide a sample of the child's behavior at a specific point in time. Thus, all tests are microexperiments (Caldwell 1972). The tester presumes that skills and/or attitudes of the young child which are being sampled are representative of a larger repertoire of skills and/or attitudes. The purpose of this sampling is but one more link of information in determining whether or not there is a problem, and if so, what kind of treatment is needed. Diagnostic testing leads to a classification decision for determining the best treatment.

A useful model for diagnostic testing is found in Figure 3–17. All testing tasks can be analyzed according to these dimensions to determine the child's strengths and weaknesses. For example, when asking the child to count, ("Count for me. You know, 1, 2, . . .") the dimensions are "rote, auditory, verbal." However, when asking the child to demonstrate understanding of numbers, ("Give me five blocks. Put them here.") the dimensions are "conceptual, auditory, and motor." This analysis will be discussed in Chapter 4, under Task Analysis.

On standardized tests, the criterion usually used for determining whether or not a particular score is significantly different is one and a half standard deviations in two or more areas of development or two standard deviations in one area of development. Elementary statistics books will clarify this criterion.

Standardized, diagnostic tests are available to assess most of the major areas of development mentioned earlier in this chapter (see Figure 3–15).

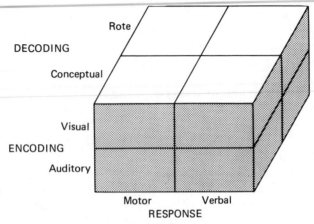

Figure 3–17   **Model for Diagnostic Testing**

Physical.   Testing in this area generally is within the realm of the physician. Specialists who may be called upon include the pediatrician, neurologist, ophthamologist, otologist, and endocrinologist. Testing would cover physical intactness, general health, activity level, vision, hearing, nutrition (eating patterns), neurological structure, and endocrine balance.

Perceptual motor.   Diagnostic tests in this area of development include

> *Ayres Southern California Battery*
> *Bruininks-Oseretsky Test of Motor Proficiency*
> *Frostig Developmental Test of Visual Perception*
> *Goldman-Fristoe-Woodcock Auditory Skills Test Battery*
> *Goodenough-Harris Drawing Test*

These tests cover gross and fine motor coordination, body image, laterality and directionality, perception of space relations, figure-ground perception, visual motor coordination, auditory discrimination, visual discrimination, perceptual constancy, and dominance. The tests are more fully described in Appendix A.

Cognition.   Diagnostic tests in this area of development are often comprehensive batteries which also assess every other area of development. The best known and most thoroughly researched tests are

> *Bayley Scales of Infant Development*
> *Cattell Infant Intelligence Scale*
> *Detroit Tests of Learning Aptitude*

> *Gesell Developmental Scales*
> *Hiskey-Nebraska Test of Learning Aptitude*
> *Leiter International Performance Scale*
> *McCarthy Scales of Children's Abilities*
> *Minnesota Preschool Scale*
> *Psychoeducational Evaluation of the Preschool Child*
> *Stanford-Binet Intelligence Scale*
> *Uzguris-Hunt Ordinal Scales of Psychological Development*
> *Wechsler Preschool and Primary Scale of Intelligence*

These tests are designed to assess intelligence, thinking processes, concept formation, auditory and visual memory, sequencing, classifying, and creativity. Most of these tests are more fully described in Appendix A.

The recent court decision in California, *Larry P.* v. *Riles,* (3 EHLR 551:295, 1980) has banned the use of IQ tests for placement on the grounds that they are discriminatory. This may have a profound effect on all diagnostic testing nationwide.

Speech and language.   Diagnostic tests in this area of development include

> *Carrow Elicited Language Inventory*
> *Carrow's Test of Auditory Comprehension of Language*
> *Hejna's Developmental Articulation Test*
> *Illinois Test of Psycholinguistic Abilities*
> *Preschool Language Scale*
> *Receptive-Expressive Emergent Language Scale (REEL)*
> *Utah Test of Language Development*

Tests in this area assess receptive and expressive language, rhythm, syntax (grammar), vocabulary, and articulation. The tests are more fully described in Appendix A.

Social-emotional.   Diagnostic tests in this area of development include

> *California Preschool Social Competency Scale*
> *Children's Apperception Test*
> *Preschool Attainment Record*
> *Vineland Social Maturity Scale*

These tests are designed to assess self-concept, motivation, adaptive behavior or coping style, social skills, level of maturity, degree of independence, aspiration level, and nervous tendencies. The tests are more fully described in Appendix A.

Some instruments listed under one area are also useful and appropriate in another area. For instance, the Goodenough-Harris Drawing Test, listed under Perceptual Motor, can also evaluate aspects of social-emotional behavior. Thus a comprehensive battery should be flexible so that as few instruments as possible are used maximally with a given child (Mardell and Goldenberg 1972, 1975).

Overtesting of young children should be avoided whenever possible. Caution must be taken by the clinician when developing a suitable battery for a particular child.

Observing the Child

Systematic observation is one of the activities which can provide significant data when drawing inferences concerning children's behavior. The purpose of noting the child's strengths and weaknesses in specific areas of behavior is twofold: it is another piece of evidence for confirming or refuting the screening results, and it reduces the need for a huge battery of formal tests. However, this is possible only when the observations are defined in terms of focus, location or setting, circumstances, length and frequency, or coding unit. Children can be observed at home in their own environment where they feel most comfortable. Interactions with parent(s), siblings, and whomever else is present in the immediate environment may be noted. The child may also be observed in a diagnostic setting where selected materials are exposed (such as toys, dolls, puppets, paints, and so on), designed to elicit a particular response. On the other hand, the setting may be left relatively unstructured to see how the child behaves under those circumstances. Settings to consider may include routine times (clean-up, toileting, snack time, rest time), adult-directed activities, and child-directed activities.

The child may be observed alone, with peers or siblings, or with adults. All of these circumstances are valuable in detecting patterns in the child's behavior. Gaps in social-affective development may be ascertained by using White's list (1975) of early childhood competencies and their normal age range of development. This list includes

- Getting and holding the attention of adults (in socially acceptable ways)
- Expressing affection and annoyance (when appropriate) to adults
- Using adults as resources after first determining a job is too difficult to handle alone
- Showing pride in personal accomplishment
- Engaging in role playing or make-believe activities
- Leading and following peers

- Expressing affection and mild annoyance (when appropriate) to peers
- Competing with peers

Children communicate in many ways besides speech—body posture, gestures, mannerisms, activity level, facial expressions, and voice quality. How they do what they do may explain the why.

There are many kinds of records such as logs, diaries, and running records (Cohen and Stern 1958). One of the most popular is the anecdotal record, a written description of an incident which is reported objectively. A good anecdotal record is free of the observer's feelings or interpretations. It is generally best to record incidents on different days and at different times in order to obtain a well-rounded picture. An attempt is made to determine the stimulus for the activity and the child's reactions. The anecdote should also describe the setting where the action occurred and how the action ended.

Other methods of recording observations of children include narrative descriptions, checklists, time samples, interactions, and rating scales (Stallings 1977). Systematic approaches to observation can be recorded by audio or videotape or pencil and paper. The central problem encountered remains the definition of a meaningful behavioral unit (Weinberg and Wood 1975). Yet, it is obvious that systematic observation is becoming more of a science and less of an art. A recording system which accurately analyzes the observational data is crucial to the diagnostic process.

Determining the Treatment Needs and Most Appropriate Services

This activity is the synthesis which was referred to earlier in this chapter—the examination and interpretation of all the information that has been gathered. If possible, all professionals involved in the data gathering stage should meet with the parent(s). Ideally, written reports of individual findings should be distributed early enough for all to read, make notes on, and formulate questions about, before the staff meeting. This saves considerable time at the actual meeting and enables everyone to have all the data accessible for relevant discussion. Reports should be written in lay terms for the convenience of the parent(s) and professionals from other disciplines. The diagnostic procedure must be explained to the parent(s) in both oral and written form in their primary language. Sattler (1974) discusses the issues involved in writing up each professional report, such as using raw scores; avoiding generalizations, ambiguities, and speculations; and presenting results clearly.

The purpose of the synthesis is the assembly of the data into meaningful patterns or constellations of behavior which avoid misinterpretation of the total child. This enables the group to develop a chart or profile of the child, listing major strengths and weaknesses. Based on the profile, all placement options are discussed so a match can be determined between the child's treatment needs and the most appropriate service(s). It is also necessary to implement the decision by relegating responsibility to particular professionals and/or the parents.

Cautions Regarding Diagnosis

With regard to diagnosis of the mentally retarded, Wolfensberger (1965) noted that "early diagnosis is desirable when it leads to prevention, early treatment, or constructive counseling; it is irrelevant if it is purely academic and does not change the course of events; it is harmful if, in balance, child or family reap more disadvantages than benefits." Surely, this statement would hold true for early diagnosis of any condition.

Differential, functional, or descriptive diagnosis as delineated in this chapter is successful *only* if it can pinpoint the kind of problem the child has, the particular strengths and weaknesses of the child, and the kind of treatment which would be most appropriate and beneficial for this particular child.

Diagnosis is never completely accurate. Therefore, one must recognize the possibility and accept the responsibility of error. Cross and Goin (1977) have charted the types of possible errors and their sources within the diagnostic process (Table 3–3).

TABLE 3–3   Sources of Error in Developmental Diagnosis

Source	Possible Errors
1. History	Failure to take a thorough history; undue reliance on the past without allowing for possibility of change.
2. Interpretation	Incorrect assumption of inability caused by child's failure to co-operate; failure to note the quality of the child's performance; failure to withhold judgment in case of doubt.
3. Observation	Limited setting (i.e., diagnostic center only as opposed to combination of multiple settings); single observations rather than observations of greater duration and frequency; decontextualization of the testing situation.
4. Instrumentation	Lack of multiple measures; administration by unskilled personnel; over-emphasis on "objective" data.
5. Placement	Lack of available options; no consideration of existing options.

From L. Cross and K. Goin, eds. *Identifying Handicapped Children.* New York: Walker & Co., 1977, p. 33.

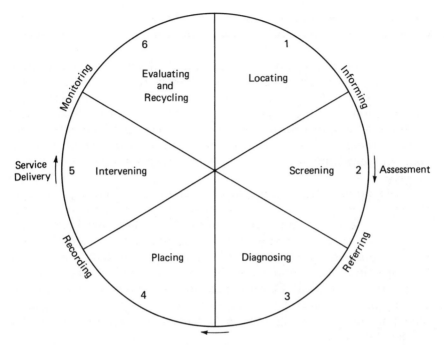

Figure 3–18 **Assessment and Service Delivery**

Testing errors may also result from using a poor test, using a technically adequate test for the wrong purpose, using a technically adequate test with the wrong child (that is, a child whose characteristics differ greatly from the population on which it was normed), interpreting the test scores incorrectly, or from clerical errors (Salvia and Ysseldyke 1978). One way to protect the child and parent from any or all of these errors is to reevaluate the findings frequently. Although this is always advisable, it is of particular importance regarding young children.

The entire assessment procedure may be illustrated in the following manner: (Figure 3–18).

Summary

Assessment of young handicapped children is a complex procedure which requires much time, preparation, and skill to be successful. The procedure can be divided into three processes: (1) locating; (2) screening; and (3) diagnosing.

Locating may include any or all of the following activities: defining the target population, increasing the public's awareness of services, encouraging referrals, and canvassing the community for children in need of services.

Screening may include any or all of the following activities: selecting conditions to be screened; selecting tests; training staff; screening children; and reporting results. There are both comprehensive screening tests and screening tests for specific areas (physical, perceptual motor, cognition, speech and language, and social-emotional). Appendix A lists screening tests in detail for use with preschool children in all areas of development. Cautions are necessary with screening procedures.

Diagnosing may include any or all of the following activities: obtaining data from all sources; interviewing the parents; testing; observing the child; and determining the treatment needs and most appropriate service(s). Standardized diagnostic tests for specific areas include those for physical, perceptual motor, cognition, speech and language, and social-emotional. In addition, Appendix A provides each diagnostic test in detail. Cautions regarding diagnosis are discussed.

Finally, the interrelationships of these three processes of locating, screening, and diagnosing and their relationship to service delivery can be illustrated diagrammatically.

Review Questions

TERMS TO KNOW

a. *assessment*

b. *locating*

c. *screening*

d. *diagnosing*

e. *validity*

f. *reliability*

g. *norm-referenced test*

h. *criterion-referenced test*

i. *false positive*

j. *false negative*

k. *etiology*

l. *analysis*

m. *synthesis*

1. Define the components of total assessment and the person(s) generally responsible for each component.
2. Why is screening such a crucial component in total assessment?
3. What are the major areas of development related to learning which are generally screened and/or diagnosed? What are the components of each?
4. Describe each of the typical areas of investigation in diagnosis and the personnel involved in each area.

5. What areas are generally covered when obtaining a case history?
6. Complete the following chart with names of tests:

Preschool Tests

	Screening	Diagnosing
Perceptual motor	_____	_____
Speech-language	_____	_____
Comprehensive	_____	-------
Cognition	_____	_____
Social-emotional	-------	_____

7. Using only a deck of playing cards, describe how to screen a three year old's development in the following areas:
   a. gross motor
   b. fine motor
   c. concepts
   d. language
   e. socioemotional
   Decide whether each task is rote or conceptual; if the input is visual, auditory, and/or haptic; and if the output is motor and/or verbal.

References

APGAR, V. Perinatal Problem in the Central Nervous System, in *The Child with Central Nervous System Deficit*, U.S. Department of Health, Education, and Welfare, Children's Bureau. Washington, D.C.: U.S. Government Printing Office, 1965.

BERMAN, A. LD Resource Materials: The Great Ripoff. *Journal of Learning Disabilities*, 1977, 10.

BRAZELTON, T. B. *Neonatal Assessment Scale*. Philadelphia: Lippincott, 1973.

CALDWELL, B. Practical Developmental Testing. *Pediatric Portfolio*, 1972.

COHEN, D., and V. STERN. *Observing and Recording the Behavior of Young Children*. New York: Teachers College Press, 1958.

CRONIN, P., and W. SCHIPPER, eds. *First National Child Find Conference*. Minneapolis, Minn.: Minneapolis Public Schools, 1976.

CROSS, L. Measurement Procedures in Early Childhood Programs. *Cycles*, 1976, 4(1), 12–16.

CROSS, L., and K. GOIN, eds. *Identifying Handicapped Children*. New York: Walker and Company, 1977.

DAVIDSON, J., and others. *Directory of Developmental Screening Instruments*. Minneapolis, Minn.: Project Search, Minneapolis Public Schools, 1977.

FALLEN, N., and J. McGOVERN. *Young Children with Special Needs*. Columbus, Ohio: Chas. E. Merrill, 1978.

FRANKENBURG, W., J. DODDS, and A. FANDAL. *The Revised Denver Developmental Screening Test Manual.* Denver: University of Colorado Press, 1970.

FRANKENBURG, W., and others. Training the Indigenous Nonprofessionals: The Screening Technician. *Journal of Pediatrics,* 1970, 77, 564.

FRANKENBURG, W., and B. CAMP eds. *Pediatric Screening Tests.* Springfield, Ill.: Chas. C. Thomas, 1975.

FRIEDLANDER, B. Screening: A State of the Art Survey, in *The Exceptional Infant,* Vol. III, eds. B. Friedlander, G. Sterritt, and G. Kirk. New York: Brunner-Mazel, 1975, pp. 603–604.

HARE, B., and J. HARE. *Teaching Young Handicapped Children.* New York: Grune & Stratton, 1977.

HAYNES, U. *Guide to Normal Milestones of Development.* New York: United Cerebral Palsy Association, 1966.

HOEPFNER, R., C. STERN, and S. NUMMEDAL, eds. *CSE-ECRC Preschool-Kindergarten Test Evaluations,* Washington, D.C.: Capitol Publications, 1971.

HOFFMAN, M. Early Identification of Learning Problems. *Academic Therapy,* 1971, 7, 23–35.

JOHNSON, H. W. *Preschool Test Descriptions.* Springfield, Ill.: Chas. C. Thomas, 1979.

JORDAN, J., and others, eds. *Early Childhood Education for Exceptional Children.* Reston, Va.: Council for Exceptional Children, 1977.

KAZUK, E., M. COHRS, and W. FRANKENBURG. *Introduction to Pediatric Screening.* Washington, D.C.: National Audiovisual Center, 1974.

KEOGH, B., and L. BECKER. Early Detection of Learning Problems: Questions, Cautions, and Guidelines. *Exceptional Children,* 1973, 40, 5–11.

KNOBLOCH, H., and B. PASAMANICK, eds. *Developmental Diagnosis.* 3rd ed. Hagerstown, Md.: Harper & Row, 1974.

KRAKOW, J., D. KELFER, and H. REINHERG. *Field Study of the Preschool Screening System.* Paper presented at the Association for Children with Learning Disabilities, Kansas City, Mo., March, 1978.

KUCIENSKI, J. *Pre-school Screening.* Northbrook, Ill.: School District 28, 1976.

Larry P. v. *Riles. Judicial Decisions* (3 EHLR 551:295), 1980.

LESSLER, K. Screening, Screening Programs and the Pediatrician. *Pediatrics,* 1974, 54, 608–11.

LILLIE, D. *Carolina Developmental Profile.* Winston-Salem, N.C.: Kaplan School Supply, 1976.

MACY, D. Evaluating Child Find Projects, in *First National Child Find Conference,* eds. P. Cronin and W. Schipper. Minneapolis, Minn.: Minneapolis Public Schools, 1976.

MARDELL, C., and D. GOLDENBERG. *Developmental Indicators for the Assessment of Learning Manual.* Edison, N.J.: Childcraft, 1972, 1975.

MARDELL, C., and D. GOLDENBERG. Instruments for Screening of Prekindergarten Children. *Research in Education,* 1973 (ED 070 528).

MATUSIAK, I., and others. *Preschool Screening for Exceptional Education Needs in a Large Urban Setting.* Milwaukee, Wis.: Milwaukee Public Schools, 1976.

MEIER, J. *Developmental and Learning Disabilities.* Baltimore, Md.: University Park Press, 1976.

NORTH, F. Screening in Child Health Care: Where Are We Now and Where Are We Going? *Pediatrics,* 1974, 54(5), 631–640.

PRESTON, M. Psycholinguistics and the Evaluation of Language Function. *Pediatric Clinics in North America,* 1973, 20, 79.

ROSENTHAL, R., and L. JACOBSON. *Pygmalion in the Classroom.* New York: Holt, Rinehart & Winston, 1968.

SAFFORD, P. *Teaching Young Children with Special Needs.* St. Louis, Mo.: C. V. Mosby, 1978.

SALVIA, J., and J. YSSELDYKE. *Assessment in Special and Remedial Education.* Boston: Houghton Mifflin, 1978.

SAMEROFF, A., and M. CHANDLER. Reproductive Risk and the Continuum of Caretaking Casualty, *Review of Child Development Research,* ed. F. D. Horowitz. Chicago: University of Chicago Press, 1975, 4, 187–244.

SANFORD, A. *Learning Accomplishment Profile.* Winston-Salem, N.C.: Kaplan School Supply, 1974.

SATTLER, J. *Assessment of Children's Intelligence.* Philadelphia: Saunders, 1974.

STALLINGS, J. *Learning to Look, A Handbook on Classroom Observation and Teaching Models.* Belmont, Calif.: Wadsworth, 1977.

STUFFLEBEAM, D., and others. *Education Evaluation and Decision Making.* Itasca, Ill.: Peacock, 1971.

THORPE, H., and E. WERNER. Developmental Screening of Preschool Children: A Critical Review of Inventories Used in Health and Educational Programs. *Pediatrics,* 1974, 53(3), 362–370.

WALKER, D. *Socioemotional Measures for Preschool and Kindergarten Children.* San Francisco: Jossey-Bass, 1973.

WEINBERG, R., and F. WOOD, eds. *Observation of Pupils and Teachers in Mainstream and Special Education Settings: Alternative Strategies.* Minneapolis, Minn.: College of Education, University of Minnesota, 1975.

WHITE, B. *The First Three Years of Life.* Englewood Cliffs, N.J.: Prentice-Hall, Inc., 1975.

WINKLER, P. Project Child: A Special Education Early Childhood Identification Project, in *Proceedings from the Child Find Conference,* 1975.

WOLFENSBERGER, W. Diagnosis Diagnosed. *Journal of Mental Subnormality,* 1965, 11, 62–70.

ZEHRBACH, R. Determining a Preschool Handicapped Population. *Exceptional Children,* 1975, 42(2), 76–83.

ZEITLIN, S. *Kindergarten Screening.* Springfield, Ill.: Chas. C. Thomas, 1976.

The Curriculum

Part **Two**

Curriculum Strategies for Preschool Handicapped Children

CONSTRUCTING A COMPREHENSIVE CURRICULUM

EARLY CHILDHOOD CURRICULUM

SPECIAL EDUCATION CURRICULUM

INTEGRATION OF EARLY CHILDHOOD AND SPECIAL EDUCATION CURRICULA

SUMMARY

Chapter **Four**

Part II deals with the second of the expanding systems model, the curriculum. The term *curriculum* describes the planned arrangement of experiences designed to bring about desired changes in the child's behavior. Each chapter in Part II concentrates on a different aspect of the curriculum. General concepts about the early childhood special education curriculum are presented in Chapter 4. Motor and perceptual skills are discussed in Chapter 5, cognitive skills in Chapter 6, communication and language skills in Chapter 7, and social-affective skills in Chapter 8.

In this chapter, the discussion of curriculum is arranged into these parts: (a) what goes into constructing a comprehensive curriculum, (b) facets of an early childhood curriculum, (c) facets of a special education curriculum, and (d) the integration of early childhood and special education curricula.

Constructing a Comprehensive Curriculum

Curriculum strategy is the functional plan through which organized educational experiences are assembled in some specific setting. Educational settings or school atmospheres are usually created to offer the most stimulating and receptive situations for teaching children. These settings are not limited to schoolrooms or classroom buildings. They may take place in any number of places, such as in parks, on school buses, on field trips to places of interest, in the immediate community, the public library or corner pet shop, as well as in the home.

The goal of every educator is to assist children to grow and develop. Teaching is one of the ways in which this is done. A variety of methods and materials are used to instruct children, and the steps for such activities are usually written in the form of a lesson plan.

A comprehensive curriculum should be a balanced combination of both content and methods. Every plan for the education of children should be balanced between the content which is to be presented and the method through which it will be received most effectively. The curriculum strategy is therefore the generalized approach or plan of educational activities designed to meet the instructional needs of each child.

Curriculum designers have emphasized four major concerns in the development of curriculum and instruction: (a) *The purposes* that the plan hopes to accomplish; (b) *the educational experiences* that achieve that purpose; (c) *the effective organization* of the experiences, and (d) *the evaluation* so that the success or failure of the plan can be determined (Tyler 1949).

Setting Purposes of the Curriculum

It is important to establish a purpose for the educational programming of children. Selection of the major purposes is a significant issue since it is the base upon which all of the future planning is built (Bloom 1956, 1964).

Much controversy has existed between subject specialists and child-centered specialists as to the correct source and purposes for education (Deardon 1968; Hirst and Peters 1970). Subject specialists, those primarily interested in the content of the lessons, are most often supportive of objectives which are subject-oriented and include the basic body of past learnings. Each child is further encouraged to acquire a competence in fundamental skills of basic subjects. The curriculum is then organized to either increase or decrease the speed and complexity with which the material is presented. This is often called a *basic skills approach.*

On the other hand, the child-centered specialists are more concerned with the child's unique interests and problems. The focus is both on the child's learning patterns and on motivation. The selection of program goals reflects an interest in providing material which will meet the child's needs, yet be attractive enough to stimulate the child to learn. This is considered a *child-centered approach* to curriculum development.

Goal determination which focuses on providing opportunities for a child to participate in a variety of experiences and which looks at the child as objectively as possible, usually follows this order: (a) an identification of interests, (b) an identification of performance gaps between the present level of skill and some standard level of expected performance in specific content areas. These gaps are sometimes called needs and can be based upon comparisons between children. The selection and order of curricular objectives and goals identifies the direction of the teacher or educational program. Understanding the differences in learning styles, effects of specialized learning conditions, and rate of instruction offers the curricular planner some variation in sequence and levels of expected competencies.

Once generalized goals have been selected for a child, these goals must be subdivided into specific objectives that will lead toward that goal. The program planner should designate each short-term objective along with the expected change in performance that is anticipated. In addition, the conditions for learning and the materials to be used to meet each objective should also be included (Mager 1962).

An illustration of the relationship between the general purpose and the contributing short-term objectives might be helpful. If a goal for a child is determined to be the increase of expressive oral language, then some short-term objectives could include (a) naming objects by imitation, (b) spontaneous naming of objects, (c) naming colors by imitation (giving an exact selection of specific colors), (d) spontaneous labeling of colors by name without cues, (e) constructing small two-word phrases in imitation, (f) spontaneous construction of phrases using a vocabulary pool from previous lessons, (g) self-initiated small phrases constructed to reply to simple questions. Further clarification of the criterion for acceptable performance would be directed to the number of times that correct terms are used, that is, 80 percent of the time, or eight out of 10 times. It would also be acceptable to limit the environment and conditions in which the behavior could be demonstrated, that is, given the visual representations for the primary colors of red, blue, yellow, and green, the child will name the colors in imitation (modeling) with 100 percent accuracy during a thirty-minute therapy session.

Selecting Experiences to Meet Purposes

The teacher must select a series of learning experiences to help the child meet each goal. Experiences are most effective when activities are dynamic; the child is the active participant. The teacher should design the settings for learning in a way that will encourage the desired behavior. The child needs ample time for practice, and opportunities to perform the skills aimed for in the lesson outlines. Such practice or drill can provide the child with a keen sense of fulfillment and satisfaction.

Sometimes two children can participate in the same activity, yet each child has a unique perception of that experience. One young child may be very much interested in the information being presented and give undivided attention to the instructions and explanations given by the teacher. Another young child may find the activities interesting at the start but become distracted by some small toy or unfamiliar sound. Even though these children have been placed in the same situation, the experience is quite different for each of them. Therefore, the teacher is responsible for understanding the individual needs of each of these children and managing the environment so as to completely stimulate and involve each of them.

There are a number of experiences which can meet specific objectives. The teacher should demonstrate flexibility in creating a wide range of methods to cover the lesson detail. It is possible for one learning experience to satisfy more than a single objective.

For preschool children, the activity itself becomes the support for other closely aligned goals. Running, jumping, crawling, and poking are fun activities for a young child and help to satisfy a need to move. The pleasure gained from the sheer physical sensation of movement is linked to the activity itself.

It is more difficult to arrange learning situations when the child thinks the particular activity is not interesting. This task requires great inventiveness on the part of the teacher. The teacher must *modify* or *alter* the method or broaden the content so as to interest the child.

Organizing Learning Experiences

The *organization* of effective learning experiences depends upon three essential components. They include (a) *continuity*, (b) *sequence*, and (c) *integration*.

Continuity is the repeated presentation of significant concepts among and within other facets of the lesson. For example, if color recognition is selected as a meaningful objective, then this concept will be presented again and again in various parts of other units. Continuity is a thread by which major concepts are supported and reinforced with continued emphasis. Sometimes continuity is referred to as a spiraling process, a method by which repetition occurs at regular intervals but at successively higher levels of complexity (Bruner 1967).

Sequence refers to successive steps of the curriculum. Each unit is built upon a previous experience but expands on the skill in a broader application. Pieces of information may be presented in succession but with each added layer of knowledge, there is greater depth to the content.

Integration is the way that all of the curriculum elements relate to each other. Experiences should be organized so that there is unity between the program elements. The skills selected for instruction should be diverse enough to offer utilization in other areas. It is important to build programs with a mind to the inclusion of experiences rather than isolation of specific components.

When the curriculum is carefully designed, continuity, sequence, and integration are woven skillfully to make a more cohesive model. The principles of organization, by which these integral facets are guided, may include chronological order of events, the increasing complexity of content, a breadth in the range of activities offered, and a description or analogy for practical illustration.

The *structure* of the curriculum plan should also be considered. It should contain (a) *a lesson,* (b) *a topic,* and (c) *a unit.* The *lesson,* the smallest element, includes all of the plans for a single day's instruction, (for example, a lesson on the individual days of the week). The *topic* includes plans for as many lessons as are needed to cover a broader area, (for example, the topic of the month of the year). A topic may require several days or weeks in presentation. The *unit* is the largest element in the structure because the information is extensive and is constructed around a major interest or purpose. A unit may be worked upon for lengthy periods of time, (for example, the unit of the seasons of the year).

In early childhood curriculum, some time is usually spent on the calendar as part of the opening of the day's general activities. This activity is aimed at an understanding of time relationships and the succession of days of the week, month, and dates for each of the days of the month. The lesson on calendars may involve correctly placing a single number on a chart of that specific month and week. It may involve counting days of the week or days of the month rotely to arrive at the correct date. The topic may be the succession of the months within a year. It may be necessary to have many lessons to complete the calendar for a specific month.

The achievement of an efficient plan is not a simple task, and it requires the careful consideration of all of the previously mentioned elements as well as the integration of creative ideas and instructional purposes.

Evaluating Learning Outcomes

Choosing, formulating, and organizing experiences are important steps in the development of an efficient model of instruction; however, the model would not be complete without a final evaluation of the outcome. Evaluation can provide the teacher with information which pinpoints the strengths and weaknesses of the curricular model. The results should locate those components which could be producing desired and undesired effects.

Popham (1970) focuses on an outcomes approach. He states that the reason for teaching is to bring about some change in the behavior of the children under the teacher's direct supervision. The criterion is not what the teacher does, but what the consequences of the lesson show as a result. If the students are unchanged or unaffected, then the purposes of the curriculum have not been met. Since a change in behavior is the hoped for outcome, it is necessary to continuously appraise a child's efforts in more than a single performance. Usually it is best to have a measure of performance prior to the instruction and a measure at the finish of that instructional program. This gives the teacher some sense of perspective for change over a specific period of time.

There are many ways to appraise children's success rates. Noting the child's typical reactions is one way to evaluate behavior. It is also possible to assemble products which demonstrate the best work of children. The drawing of these behavior samples is called *sampling*. Once instructional objectives have been established for a child's educational program, the evaluation procedure should provide some tangible evidence of the accomplishment of that behavior. The technique decided upon should sample performances which document skill mastery. This means that the teacher should give children opportunities to demonstrate the behavior under question. If the objective for instruction was to increase the ability to express ideas orally, then the situations for evaluating the objective must give the child the opportunity to demonstrate that type of behavior. Behavioral evaluation methods are discussed later in this chapter under criterion-referenced measures.

Early Childhood Curriculum

Most early childhood programs emphasize a curriculum that encourages total development. Each facet of a child's growth and development is considered an integral part of that program.

Essential Components in an Early Childhood Curriculum

The construction of a curriculum for young children should include *physical, emotional, social, creative, cognitive,* and *language* elements. The *physical* elements include the development of large and small muscle skills as well as self-help skills which include eating, dressing, and toileting skills (Fallon 1973). Sustaining a good mental attitude and being able to cope with other children are included for *emotional* considerations. *Social* skills include sharing in group activities and general cooperation, since young children need to learn to assume responsibilities and value the efforts of others. *Creative expression* addresses abilities of the child in the formulation of artistic projects, building and using constructive games, music, and thinking skills. Creative expression is also developed through artistic projects which build and use art, games, music, and thinking skills. *Cognitive* elements run through all activities in the building of concepts, making judgments, and organizing skills (Spodek 1973). Along with all of the other components, *oral language* should be emphasized as an integral part of all early childhood activities.

Early Childhood Curriculum Models

From the time of the McMillan sisters' first nursery schools in London to Freud's focus on the critical relationships of emotions and behavior, to Dewey's emphasis on the importance of first-hand experience, early childhood curriculum has seen programmatic changes come and go (Dewey 1962; Freud 1965; Weber 1971; Whitbread 1972). Basically, preschool curriculum approaches fall into four categories. First, there is the basic enrichment model, designed for the expansion of experiences. Second, there is the directed teaching model in which remediation or acceleration is emphasized, such as Head Start (Westinghouse 1969). Third, there is the caretaking or custodial model for the working parent. This model may be nothing more than placement with a daycare center, a neighbor, or a good friend. The fourth possibility would be any combinations of the above three. The direction of the curriculum will depend, in part, on the nature of the program.

Enrichment curriculum.   The enrichment program emphasizes giving a child a great number of experiences for a variety of purposes. The enrichment classroom has special activity areas which include large blocks, dress-ups and playhouse materials, a quiet play area, and a creative arts area. The children also have periods of the day assigned to outdoor play and to field trips to broaden their experience levels. Enrichment curriculum provides field trips to the outer world, places like museums, the post office, stores, and parks. The teacher may arrange a generalized flexible time schedule for the day, but most often activities are child selected, and exploration is encouraged.

Directed teaching curriculum.   A directed teaching curriculum concentrates on the direct teaching of skills selected by the teacher. This

approach is sometimes included as a compensatory model of curriculum because it attempts to aid disadvantaged children by providing learning activities they may not have had an opportunity to experience. Materials and activities are carefully selected to help children learn skills that are cognitive or academic in nature. For example, in the Bereiter and Engelmann curriculum (1968), children are taught language, reading, and arithmetic skills. In the Perry Preschool Project (Weikart 1972), the teaching activities that are selected are done for the purpose of developing cognitive skills. The Montessori-type curriculum can also be viewed in this context because the child's learning materials are structured to ensure the learning of specific tasks. The direct teaching curriculum thus provides a carefully structured learning environment for the teaching of very specific skills. The teacher, rather than the child, is the key decision maker.

Custodial care curriculum.   In some cases, parents who work need to arrange for custodial care for their child. This may be done in a daycare center or private home. Here, children are supervised for the portion of the day that the parent needs to be away. This may be the entire day or parts of a day. The child may arrive as early as 7:30 in the morning and stay as late as 6:00 in the evening. The curriculum planning for children in this type of setting is dependent upon the level of expertise of the supervisory staff, the age of the child, and the numbers of children within the facility. Most often custodial care is fairly loosely structured with much of the day being taken up in napping, feeding, and toileting schedules.

Combination curriculum. In practice, most programs for young children combine elements of several curriculum models. They provide some open experiences that are child selected, they offer directed teaching of specific skills, and they may even extend day services to meet the needs of the working parent(s).

Special Education Curriculum

The special education curriculum is flexible, permitting teachers to take advantage of selective teaching techniques and methods to meet and solve the varied instructional demands of handicapped children. Special services of related personnel are often used in special programs to provide support and assistance for children with exceptional needs. The use of related personnel is discussed more fully in Chapter 10.

Among the unique contributions of special education to curriculum development, two are discussed in this section: (1) the emphasis on individual differences and (2) the intensive examination of tasks to be learned, that is, task analysis.

Intra- and Interindividual Differences

The special education curriculum should be designed to take into account individual differences. These differences can be *intraindividual* differences, that is, differences in ability in various areas of functioning within a single child, or *interindividual* differences, that is, differences found between children. Both intra- and interindividual differences are important considerations in planning curriculum for the exceptional preschool child (Kirk and Kirk 1971).

Intraindividual differences are seen by looking at an individual child's developmental delays or demonstrated lags in skill levels. Some abilities are adequate or even superior, while other abilities appear to be weak. Greater and lesser abilities are observable within the child.

Interindividual differences are seen by comparing the performances of one child with a group of children of similar age. It is found that at a specific age, some children have acquired less of a trait while others have acquired more of the same trait. These differences may be measured by percentile ranks, stanines, or other age-correlated scores. In interindividual comparisons, the child is often placed according to age-related scales. For example, the child's language score may be 5–6, meaning the child's scores on a language test are as an average child of five years and six months. The age score indicates how children in the normal sample population scored. These tests are usually constructed so that the child is given simple tasks to begin with and moves upward to more difficult items as the evaluation progresses. If the scales are accurately designed, it would be expected that as a child progresses in chronological age, so would performance improve proportionately on the test. Evaluation of the intraindividual differences tends to be more descriptive while the differential diagnosis of skill gap between the child and other children tends to be more categorical (Suran 1979).

Task Analysis

There are two ways in which special education uses the term *task analysis*. One focuses on the child and one focuses on the task that is to be learned.

Analysis of the child. One method analyzes the task from the way that the child understands and performs the task. From this perspective, the analysis is on how the child receives, stores, and retrieves the information. An analysis is made as to which sense modality is being used. Is the activity visual, auditory, or tactile?

The teacher also analyzes whether the task is one of reception or expression. If the child is to receive some information from the outside world, such as the stimulation of "Sesame Street" on television, this is analyzed as *reception*. If the child is required to respond by following a direction or making an oral reply, this would be considered *expression*.

To illustrte the child-analysis perspective, the task of answering a telephone call will be examined. The sensory modalities involved are the auditory sense (hearing the ring); the visual sense (seeing the object of a phone and relating to it as the object to talk into); the tactile and kinesthetic sense (touching and moving in picking up the receiver). The use of all of the senses makes the task intersensory. Hearing the sound can be analyzed as receptive while the response of picking the phone up is an expressive act.

The exceptional child's specific handicap may affect the child's ability to handle the task. For example, the child with a visual handicap may not see the phone clearly; the child with an auditory handicap may not hear the ring; the child with a motor handicap may not be able to pick up the phone, and a child with a cognitive deficit may be unable to associate the sound of a ring with the phone. The analyses of the components of the task in terms of the child's abilities and disabilities help the teacher understand the limitations imposed on any curricular design.

Analysis of the task.   The second type of task analysis is the examination of the structure of the task. In this sense, the term task analysis is used by special educators to indicate a careful scrutiny of the task that children are expected to learn. This is accomplished by looking at the steps that are needed to learn a specific task. Once the steps are determined, they are placed into an ordered sequence. This is essentially a behavioral approach to curriculum construction; it places importance on more accurate measurement of actual behavioral outcomes.

Analysis of the task, thus, is the reduction of the performance into successive steps. In the task of brushing teeth, a preschool activity, the task can be analyzed into the following steps:

1. Walk up to the sink, turn on the water, and reach for the toothbrush and paste.
2. Unscrew the cap of the toothpaste.
3. Place the cap on the sink surface.
4. Pick up the brush, and get it wet.
5. Put the paste on the toothbrush.
6. Put the tube of toothpaste down on the sink.
7. Brush teeth.
8. Put the brush down.
9. Rinse mouth out with water.
10. Turn the water off, and put the brush away.
11. Replace the cap on the toothpaste.

Program development of handicapped children should reflect both types of task analysis. In the first use, the young child should have been subject to a comprehensive case study to help determine difficulties in the acquisition of information. In the second use, once the major difficulties are found, the next step is to determine the child's functional skill levels according to the curriculum pattern.

Integration of Early Childhood and Special Education Curricula

In developing a curriculum for the young handicapped child, elements are needed from both early childhood and special education (Spicker and others 1976). The early childhood contribution is the focus on the totality of the child, the "whole child". The special education contribution is the focus on the individual differences and task analysis.

To appreciate an integrated program we will look at (a) placement of preschool handicapped children and (b) criterion-referenced teaching.

Placement in Early Childhood Special Education Settings

The design of a preschool child's educational program should be the result of a careful review of all of the factors which contributed to a comprehensive case study. Figure 4–1 depicts the contributing structures of integrated performance. A comprehensive case study usually includes interview data, assessment scores, observational records, current teacher's anecdotal records, achievement information, and other assessment results.

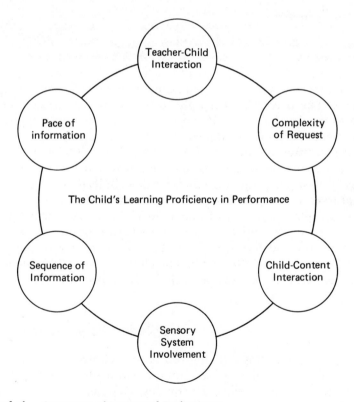

Figure 4–1   Structures of Integrated Performance

Once a determination is made that a child is eligible for a preschool program, there are various placement alternatives. The child may be placed in a regular nursery school program and receive partial service, such as a speech therapist. This means for a part of the day there is interaction with nonhandicapped children, and for a portion of the day the child has service with a trained professional who provides special education instruction.

Another possibility is placement within an itinerant hospital program or an agency directed facility. The child may be at home for the major portion of the day and with the specialist for as little as an hour or as much as a full day per week.

Head Start is another placement option for disadvantaged children (see Chapter 10). At least 10 percent of the children in Head Start programs are required to be identified as handicapped.

A noncategorical diagnostic class placement is yet another option used by the school systems. In such classes, children are screened and if found to be high risk, they receive futher assessment through case study and direct observation. Decisions are tentative in such case studies to be resolved in the diagnostic classroom. Here the teacher can interact with the child and also observe other child interactions so that later decisions regarding placement and teaching can be made.

Even though the school identifies a young child with a potential handicapping condition, the school cannot mandate placement in special programs. The parent has the right to refuse special services and may choose to invoke that right. Parents are the adults who are given the right to make decisions for the child under their direct supervision. In many cases, after a case conference has been completed there are significant delays. Sometimes parental acceptance of the problem takes months or even years, and it is a difficult time, indeed, for all concerned.

Intervention in the home environment is one way in which a gradual acceptance and involvement in child management has been instituted for handicapped children. In such programs as the *Portage Project* (Shearer and Shearer 1976), the child is seen with the parent, and this is begun soon after birth. The children most often involved in these programs are the more severely handicapped children.

Criterion-Referenced Teaching

Because young handicapped children have such unique needs, curriculum planning must take into account these individual needs. Criterion-referenced teaching is well suited for this purpose.

Criterion-referenced teaching does not focus on peer comparison.

Instead, a standard or criterion of performance is established, and tasks are chosen to measure the mastery of that skill. The child is assessed by a criterion-referenced test to determine competence or the level of mastery in that skill.

This knowledge can offer additional information useful in planning for young children with special needs. There is much to be gained from both the inclusion of criterion-referenced assessment information as well as the more popular norm-referenced measures. Very often the teacher finds that norm-referenced data is limited in use because it describes average groups of children. Criterion-referenced measures allow the teacher to look at the individual child's skill mastery without a peer comparison. It is an intra-individual analysis. The child has an opportunity to perform tasks, and those that are mastered are recorded as such. Those skills not mastered then become the prime targets for instructional programming and individualized education program (IEP) goals. The IEP is part of special education legislation (PL 94–142) and is explained in detail in Chapters 10 and 11.

The use of criterion-referenced measures does not exclude the use of norm-referenced data. Norm-referenced measures offer the curriculum planner an opportunity to compare a child's performances to those of age-related peers. There may even need to be some prescriptive teaching along the way. Prescriptive teaching is accomplished through the teacher-child interaction during an actual lesson.

TABLE 4–1   Early Childhood-Special Education

Class Schedule

A.M. TIME	P.M. TIME	ACTIVITY*
8:45– 9:00	12:30–12:45	Calendar: days of week, weather
8:45– 9:00	12:30–12:45	Show and Tell
9:00– 9:30	12:45– 1:15	Movement activity—Wednesday and Friday
9:00– 9:30	12:45– 1:15	Gym—Tuesday and Thursday
9:30–10:15	1:15– 2:00	Individual work: includes free choice of activity, a fine-motor project, cognitive activities, and socialization.
10:15–10:20	2:00– 2:05	Clean up
10:20–10:40	2:05– 2:25	Snack: set table, wash hands, brush teeth.
10:40–10:45	2:25– 2:30	Reading: children choose a book and "read" to themselves, to each other, or with an adult.
10:45–11:05	2:30– 2:50	Group: activities vary daily to include review of cognitive concepts, music, fingerplays, discussion of pertinent events, and group decisions.
11:05–11:15	2:50– 3:00	Dismissal: put on coats, distribute notes.

* Therapist works one-to-one or in groups with select children.

The teacher changes or alters the task to determine what adjustments of pace or method can change the negative score to a more positive one. The teacher must make use of each and every tool to understand the child's performance in order to plan appropriate curriculum experiences. An example of an early childhood-special education class schedule is shown in Table 4–1.

Summary

Curriculum is a term used to describe a planned arrangement of experiences which are designed to bring about changes in a child's behavior. The strategy for developing appropriate curriculum is dependent upon four major concerns. These concerns include setting purposes of the curriculum, selecting experiences to meet those purposes, organizing learning experiences, and evaluating the outcomes.

Setting purposes for curriculum can be accomplished with either a basic skills or child-centered approach. Selecting experiences is important because there are a number of experiences which can meet a specific objective. Organization of the learning experiences should include a consideration of *continuity, sequence,* and *integration.* The structure of the teaching format should contain a *lesson, topic,* and *unit* outline for content. Evaluation for outcome performances can be collected with typical responses and best performance sampling techniques.

The essential components of the early childhood curriculum should include *physical, emotional, social, creative, cognitive,* and *language* elements. The models upon which the programs are planned could include enrichment, directed teaching, custodial, or combination curricula.

A special education curriculum must be flexible while taking advantage of unique teaching methods and materials to meet the instructional needs of the exceptional children in question. Special education has made a unique contribution to curriculum development through an emphasis on individual differences and the use of task analysis.

Intraindividual differences are determined by looking at the child's skill levels to determine lags and competencies.

Interindividual differences are derived from the comparison of a single child's performance with a group of children of similar age.

In planning curricular experiences, it is also important to evaluate the complexity of the task given to a child. This is done with task analysis. The analysis of the child will review the way that the child responds to a stimulus and the use of senses for receiving, storing, and retrieving the information. An analysis of the task will allow a reduction of the most complex task into a series of steps in some ordered sequence.

In planning a program of educational intervention for a young handicapped child, it is important to integrate elements from both early childhood and special education. Placement is made into programs which can support full- or part-time educational involvement. Young children can be placed in any number of settings which will give increasing amounts of direct service. The integration of nonhandicapped and handicapped children in early childhood programs is encouraged by state and federal agencies.

Placement is made following a comprehensive case study. The accurate documentation of a young child's exceptional needs can be improved with the use of both criterion-referenced assessment and teaching as well as norm-referenced measures. Each of these tools can offer additional pieces of important information which will help the teacher to better understand the young child's developmental performances.

Review Questions

TERMS TO KNOW

a. *curriculum*	e. *directed teaching curriculum*
b. *basic skills approach*	f. *interindividual differences*
c. *child centered approach*	g. *intraindividual differences*
d. *enrichment curriculum*	h. *task analysis*

1. Give an example of a coordinated *lesson, topic,* and *unit* for early childhood special education.
2. What elements are included in constructing a comprehensive curriculum?
3. Three components to be considered in organizing learning experiences are *continuity, sequence,* and *integration.* How does each contribute to the organization of learning experiences?
4. Give an illustration of a way to evaluate a curriculum activity.
5. Four early childhood curriculum models were discussed in this chapter. What is the distinguishing feature of each?
6. What are some of the contributions of special education and early childhood education to the integration of early childhood-special education?
7. Do a task analysis of making a peanut butter and jelly sandwich:
   a. from an analysis of the child perspective.
   b. from an analysis of the task perspective.

References

BEREITER, C., AND S. ENGELMANN. *Teaching Disadvantaged Children in the Pre-school.* Englewood Cliffs, N.J.: Prentice-Hall, Inc., 1968.

BLOOM, B. S., ed. *Taxonomy of Educational Objectives: The Classification of Educational Goals.* New York: Longmans, Green, 1956.

BLOOM, B. *Stability and Change in Human Characteristics.* New York: Prentice-Hall, Inc., 1964.

BRUNER, J., AND OTHERS. *Studies in Cognitive Growth.* New York: John Wiley, 1967.

DEARDEN, R. F. *The Philosophy of Primary Education.* London: Routledge & Kegan Paul, 1968.

DEWEY, J., AND E. DEWEY, *Schools of Tomorrow.* New York: Dutton, 1962.

FALLON, B. J., ed. *40 Innovation Programs in Early Childhood Education.* Belmont, Calif.: Lear Siegler, Inc.-Fearon Publisher, 1973.

FREUD, A. *Normality and Pathology in Childhood.* New York: International Universities, 1965.

HIRST, P. H., AND R. S. PETERS. *The Logic of Education.* London: Routledge & Kegan Paul, 1970.

KIRK, S., AND W. KIRK. *Psycholinguistic Learning Disabilities.* Urbana, Ill.: University of Illinois Press, 1971.

MAGER, R. F. *Preparing Instructional Objectives.* Palo Alto, Calif.: Fearon, 1962.

POPHAM, W. J., AND E. L. BAKER. *Systematic Instruction.* Englewood Cliffs, N.J.: Prentice-Hall, Inc., 1970.

SHEARER, D., AND M. SHEARER. The Portage Project: A Model for Early Intervention, in *Intervention Strategies for High Risk Infants and Young Children,* ed. T. Tjossem. Baltimore, Md.: University Park Press, 1976.

SPICKER, H., N. J. ANASTASIOW AND W. L. HODGES. *Children With Special Needs: Early Development and Education.* Minneapolis Leadership Training Institute, 1976.

SPODEK, B. *Early Childhood Education.* Englewood Cliffs, N.J.: Prentice-Hall, Inc., 1973.

SURAN, B. G., AND J. V. RIZZO. *Special Children: An Integrative Approach.* Glenview, Ill.: Scott Foresman, 1979.

TYLER, R. W. *Basic Principles of Curriculum and Instruction.* Chicago, Ill.: University of Chicago Press, 1949.

WEBER, L. *The English Infant School and Informal Education.* Englewood Cliffs, N.J.: Prentice-Hall, Inc., 1971.

WEIKART, D. P. Relationship of Curriculum Teaching and Learning in Preschool Education, in *Preschool Programs for the Disadvantaged. Five Experimental Approaches to Early Childhood Education,* ed. J. C. Stanley. Baltimore, Md.: Johns Hopkins, 1972.

WESTINGHOUSE LEARNING CORPORATION AND OHIO UNIVERSITY. *The Impact of Head Start on Children's Cognitive and Effective Development.* Washington, D.C.: Office of Economic Opportunity, 1969.

WHITBREAD, N. *The Evolution of the Nursery-Infant School.* London: Routledge & Kegan Paul, 1972.

Teaching Motor
and Perceptual Skills

Chapter **Five**

Motor and perceptual abilities are integrally involved in the process of learning. While the learning process comprises many kinds of experiences, motor and perceptual abilities are basic components of the child's total development (Bruner 1973; Gesell and Ames 1973; Shirley 1931).

This chapter provides information relative to sensorimotor and perceptual development of the child, describes atypical manifestations of this development and presents ways of teaching motor and perceptual skills to the young handicapped child. Specifically, this chapter considers: (a) components of motor and perceptual skills, (b) sensorimotor development, (c) atypical motor development, (d) sensorimotor integration, (e) characteristics of children with sensory integration disorders, and (f) instructional strategies for teaching perceptual motor skills.

Components of Motor and Perceptual Skills

Because many different terms and definitions are used in the broad explanation of motor and perceptual learning, they may appear to be confusing. Sensorimotor and perceptual skills are integral components of the learning process. While theoretical positions on the primary sources for the acquisition of information and learning differ, there is general agreement that human beings acquire knowledge through the use of their senses and with the incorporation of environmental experiences (Clark and Clark, 1976; Hunt 1972). Sensorimotor and perceptual competencies serve to enhance the incorporation of these experiences and promote intellectual growth.

Sensations

Generally, the young child displays a variety of active movements which are primarily derived from *sensations* (Conner and others 1978; Liley 1965; Piaget 1952). Sensations are impressions which are received through the five sense organs; the eyes, ears, nose, mouth, and skin.

The *sensory system* is composed of the five sense organs which conduct the impressions inward to the nervous system and then to the brain. Thus, sights, sounds, smells, tastes, and touch are incoming pieces of information which are funneled through the nervous system pathways. These sensations make their way to the brain and are coded and stored for later use.

Motor Acts

Once the brain receives the sensory information and identifies the content, proper follow-through action is dispatched. The response information is carried back through the same nervous system pathway (Gardner 1975; Grayson 1960). The demonstration of the completion of the process is an observation of the young child performing some noticeable motor act.

A *motor act* is a skill involving movement (Wickstrom 1970). It is a physically expressed movement of the human body and its parts (Connolly 1970; Robb 1972). Motor performance suggests large muscle action, muscles and bones moving together in a purposeful manner.

Muscle Activity

Individual muscles are really limited in their performance. A muscle can perform only two actions. It can contract, and it can relax. When it contracts, the muscle becomes shorter. When it relaxes, the muscle lengthens. *Muscle activity* is dependent upon the position of the bones of the body (posture) and the attached muscle. The energy for this muscle activity is transmitted through nerves. Electrical impulses emanate from the brain and are transmitted through the spinal cord and outer nerve endings to the muscles. All muscle action is controlled by the specialized centers of the brain.

Perception

Perception is an interpretive function of the brain. It is the translation of sensory impressions into some representational level that is easily stored and recalled. The interpretation is dependent upon previous experience and information. In reality, the functions of sensation, motor activity, and perception are so closely related that it is difficult to separate one from another.

From infancy through the early months of life, the young child is bombarded by environmentally stimulating sensations which have to be perceived. How does the infant and young child learn to develop perception from sensations? Learning theorists explain this process in different ways. Bower (1969, 1977) describes the process as intersensory differentiation. Piaget (1969) lists the dual processes of assimilation and accommodation. Bruner (1968) cites movement with precision as the means by which the child demonstrates an understanding and interpretation of the environment. Cratty (1970, 1979) has developed a series of axioms and postulates which attempt to classify early perceptual patterns as latticed behaviors and attributes.

Each of these writers describes interconnecting bonds between levels of perception and the child's developmental performance. The increasing adeptness of the child to use and direct the body in perceptual-motor activity is seen as a progressive development and one in which both sensory and motor systems interface (Diamondstein 1971).

Since motor and sensory responses are interrelated and difficult to separate in the early years of a child's life, the term *sensorimotor* is often used to describe the intergrated result of sensation and motor interactions as they relate to early childhood development.

Sensorimotor Development

From the time of conception, human creatures experience varying forms of physical movement (Carmichael 1970; Cratty 1970, 1979; Kephart 1960). The rate, sequence, and complexity of motor development are usually judged by direct observation of physical landmark performances. Therefore, children's normal physical development is catalogued by the speed in which grasping, sitting, walking, and self-feeding accomplishments are made.

The Newborn Infant

There is currently a rebirth of interest in the sensorimotor development of the newborn. Landmark studies in this area were made by Kagan (1971), Piaget (1952), Provence and Lipton (1962), Schilder (1935), and Spitz (1950). The current research studies, using carefully controlled behavioral conditions, are gathering highly detailed data which are descriptive of the developmental progressions and observable changes in newborn infants. Some of the developmental areas which have received attention are: the various states of awareness of the infant (Wolff 1965, 1973); patterns of vision in newborns (Fantz 1956, 1966); and measurement of temperament (Thomas, Chess, and Birch 1965; Thomas and Chess 1977).

The newborn infant is a fairly competent creature at birth. Although dependent upon the adult for food and protection for a period of time, the infant has adaptive abilities which will eventually provide for survival (Lipsitt and Kaye 1964). The first reactions to the environment may seem clumsy and uncoordinated, but these activities will be repeated and soon become well integrated (Kagan 1970; White 1975).

The first actions, mostly reflex in origin, are lower nervous system-based functions. These are involuntary movements which are prime supports for survival. Through consistent practice, the lower-level functions become automatic, and higher-level functions are performed through an integration of repeated experience and some selective choice.

Total flexibility of the sensorimotor system requires an adequate physical constitution, opportunity to practice, and an environment which encourages and supports functions of the total body. In most children, the sensorimotor system is fully operable at birth with refinements increasing as the body is capable of more specialized functions. Integration of sensory and motor activities is accomplished in a segmental fashion over time. Average children reach locomotor competence, the complete integration of sensory and motor components, by the age of six or seven (Halverson 1966).

Basic components of the motor system are established at the critical moment of conception and continue through the formative years (Coghill 1929; Gardner 1975). In the developing embryo the motor areas of the nervous system are the first in development. The prenatal period of growth is one in which great cellular changes occur in rapid succession. The culmination of the prenatal growth period is seen in the active and resilient movements performed by the newborn.

Reflex Behaviors

The responses made by the newborn infant take the form of reflexive behaviors. *Reflex behaviors* are automatic actions which enable newborn infants to practice those motor patterns over which they will have voluntary control. The reflexive behaviors include *rooting, sucking, swallowing*, the *Moro reflex*, the *Babinski reflex*, and *stepping*. Evaluations of reflexive behaviors have been used as components of neonatal assessment scales (Brazelton 1969; Prechtl and Beintema 1964).

It is expected that these reflexes will diminish in occurrence as the child develops greater voluntary control of the motor response system. Rooting, swallowing, and sucking are necessary for the location of food. *Rooting* is the turning of the head and mouth searching for the breast nipple. A soft touch to the awake infant's cheek will set this reflex into motion. *Sucking* allows the ingestion of liquids for nourishment. It also can be initiated by a soft touch to the mouth or cheek. The lips purse and make inundating motions. *Swallowing* follows sucking but is in operation even during sleep. There is a need to keep the throat and nasal passages clear for breathing, so swallowing also helps to move any mucus or fluid drainage of the sinuses.

The *Moro reflex* is a startle response, a sharp jolted action which follows a sudden change in sensation for the young infant. The head falls back, the arms are thrust out to the sides of the body, and the legs stretch and extend. The infant cries and brings both arms together. Startles diminish in number and intensity as the infant nervous system matures, until the residual remains are observed as a minor body flinch (McGraw 1969).

Another reflex which diminishes in normal development, the *Babinski reflex,* can be initiated by stroking the sole of the infant's foot. The result is the spread or fanning of the toes. This reflex usually disappears four to six months after birth.

Stepping reflexes are seen when the newborn is supported in an upright position and the feet are placed on a hard surface. The infant will make walking steps, alternating feet, but these reflexes also disappear a few weeks after birth.

Principles of Motor Development

There are five major principles of normal sensorimotor development (Conner 1978; McGraw 1969). These include

1. *Sequential Development*: Foundations of movement occur in a definite pattern and are integrated to combine and form new motor acts. The rate may vary but the sequence is usually fixed.

2. *Overlapping Sequences*: Babies are in a constant state of change. One skill may be in the process of being mastered along with the introduction of succeedingly difficult tasks.

3. *Dissociation*: Sensorimotor maturity is demonstrated by independent body movement patterns. Gradually the infant moves from a total responding organism to one which can separate body parts and can select independent movement. The infant progresses from using the whole arm

action to swipe at an object to the limited grasp of the object with only the fist or fingers.

4. *Cephalocaudal Development*: Development proceeds from the head to the feet. Motor control and coordination are achieved in the upper parts of the body and then progress down to the lower extremities. Head and trunk control precede leg control.

5. *Proximal-Distal Development*: Development also progresses from the center of the body to the periphery or extremities. There is greater control of the shoulder and arm actions before there is individualized finger dexterity.

Muscle Control and Capacity

Normal motor development is a continuous progression of muscle control and capacity (Table 5–1). Internal bodily processes are stabilizing. Breathing, digestion, and elimination become automatic processes. As external reactions of the infant are integrated, there is an increase of voluntary motor efficiency.

Flexor tone and flexion are predominant characteristics of the normal full-term baby. The arms and legs are somewhat fixed in a partial flexion and are rarely seen fully extended. This means that the extremities are positioned close to the body and are not easily straightened.

Looking at sensorimotor skills in the order of increased control, a hierarchy of skills begins to form, and there is the verification of the previously mentioned principles of development. The left side of the hierarchy listed in Table 5–2 describes motor behavior while the right side enumerates methods for the stimulation of such behaviors.

TABLE 5–1   Sensorimotor Development

Months	Trunk and Limb Control	Hand and Finger Control
0–4	Head turning-control Head lifting on forearms	Flexion of arms and legs Partial extension Hand to mouth-finger sucking Unilateral arm-leg movement

4–6	Supports body weight with arms
	While on stomach supports weight
	  by stretching arms and legs out
	  from support
	Dissociation of head-limbs
		Reaches for visual objects
		Brings hands together
		Brings objects to mouth
		Feet to mouth
		Bilateral arm-leg movement

6–8	Prone pivot Trunk extension Backward push Trunk control Supported upright sitting	Radial hand grasp Shakes objects Bangs objects

TABLE 5–1   (continued)

Months	Trunk and Limb Control	Hand and Finger Control
8–12	Trunk rotation	Thumb-index finger grasp
	Segmented body movement	Voluntary grasp-release
	Chest off floor (support on hands-knees)	Purposeful squeeze
		Inferior pincer grasp
	Propels body forward	Individualized finger agility
	Belly crawling-creeping	
	Unsupported upright sitting	
	Body rocking-bouncing (Flexion and Extension)	
	Pull to stand	
	Cruising	
12–18	Creeping	Plantar flexion
	Forward walking supported	Hip extension-toes extension
	Forward walking unsupported	Superior pincer grasp
18–24	Independent erect standing	Independent use of thumb
	Changes positions from sit to stand	Releases object at target
	Changes positions from prone to supine	Pours objects from container
		Uses whole arm movements in painting
	Fast walking	
	Wobbly gait	Throws ball overhand-two hands
	Walks upstairs assisted	
	Walks downstairs assisted	
	Kicks ball forward	
24–36	Pedals trike	Dresses self
	Reciprocal walk-alternate arm swing	Attempts buttoning
	Ascend and descend stairs (nonalternate of feet)	Zippers
		Buckles
	Running	Strings beads
	Jump holding on	Uses scissors-pencils
	Step-jump	
	Hop	
36–48	Fast run	
	Skillful jump continuous-forward	
	Skillful hopping	
	Can walk a balance beam	

TABLE 5–2   Hierarchy of Motor Behavior and Methods of Stimulation

Motor Behavior	Method of Stimulating Motor Behavior
HEAD AND NECK CONTROL	Stimulate the infant to raise head with the
To turn head to side	use of a moving light or noisy toy.
To raise head from prone position	
To support head in an upright position	
SITTING WITH SUPPORT	Gradually reduce the need for support and
To sit in a lap with minimal support	increase the length of time for nonsupport.
Independent sitting with prop (pillow)	
Independent sitting in objects with reduction of support	Increasing reduction of support gives the infant new situations to adjust to.

TABLE 5–2 (continued)

Motor Behavior	*Method of Stimulating Motor Behavior*
ROLLING OVER To roll over from back to stomach	Place infant on back and guide roll to left or right.
RAISING BODY To support the upper body on forearm	Stimulate the infant by placing on stomach and using a noisy toy or colorful object to draw attention.
SITTING WITHOUT SUPPORT To sit in chair independently To sit on the floor independently	Gradually increase the length of time for nonsupported sitting and alternate a variety of places for sitting: floor, chair, highchair, swing, and jumperseat.
PRECRAWLING To initiate forward movement—prone	Use a toy or food as an incentive and draw the infant's attention toward it.
PULL TO A SITTING POSITION To pull to a sitting position—prone To require less adult support in task	The adult is an assist and support for the child. The adult will support the child in attempts to accomplish the task.
CREEPING To locomote forward on hands and knees	Offer objects to infant to increase distance accomplished.
PULL TO STANDING POSITION To pull to standing position with support To pull to stand with less physical support To use objects as assist for pull to stand	Offer infant the use of adult support to pull to stand from a sitting position, and reduce amount of support. Also make objects available for use as supports.
SIDESTEPPING WITH SUPPORT To sidestep around objects while standing	Encourage moving to left and right in moving around objects.
STANDING WITH SUPPORT To stand with minimal adult assistance To stand using objects for adult support To stand without any support	Begin with physical support, and then the adult will gradually reduce support. First, hold with two hands and reduce to one hand and then to fingers.
WALKING To walk with back support To walk with front support To walk with object support To walk with support from side To walk without support To practice walking skills	Begin with front and back support of infant, and gradually reduce physical support. Practice the skill with regularity.
STAIRWALKING To creep upstairs To creep downstairs To walk upstairs with support To walk downstairs with support To walk upstairs without support To walk downstairs without support To practice stairwalking skills To use alternate feet in stairwalking To walk stairs in a continuous alternation of feet	Provide safe opportunity for child to attempt to accomplish the skill. Small set of stairs is a good start. Provide supervision for the practice of this skill. The adult should be physically near the child while this skill is being practiced until such time as it is mastered.
RUNNING To alternate feet To alternate feet and have both in air To increase tempo of running and length of time in midair	Establish an area which is free of objects and which will allow the child an opportunity to practice the task. Playgrounds, parks, walks, and hallways are good areas. Be sure that shoes are not slippery or new.

TABLE 5-2 (continued)

Motor Behavior	*Method of Stimulating Motor Behavior*
LEAPING To leap forward To increase height of leap To increase distance of leap To leap continuously	Provide an opportunity to move freely. Give the child a model to follow or a set of actions to copy.
JUMPING To jump from step holding on to support To jump from one foot to the other foot To jump up from two feet To jump down from two feet To run and jump forward from one foot to other To jump forward from two feet To jump down from one foot to two feet To run and jump forward from one foot to two feet To jump over object from two feet To jump from two feet in a continuous manner	Provide situations which will induce the child to use the skill. Offer models for the child to copy. Set a special time for practice of the skill. Offer physical support to initiate the action. Place objects down in an obstacle path for the child to jump over. Show the child that you are pleased with any effort. Encourage practice. Play games that use the skill.
HOPPING To hop on one foot To hop on the other foot To hop continuously on either foot To hop alternating feet	Give physical support for balance. Remove the support as the child can manage alone. Encourage practice, and show the child that you are pleased with any effort. Young children begin this task by holding on to the foot that is not used and then progress to independently lifting the one foot off the ground during the hop. Play games that use the motor skill.
SKIPPING To move forward using a step and hop To step and hop using step on one foot and hop on other (gallop) To step and hop using step on one foot and hop on the same foot (skip)	Provide a model for the child to copy. Separate the parts of the skip into a step and a hop. Integrate the two steps into a smooth pattern. It may require extended practice. Encourage the child to practice. Encourage the child to practice, and show that you are pleased with any effort. It may help for the child to say "step-hop-step-hop" while doing the task.
THROWING To use the whole arm prior to the release of the object To release object with backward or forward thrust with no body rotation To release object with rotation of trunk and step off one foot To release object with step, pivot, and timed throw	Offer small objects that can be easily grasped, such as beanbags or soft toys. When using balls, use a small ball that the child can hold easily if you plan to throw for accuracy. If you are going to throw for distance, use a large ball—inflated but soft. Provide a target for the throw, and alternate accuracy and distance priorities. Begin with a large ball and decrease size of ball to accommodate the child's hand and grasp.

134

TABLE 5–2 (continued)

Motor Behavior	*Method of Stimulating Motor Behavior*
CATCHING To roll a ball to another person To receive a ball (small object), body cradling for the catch To receive an object with arms clasped to grasp To receive an object with arm preparation	Begin with rolling activities, and increase to toss at a short distance. Throw to the child at the middle of body height so as to make the catch possible. Observe the child's stance to catch, and alert the child to prepare arms for the catch. Plan activities that use catching skills for practice.

Atypical Motor Development

Differences in the quality of motor performance and variances in the rate of motor skill proficiency in young children are often viewed as atypical developmental patterns and may be signs of later problems.

There has been a growing interest to link the significant factors in motor growth and in motor lags to future academic performances (Balow 1969; Birch 1973; Gesell and Amatruda 1954).

However, Wickstrom (1970) cautions that developmental performance of motor patterns shows normal variance, and children frequently make large and uneven growth spurts. Stages are not attained by all children, and at equal intervals uneven increments in growth and motor development may only indicate the range and variance in human development.

Kinds of Atypical Motor Development

The child whose motor development is different from the established norm may show one of the following patterns:

Stage Skipping: A child may skip one or several of the regular stages and achieve a mature motor pattern at an earlier age than expected.

Stage Deviation: A child may fail to make significant progress and remain at an immature stage indefinitely.

Partial Stages: A child may acquire partial skills and not fit into a particular stage.

Stage Lag: A child may linger at an early stage of skill development for a while, then quickly pass through several stages to a mature pattern.

Motor Deviations

Atypical motor development can take many forms (Birch 1973; O'Brien 1971). A motor system must be intact and free from deviations in order for normal progression to occur. Defective chromosomes can alter growth patterns as can maternal diet during pregnancy. Drug use and illness at critical stages of pregnancy have also demonstrated disastrous results in the newborn (Meier 1976). Minor muscle weaknesses, joint formation problems, or malformations can also increase the possibility for motor differences and abnormalities.

Delays or deviations in muscle development can be classified by the elements of *muscle tone, muscle control,* and *muscle strength*.

Deficits in muscle tone.   Tone deficits are muscle tension related, and the stretching capacity of muscles is of great importance. A tense child will have increased tone while a sleeping child will have decreased tone.

An exaggeration to either extreme on a regular basis creates a condition called *hypotonicity* or *hypertonicity*.

When muscles are limp and do not demonstrate resistance to a stretch, a loss of tone is said to create *hypotonicity*. The child experiencing this problem will probably have little effectual movement and a lack of postural stability. Just the support of the body in an upright fashion may be taxing for such a child.

Tight muscles, on the other hand, are muscles constantly excited and stretched, a condition called *hypertonicity*. In order to accomplish efficient movement, an overexertion of force is necessary.

Two types of hypertonicity are *spasticity* and *rigidity*. Muscles which are *spastic* require force to overcome the resistance to stretch, but there will be some movement. Sometimes the resistance is overcome, but the resulting movement is erratic. On the other hand, *rigid* muscles resist any movement.

Deficits in muscle control.   Rapid, jerky, involuntary movements of the arms and legs are called *tremors*. Involuntary muscle vibrations impair the child's use of balance and coordination. These movement disturbances may be seen as poorly controlled sets of subskills. In some children, the motor abilities appear to resemble normal children's performance but at younger or less mature levels of motor coordination.

Deficits in muscle strength.   There may be differences in muscle strength within a child's body. Greater or lesser muscle strength may be found on the right or left side of the body. Also, muscle involvement may affect one side of the body more than the other. A muscle weakness is called a *paresis,* while a total inability to move is called a *plegia.*

The causative basis for deviant motor development is often connected with damage or lack of control in one or more of the centers of the brain (Johnston and Magrab 1976; Penfield and Roberts 1959). However, observable differences in early motor integrations can signal deviant patterns and offer the possibility for intervention, remedial suggestions, and potential changes in motor integrations.

Sensorimotor Integration

Kephart

Newell Kephart (1960) adapted concepts of learning and motor theory to build an understanding of the handicapped child. He viewed development as a sequential refinement of basic motor generalizations rather than as a sequence of skills (Chaney and Kephart 1968). Kephart defined the development of motor coordination into four basic subcategories: (a) balance and posture, (b) locomotion, (c) contact-manipulation, and (d) receipt and propulsion.

According to Kephart, the orderly development of motor skills relies upon a perceptual motor matching. Inaccuracies of the motor perception match are considered prime causes for children's learning problems. Therefore, Kephart strongly endorsed the intensive remediation of perception-motor skills as the foundation for all other learning problems. Giving a child a more secure and trustworthy sense of the qualities of the physical universe which are met on a daily basis was suggested as the means by which further academic success could be reached.

Ayres

Ayres (1972), an occupational therapist, contends that the learning problems of handicapped children are related to deficits in sensory integration. Further, Ayres believes that special sensorimotor activities which are designed to provide tactile and vestibular stimulation can enhance sensory integration and thereby ameliorate the learning disorders of handicapped children.

By definition, *sensory integration* is a neurophysiological process by which sensory information is organized and interpreted. It involves the central nervous system, taking in, sorting out, and connecting information from our environment. The sensory systems take in the information, the brain integrates the information with older behavior, and feedback from this behavior circles back to the brain, so it can decide if a higher-level behavior is needed.

The sensory systems involved in sensory integration are: (a) tactile, (b) vestibular, (c) proprioceptive, (d) olfactory, (e) visual, and (f) auditory. The visual and auditory systems receive much educational emphasis because of their obvious classroom application. Even though the tactile and vestibular systems are the oldest systems (they develop first in utero), they have received less emphasis in instructional planning. Sensory integration deals with stimulating the *tactile* and *vestibular systems*. These two systems are expected to help provide the foundation for the auditory and visual systems.

To understand how influential these two systems are on the learning process, it is necessary to look at them closely and begin to understand them both functionally and anatomically.

The *vestibular system* provides a sense of balance. Research shows that at twenty weeks in fetal life, the vestibular system has developed, is receiving information, and is acting on the stimulation it receives. Some researchers believe that it may be this system that tells a baby to invert itself in utero to ready itself for passage through the birth canal.

The receptors of the vestibular system are located in the inner ear. Depending on the type of vestibular stimulation, one or more of the receptors will be stimulated, and the information will be relayed on to other centers. The vestibular system has many functions and influences many other areas of the brain, such as sending direct messages to the cranial nerves that control eye muscles.

Just as a child can be overstimulated by vestibular input, a child can also be overinhibited. Vital functions that are controlled at the brain stem level can be depressed to a dangerous state. An overinhibited child can experience decreased respiration, decreased heart rate, or various vasomotor responses, such as blanching, nausea, or perspiration. These will be considered further in the discussion regarding precautions.

Although little is known about how sensory integration can affect personality directly, it is known that all sensory modalities send impulses to the brain's limbic system which has a central role in emotional development. The limbic system is responsible for gut-level emotions, such as anger, rage, and motivation.

The vestibular system both receives and interprets movement information. As such, it is central to learning and to central nervous system maturation.

The *tactile system* is another influential system. The tactile system refers to sensations received through the skin—the sense of touch. Tactile sensation influences a wide range of human behaviors. It provides a major source of information about environmental conditions, telling us what is dangerous and what is not.

The receptors for the tactile system are in the skin. Along with its receptors, the tactile pathways and other brain structures make up the complete tactile system. Information concerning tactile stimuli is relayed in two major pathways: the *spinothalmic* and the *lemniscal*. The *spinothalmic* pathway carries protective information that tells the organism about dangerous stimuli; it readies the organism for a response that is usually motor. This pathway system has a large receptor field so that no information is missed or overlooked that could be potentially harmful. This protective pathway transmits information about potential harm, light touch, hair displacement, pain, and temperature. The *lemniscal system* is more discriminative. It initiates desire in the individual and allows purposeful movement to explore the environment. These pathways relay information regarding (a) pressure, (b) proprioception and kinesthesia, and (c) spatial and temporal aspects of touch, such as size and stereognosis. In the normal person, these two systems maintain a delicate balance in assisting a child to learn about the environment (Johnson, Haugh and Topper 1979).

Other sensory systems are also involved in sensory integration, but the tactile and vestibular systems provide the foundation noted earlier for other sensory systems. Problems in either of these sensory systems can hinder the development of other systems.

To summarize, sensory integration follows a developmental process. Rather than a ladder system, however, it is a spiraling chain whose levels overlap and build on each other. As the child develops, information absorbed through different sensory systems provides knowledge about the self and the environment.

Characteristics of Children with Sensory Integration Disorders

Children with disorders in the tactile and vestibular systems can display a wide range of characteristics. It is important to recognize how these characteristics interfere with learning.

A well-integrated tactile system will provide the child with the ability to use touch for object discrimination, motor planning, and also as a protective system to withdraw quickly from potentially harmful stimuli. When the tactile system is unbalanced and the protective system predominates, touch is often perceived as a threat, resulting in withdrawal. To varying degrees, children with this problem, called *tactile defensiveness*, will dislike having their hair combed, hugging or touching, playing with fuzzy textures, and rolling up their shirt sleeves. In some cases, children will only manipulate objects with the tips of their fingers, avoiding the palms of their hands, or will walk on their toes, rather than on the whole sole of their foot. These children may have difficulty relating to other children because they will interpret the typical jostling play of children as aggressive or attacking and will respond accordingly. Some children may touch or explore the environment and seek out tactile stimuli but they must be the ones to initiate and control the stimuli, and if touched by someone, they may react negatively.

Hyperactivity and distractability are frequently seen in children with tactile defensiveness. However, not all cases of hyperactive and distractable behavior can be attributed to tactile defensiveness. If the protective tactile system overrides the discriminative tactile system, the child may interpret some tactile information as potentially harmful. As a result, the child may fail to inhibit responses to many stimuli which others consider irrelevant. When children respond to the irrelevant stimuli, the teacher may label them distractable.

Equilibrium reactions can also be effected by vestibular system dysfunction. Equilibrium reactions help us maintain or regain a given posture, such as quadruped, kneeling, sitting, or standing. By changing the body's center of gravity, or the surface supporting the body, equilibrium reactions are elicited. These reactions involve moving the body's center of gravity to maintain balance; this includes moving the extremities to assist in that maintenance.

Postural insecurity may be present with poor equilibrium reactions. This may be displayed by children who have rigid postures and demonstrate adverse reactions to movement. These children lack a feeling of security when moving through space and changing positions in relation to gravity. They are fearful when their feet are not firmly on the ground. Such children are also fearful of playground equipment and tend to avoid roughhouse playing.

Postural background movements place the extremities in a more appropriate position for fine motor tasks. Children with poor postural background movements rely on trunk movements, rather than isolating arm movements, for fine motor tasks.

Also related to vestibular dysfunction is *poor ocular control*. If eye muscle control is poor, children may fatigue or skip letters, words, or lines. One classroom problem that results is that the children have difficulty locating a visual stimulus and focusing in on it. They may lose their place when glancing from their book to the blackboard. Poor ocular control may also be evidenced by poor tracking abilities, especially when tracking across the midline. The children may blink, or turn the head to avoid the midline, and thus lose the object that they were tracking.

Also related to poor interhemispheric communication is *difficulty with bilateral motor coordination*. In order to perform smooth, automatic movements involving the two body sides, the child must first develop adequate coordination in each individual body side. Observations in the classroom that could indicate poor bilateral coordination are a child failing to hold down the paper with the nondominant hand when writing, or a child having trouble jumping with two feet together. Clapping games and skipping are also impeded by poor bilateral motor coordination.

Self-stimulation is behavior in which the child stimulates one of the senses which has not matured properly. This may take the form of tapping fingers, hand flipping, finger clicking, rocking, head banging, twirling, or watching circular motions, to name a few. This child is using these socially unacceptable behaviors to provide the nervous system with stimulation that cannot be obtained through normal behaviors.

Instructional Strategies for Teaching Perceptual Motor Skills

Children with tactile or vestibular system dysfunction can display a wide variety of characteristics that may interfere with their classroom performance. When these characteristics do interfere with learning, it is important for the therapist and teacher to work together in providing help for the child. Any remediation done by an occupational therapist (OT) requires a prescription from the physician in charge of the case.

The occupational therapist uses a multisensory approach along with careful control of specific sensory stimuli to elicit an adaptive response while also following the developmental sequence. The therapist employs tactile and vestibular stimuli carefully because of widespread influence on the nervous system, and especially because of the influence on the visual and auditory processes.

Tactile activities should encompass a variety of touch stimulations over as much of the body as possible. Watch the child's reaction, and strive for pleasurable touch. It should be noted that a tactually defensive child will respond best to firm touch and deep pressure. Light touch and furry textures are most likely to elicit aversive reactions, triggering the protective "flight" system. Imposed tactile stimulation is more threatening than input controlled by the child. These are important points to remember when dealing with young children.

Activities for Sensory and Movement Stimulation

General sensory and movement stimulation can be accomplished through many developmental experience designed activities (Clifton 1970; Connolly 1970). Rolling on textured surfaces, such as grass and sculptured carpeting, provide added stimulation (Conner and others 1978). Playing with water, dough, and sand are also texture-stimulating activities. Rubbing the body with powder and lotion is cutaneous stimulation. Bouncing on inflatable equipment, playing with musical toys, and negotiating an obstacle course are more physically involved exercises. In each instance, the activity is designed to increase sensorimotor input. Only when the muscle tone requires carefully altered patterns of stimulation are those techniques instituted.

Spastic muscle tone may require controlled sleeping situations, use of an inflated air mattress, bolsters, and rolled towels to reduce the effects of limited muscle response to a resting state. In some cases, sustained pressure on particular joints and muscles will increase muscle response. A light embrace, meant to be a sign of approval, may actually be a very unpleasant experience for a child, while a spanking may turn out to be reinforcing.

Tactile stimulation can be provided in a variety of ways, for example, rubbing hands, feet, or the body with a blanket or towel; lying in a hammock that wraps around the body; writing on a carpet square with chalk, then erasing it with the arms, elbows, or feet; reaching for toys in a carpeted barrel, or lying or rolling on a carpeted surface; rolling up in a blanket, then unrolling; walking barefoot in sand, grass, or leaves; playing with water; playing with play dough or clay; painting with finger paints or shaving cream; engaging in puppet games; and digging for objects buried in sand.

Initially, the tactile system is best developed in the mouth. Babies often explore objects by placing them in the mouth. We might see older children inappropriately mouthing toys and the possibility that the child might not be receiving adequate sensory information through the hands should be considered. Children might benefit by manipulating materials which provide extra tactile input when they hold them, such as blocks covered with sand or other more defined fabrics.

Vestibular stimulation can be both active and passive. Children can have stimulation imposed upon them, or they can actively control the movement themselves. If the child shows little response to motion input, and likes it, activities should stress rapid acceleration of motion or change of speed. Upside down is also a good position, even though it is not accelerated motion. If the child seems frightened by, or overly dizzy from, the motion, the activities should be given slowly and with the child actively controlling the motion.

Active vestibular stimulation can be achieved through any of the following: "sit and spin"; spin and unwind on a twisted swing or single rope swing; spin on scooterboard; push off fast from a wall while on a scooterboard; upside down on a barrel; rock on barrel or inflated big beach ball or use rocking chair; spring horse; somersaults; roll down an incline; inverted football hiking games; ride scooterboard down a ramp.

The following precautions should be observed when using sensory integrative activities:

1. Never maintain a high rate of speed.
2. Stop when children indicate that they have had enough—either verbally or by watching body signs.
3. Never stay on spinning activities for more than two minutes.

The prone position (lying flat, face down) has been demonstrated to play an important role in enhancing sensory integration when the deficits are associated with the brain stem. Activities using movement prone on a scooterboard are frequently seen in a sensory integrative therapy session. This treatment principle can be incorporated into a classroom program by positioning children prone on their stomachs during certain activities.

The development of a good *body scheme* is paramount to developing perceptual-motor skills. When perceptual difficulties are encountered, it is wise to carefully evaluate the child's body scheme development. Even though a child can correctly identify body parts, he or she may not have any idea of how those parts work together as a whole. Many gross motor games and activities can assist in the development of body scheme. *Charades* is a game that can easily be used with a large group of children and also graded to specific levels of difficulty.

Once children have developed an intact body scheme, they can begin to regulate or monitor motor skills. They learn to "think through" or plan new motor tasks. In order to motor plan effectively, information from the touch, proprioceptive, vestibular, and visual systems are needed. Think about how much effort children use when learning to motor plan activities such as tying shoes—they need all the help they can get from numerous sensory systems. Once children learn to tie shoes, the process should become automatic. They should no longer need to put all that initial effort into tying the shoes. Children with sensory integrative dysfunction, however, often cannot rely on efficient processing of sensory information and motor planning tasks may not readily become automatic.

The treatment plan for children with poor motor planning skills entails providing them with a variety of motor tasks that have not been previously learned and thus requires them to focus attention on the tasks.

Although all sensory integrative activities should be planned under the supervision of a trained therapist, there are a number of principles that can be followed in the classroom. It is not realistic to expect that a total therapy program can be implemented in the classroom. Rather, by knowing about behavioral characteristics of children with sensory integrative dysfunction, a teacher may be better equipped to understand the child, the needs for sensory input, and be better able to meet some of those needs in a group setting.

Children who engage in self-stimulating behaviors are relaying information. Hand flapping, bouncing in the seat, or rocking back and forth may not be appropriate in certain situations. However, these children are seeking out specific sensory input—possibly to help organize the nervous system so they can handle school work better. This should not be ignored. It might be more efficient in the end to let the child get up and out of the seat and do some work prone on a mat or let the child engage in gross motor games periodically during the day in order to enhance the ability to organize sensory systems. Often the child's attention span will lengthen and school work will be completed with much less effort.

Sensory integrative therapy is aimed at enhancing the nervous system's ability to organize and interpret sensory input in order to improve the efficiency of motor output. It is not aimed at directly improving certain developmental motor tasks.

Adaptive Supports

The handicapping condition can present some motor involvement for young children. The age of the child at the onset of the condition and the degree of severity affect the motor needs of that child. The severity of the handicap may necessitate the use of specialized equipment to compensate for motor deficiencies. Muscular incoordination may require the use of special chairs, tables, braces, or wheelchairs.

A young child who is not able to sit well can be supported with rolled bolsters or be placed in a chair supported with footrests, harnesses, cloth tie-ins, or straps. This can offer additional support to compensate for the inability of the muscles to support the body.

Fine motor teaching strategies can be assisted with the use of foam, wood, plastic, and tape additions to the pencils or crayons used with young children. Reducing the slippery surface helps the child with grasping problems. Using foam and placing the writing tool through foam gives the child a larger mass to hold. Also, specialized pencil grip holders are available for strapping the pencil to the hand, should grasp be difficult.

Fine Motor Activities

There are many instructional activities which can be used to enhance fine motor and eye-hand coordination.

1. *Preschool Games*: Many preschool games and toys, such as pounding pegs with a hammer, hammer and nail games, and dropping forms into slots, can be useful to practice fine motor control.

2. *Clipping Clothespins*: Clothespins can be clipped onto a line or a box. Children can be timed in this activity by counting the number of clothespins clipped in a specified time.

3. *Water Control*: Carrying and pouring water into measured buckets from pitchers to specified levels can be encouraged. Use smaller amounts and finer measurements to make the task more difficult. Use of colored water makes the activity more interesting.

4. *Lacing*: A cardboard punched with holes or a pegboard is suitable for this activity. A design or picture is made on the board, and the child weaves or sews with a heavy shoelace, yarn, or similar cord through the holes to follow the pattern.

5. *Tracing*: Trace lines, pictures, designs, letters, or numbers on tracing paper, plastic, or stencils. Use directional arrows, color cues, and numbers to help the child trace the figures.

6. *Cutting with Scissors*: Have the child cut with scissors, choosing activities appropriate to needs. Be sure to have left-handed scissors available. There are also "guiding scissors" which allow the teacher to hold on the scissors simultaneously with the child. Easiest to cut are straight short lines marked near the edges of the paper which make a fringe. Then cut along straight lines across the paper. Some children might need a cardboard attached to the paper to help guide the scissors. Cut out marked geometric shapes, such as squares, rectangles, and

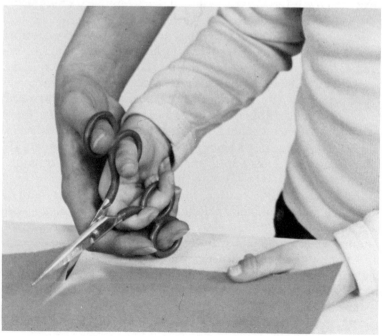

triangles. Draw a different color line to indicate change of direction in cutting. Cut out curving lines and circles. Cut out pictures. Cut out patterns made with dots and faint lines.

7. *Paper Folding*: Simple paper folding activities are useful for the development of eye-hand coordination, following directions, and fine motor control.

8. *Stencils or Templates*: Have the child draw outlines of patterns of geometric shapes. Templates can be made from cardboard, wood, plastic, old X-ray films, or containers for packaged meat. Two styles can be made: a solid shape or frames with the shape cut out.

9. *Paper and Pencil Activities*: Simple coloring books, readiness books, and dot-to-dot books frequently provide good paper and pencil activities for fine motor and eye-hand development.

10. *Copying Designs*: Children look at a geometric design and copy it onto a piece of paper.

Limitations of a Perceptual Motor Training Program

Learning theorists, such as those described in this chapter, believe that sensorimotor and perceptual development provide the essential foundation for other kinds of learning. A question that must be asked, however, is how effective are motor and perceptual training activities in improving other kinds of skills, particularly academic skills.

Motor and perceptual training programs have been criticized because they have not been proven to lead to academic improvement. Programs which concentrate on motor training *only* are questioned because of the limitations that such remediation offers in transfer to academic subjects. Also, statistical evaluation is not easy to perform given the differences found in the statistical designs among the programs, the size of each group of subjects, the criterion for achievement, and the level of motor proficiency expected (Hammill and others 1975).

Evaluation to determine the effectiveness of motor training has relied on change in IQ scores or improvement in reading level as measures of progress. However, both types of measures have been questioned as valid evaluation criteria (Meier 1976). There *are* positive gains from motor programs; but, those gains are but *one* part of an educational plan for a child with developmental problems (Herkowitz 1970). Attempting to correlate increases in perceptual motor skill with intelligence and achievement increases may be unwarranted. In viewing infants and young children's normal development, intelligence has been equated with reflex and motor efficiency (Bayley 1935, 1949, 1956; Peiper 1963). Most items for children below the age of two are motor items due to the fact that expressive language does not emerge until the second year of life. Little correlation has been found between these motor-rated measures of intelligence taken at younger ages of development and later measures of academic excellence.

It may be that we need to select appropriate measures to determine the effectiveness of motor training. Further, current studies suffer from inappropriate statistical design (Campbell and Erlebacher 1970). The sensorimotor process is such an intricate system, it might be important to carefully document the establishment of each of the levels of cortical functioning in normal children and then apply that model to atypical children to determine specific differences in sequence and rate and the effects of a remedial plan to both normal and atypical children.

Summary

Perceptual motor learning and development is best described as one of the integrated processes of generalized learning. The young child receives sensory impressions which are transformed into symbolic representations. The impressions are stored within the central nervous system and are carried in and out of those internal structures through muscle and nerve connections. The completion of the process results in a motor act. The nervous system has a hierarchy of function which permits an increasingly complex integration of sensation and motor-produced responses. The lower the level of integration is, the more specific the response. The more generalized responses result from a higher level of neurological integration.

The principal features of motor development are found within the embryo's development. The first developing system, the nervous system, controls motor activity and body movements. These motor actions are initiated with reflexive actions, such as sucking and swallowing. Involuntary activities are followed by more complex voluntary actions, such as grasping, walking, skipping, or writing.

Children grow and develop in numerous ways, including physical size and motor capacity. The normal maturation of internal structures along with day-to-day experiences merge to result in motoric performance. The ability to perform changes as the child becomes more proficient in the voluntary control of individual body parts and movement patterns. Development is sequential, but skills can overlap. Motor control proceeds from the head to the toes and from the center of the body to the periphery. Beginning with a flexor strength, the muscles increase in flexibility until they can extend as well as flex. Flexion and extension give greater trunk and joint rotation and increase the range of movement.

Deviations in motor skills result in atypical behavior. Children with central nervous system damage or with maturational lag can demonstrate difficulties in motor processing.

Sensory stimulation and motor intervention are suggested as components in the educational program designed to aid a child with developmental motor delays. The remedial plan should consider physical readiness and the limiting motoric capacity of a specific handicap, should there be a severe effect. Categories of sensorimotor skills can be instituted using a regular physical education program to provide the organizational format. Independent techniques can also be designed to facilitate bilateral manipulation, lateral alternation, and integrated lateral action of arms and legs.

Review Questions

TERMS TO KNOW

a. *sensation*	f. *perception*
b. *hypotonicity*	g. *principles of motor development*
c. *sensorimotor development*	h. *hypertonicity*
d. *Ayres*	i. *reflexes*
e. *motor act*	j. *Kephart*

1. List the five principles of motor development, and describe each. How would these differ in an average six year old compared to a TMH child?
2. What is cephalocaudal and proximal distal development? Give an example of each at ages one and three years.
3. Atypical motor development can be identified in different ways. Describe one kind of atypical motor development and a brief plan for remediation using therapeutic strategies.
4. If a child requires occupational therapy, what does it involve?
5. List three characteristics of a child with a disorder in the tactile system.
6. Tactile defensiveness may be combatted. What is it, and how is this done?
7. Name three precautions for sensory integration therapy.
8. Adaptive supports may be necessary for an early childhood program. Describe what one may be.
9. Plan an instructional activity for a child with a gross motor problem.

10. Competent fine motor skills are necessary in preparation for regular classroom success. List a developmental hierarchy for the skill of cutting and two techniques to assist a child in acquiring competence in this task.

References

AYRES, J. *Sensory Integration and Learning Disorders.* Los Angeles: Western Psychological Services, 1972.

BALOW, B., AND OTHERS. *Educational and Behavioral Sequelae of Prenatal and Perinatal Conditions.* Unpublished report, University of Minnesota, 1969.

BAYLEY, N. The Development of Motor Abilities During the First Three Years. *Monographs of the Society for Research in Child Development,* 1935, 1, 1–26.

BAYLEY, N. Consistency and Variability in the Growth of Intelligence From 0 to 18 years. *Journal of Genetic Psychology,* 1949, 75, 165–196.

BAYLEY, N. Individual Pattern of Development. *Child Development,* 1956, 27, 45–74.

BIRCH, H. G. Perinatal Factors: Minimal Brain Damage, in *The Competent Infant,* eds., L. J. Stone, H. T. Smith, and L. B. Murphy. New York: Basic Books, 1973.

BOWER, T. G. R. *A Primer of Infant Development.* San Francisco: W. H. Freeman & Company, Publishers, 1977.

BOWER, T. G. R. Perceptual Functioning in Early Infancy, in *Brain and Early Behavior,* ed. R. J. Robinson. London: Academic Press, 1969.

BRAZELTON, T. B. *Infants and Mothers.* New York: Dell Pub. Co., Inc., 1969.

BROMWICH, R. M. Stimulation in the First Year of Life. *Young Children,* 1977, 32, 71–82.

BRONFENBRENNER, U. *Is Early Intervention Effective?* Vol. II, DHEW Publication No (OHD) 7425, 1974.

BRONFENBRENNER, U., AND M. A. MAHONEY, eds. *Influences on Human Development.* Hinsdale, Ill.: Dryden Press, 1975.

BRONSON, G. W. The Postnatal Growth of Visual Capacity. *Child Development,* 1974, 45, 873–890.

BROWMAN, S. H., P. L. NICHOLS AND W. A. KENNEDY. *Preschool IQ: Prenatal and Early Developmental Correlates.* New Jersey: Lawrence Erlbaum, 1975.

BRUNER, J., AND OTHERS. *Studies in Cognitive Growth.* New York: John Wiley, 1967.

BRUNER, J. Processes of Cognitive Growth: Infancy. *Heinz Werner Lecture Series No. 3.* Massachusetts: Clark University Press, 1968.

BRUNER, J. *Beyond the Information Given.* New York: W. W. Norton, 1973.

CALDWELL, B. M. The Rational For Early Intervention. *Exceptional Children,* 1970, 36, 717–726.

CALDWELL, B. M., AND D. J. STEDMAN, eds., *Infant Education: A Guide For Helping Handicapped Children in the First Three Years.* New York: Walker & Co., 1977.

CAMPBELL, D. T., AND A. ERLEBACHER. How Regression Artifacts in Quasi-Experimental Evaluation Can Mistakenly Make Compensatory Education Look Harmful, in *Disadvantaged Child,* Vol. 3, ed. J. Hellmuth. Seattle: B. Straub and J. Hellmuth Co., 1970.

CARMICHAEL, L. Onset and Early Development of Behavior, in *Carmichael's Manual of Child Psychology,* ed. P. H. Mussen. New York: John Wiley, 1970.

CARTERETTE, E. C., AND M. P. FRIEDMAN. *Handbook of Perception.* New York: Academic Press, 1973.

CHANEY, C. M., AND N. C. KEPHART. *Motoric Aids to Perceptual Training.* Columbus, Ohio: Chas. E. Merrill, 1968.

CLARK, A. M., AND A. D. CLARK, eds. *Early Experience: Myth and Evidence.* New York: The Free Press, 1976.

CLIFTON, M. A Developmental Approach to Perceptual Motor Experiences. *Journal of Health, Physical Education Recreation,* 1970, 41, 34–38.

COGHILL, G. E. *Anatomy and Problem Behavior.* Cambridge: Cambridge University Press, 1929.

CONNOLLY, K., ed. *Mechanisms of Motor Skill.* New York: Academic Press, 1970.

CONNOR, F. P., G. G. WILLIAMSON, AND J. M. SIEPP. *Program Guide for Infants and Toddlers with Neuromotor and Other Developmental Disabilities.* New York: Teacher's College Press, 1978.

CRATTY, B. J. *Perceptual and Motor Development in Infants and Children.* London: Macmillan, 1970.

CRATTY, B. J. *Perceptual and Motor Development in Infants and Children.* Englewood Cliffs, N.J.: Prentice-Hall, Inc., 1979.

DIAMONDSTEIN, G. *Children Dance in the Classroom.* New York: Macmillan, 1971.

FANTZ, R. L. A Method for Studying Visual Development. *Perceptual Motor Skills,* 1956, 6, 13–15.

FANTZ, R. L. Pattern Discrimination and Selective Attention as Determinants of Perceptual Development From Birth, in *Perceptual Development in Children,* eds. A. H. Kidd and J. J. Rivoire. New York: International University Press, 1966.

GARDNER, E. *Fundamentals of Neurology.* Philadelphia: Saunders, 1975.

GESELL, A., AND L. AMES. Early Evidences of Individuality in the Human Infant. *Scientific Monthly,* 1937, 45, 217–225.

GESELL, A., AND C. S. AMATRUDA. *Developmental Diagnosis.* New York: Hoeber, 1954.

GLAVIN, J. P., ed. *Perceptual Motor Training for Handicapped Children.* New York: MSS Educational Publishing Co., 1975.

GRAYSON, J. *Nerves, Brain & Man.* New York: Taplinger Publishing, 1960.

HALVERSON, L. Development of Motor Patterns in Young Children. *Quest,* 1966.

HAMMILL, D., L. GOODMAN, AND J. WIEDERHOLT. Visual Motor Processes—Can We Train Them? in *Perceptual Motor Training for Handicapped Children,* ed. J. P. Glavin. New York: MSS Educational Publishing Co., 1975.

HERKOWITZ, J. A Perceptual Motor Training Program to Improve the Gross Motor Abilities of Preschoolers. *Journal of Health Physical Education Recreation,* 1970, 41, 38–41.

HUNT, J. M., ed. *Human Intelligence.* New Jersey: Transaction Books, 1972.

JOHNSON, E., S. HAUGH AND C. TOPPER. Implementation of Sensory Integrative Therapy. ICEC Conference, Chicago, November 1979.

JOHNSTON, R. B., AND P. R. MAGRAB, eds. *Developmental Disorders: Assessment, Treatment, Education.* Baltimore, Md.: University Park Press, 1976.

KAGAN, J. The Determinants of Attention in the Infant. *American Scientist,* 1970, 58, 298–306.

KAGAN, J. *Change and Continuity in Infancy.* New York: John Wiley, 1971.

KEPHART, N. C. *The Slow Learner in the Classroom.* Columbus, Ohio: Chas. E. Merrill, 1960.

LILEY, A. W. *Studies in Physiology.* Berlin: Springer-Verlag, 1965.

LIPSITT, L. P., AND H. KAYE. Conditioned sucking in the human newborn. *Psychonomic Science,* 1964, 1, 29–30.

McGRAW, M. *The Neuromuscular Maturation of the Human Infant.* New York: Hafner, 1969.

MEIER, J. *Developmental and Learning Disabilities.* Baltimore, Md.: University Park Press, 1976.

O'BRIEN, J. S. How We Detect Mental Retardation Before Birth. *Medical Times,* 1971, 99, 103–108.

PEIPER, A. *Cerebral Function in Infancy and Childhood.* London: Pitman Medical Publishing Co., 1963.

PENFIELD, W., AND L. ROBERTS. *Speech and Brain Mechanisms.* Princeton, N.J.: Princeton University Press, 1959.

PIAGET, J. *The Origins of Intelligence in Children,* trans. M. Cook. New York: International University Press, 1952.

PIAGET, J. *The Mechanisms of Perception,* trans. G. N. Seagrim New York: Basic Books, 1969.

PRECHTL, H., AND D. BEINTEMA. *The Neurological Examination of the Full Term Newborn Infant.* London: Heineman, 1964.

PROVENCE, S., AND R. C. LIPTON. *The Infants in Institutions.* New York: International Universities Press, 1962.

ROBB, M. D. *The Dynamics of Motor Skill Acquisition.* Englewood Cliffs, N.J.: Prentice-Hall, Inc., 1972.

SCHILDER, P. *The Image and Appearance of the Human Body.* New York: International Universities Press, 1935.

SHIRLEY, M. M. *The First Two Years: A Study of 25 Babies.* Minneapolis, Minn.: University of Minnesota Press, 1931.

SPITZ, R. A. Anxiety in Infancy: A Study of Its Manifestations in the First Year of Life. *International Journal of Psychoanalysis,* 1950, 31, 138–143.

THOMAS, A. S., S. CHESS, AND H. G. BIRCH. *Temperament and Behavior Disorders in Children.* New York: New York University Press, 1965.

THOMAS, A., AND S. CHESS. *Temperament and Development.* New York: Brunner-Mazel, 1977.

WICKSTROM, R. L. *Fundamental Motor Patterns.* Philadelphia: Lea & Febiger, 1970.

WHITE, B. *The First Three Years of Life.* Englewood Cliffs, N.J.: Prentice-Hall, Inc., 1975.

WOLFF, P. H. Observation on Newborn Infants. *Psychosomatic Medicine,* 1959, 21, 110–118.

WOLFF, P. H. The Development of Attention in Young Infants. *Annals of the New York Academy of Sciences,* 1965, 118, 815–830.

WOLFF, P. H. The Classification of States, in eds. L. J. Stone, H. T. Smith, and L. B. Murphy. *The Competent Infant,* New York: Basic Books, 1973.

Teaching
Cognitive Skills

Chapter **Six**

The ability to think has been called the essence of being human. "I think—therefore I exist," the oft-quoted premise of the philosopher, Descartes, reflects the inseparable relationship between the essence of the human species and the thinking process.

What Cognitive Skills Are

Cognitive skills are a collection of mental abilities related to thinking activities, such as knowing and recognizing, developing concepts, organizing ideas, remembering, problem solving, labeling and naming, understanding cause and effect relationships, drawing inferences, developing rules and generalizations, judgments or evaluations. Cognition is a pervasive term involved in all forms of learning; therefore, the need for cognitive abilities exists in every area of the curriculum in early childhood programs—language, perceptual pre-academic, social, and reasoning activities (Lillie 1975).

Because various researchers and writers have defined or used cognition in different ways, there is some confusion about the term. Bloom (1956), in his taxonomy of educational objectives, divides all curriculum activities into three major categories: cognitive, affective, and psychomotor. According to Neisser (1967), cognition is the process by which sensory input is transferred, reduced, elaborated, stored, recovered, and used. Kagan (1973) defines cognition as a set of mental *units* and a coordinated set of *processes* that manipulates these units in the intricate ballet of thought. The primary *functions* of cognition are to allow the child (1) to recognize the past, (2) to understand new experiences, and (3) to manipulate symbols, concepts, and rules in order to solve a problem. Kagan further specifies the basic *units* of cognition as including schemata, images, symbols, concepts, and rules. The basic *processes* of cognition are perception, memory, inferences, evaluation, and deduction.

It is evident that thinking and cognition are an integral part of all aspects of human learning and behavior. As a consequence, cognition is difficult to examine as an entity apart from other kinds of learning.

Cognitive abilities develop during all of the individual's life, beginning with infancy and early childhood. For example, the apperception of a nipple or the recognition of a mother's face indicates the child's growing ability "to know." The young child's play, such as putting pots and pans inside each other, represents the development of certain cognitive skills. The realization that pushing a button or bell results in a ringing noise or buzz illustrates the development of other cognitive skills. The learning of language cannot be separated from cognitive growth and is perhaps the most important area of cognitive learning for the human being.

Impact of Early Intervention on Cognitive Development

Historically there have been two views concerning the improvement of cognitive abilities and intelligence. One view is that *heredity* sets the limits of cognitive growth and intelligence; consequently home and school training cannot develop the child's intelligence beyond those limits set by inherited biological characteristics. One of the most outspoken proponents of the heredity viewpoint is Arthur Jensen (1969, 1979), who contends that early tests predict intellectual and educational abilities and that educational efforts cannot modify these predictions. The other viewpoint about improving cognitive abilities and intelligence is an *environmental* perspective, which suggests that school success is at least partly the product of early home and school training. Consequently environmental experiences can accelerate mental growth.

Studies on the inheritance of mental deficiency led Goddard (1916) to conclude that mental deficiency is inherited in about 80 percent of the cases he investigated and that training would not alleviate mental deficiency. In more recent years, Goddard's view, which had been widely accepted, has been challenged. The crucial import of the early childhood years to the development of thinking skills and cognitive growth is demonstrated in research stemming from cognitive psychology and special education.

Hunt (1961) in his famous work, *Intelligence and Experience,* disputed the notion that intelligence, or cognitive ability, is a fixed entity and argued that a person's intellectual level can be changed by environmental experiences. Bloom (1964) supplied further evidence of how critical the early years are to cognitive growth. Finding that 80 percent of the child's cognitive development is completed by age four, Bloom warned that waiting until the child reaches age six is perhaps too late. Special education research of changes in the cognitive abilities of retarded babies under favorable environmental conditions gives further evidence of the impact of early intervention on cognitive growth.

Skeels and Dye (1939) reported on an experiment in Iowa in

which thirteen children less than three years of age were removed from an orphanage and placed in an institution for mental defectives. These infants were placed, only one to a ward with adolescent mentally retarded girls, who gave them attention and training. There was also a comparison group that remained in the orphanage and received no special training or care. Two years later both groups were tested, and the babies who had received a great deal of attention and stimulation from the retarded girls in the institution increased their scores on intelligence tests an average of 27.5 points. The children who remained in the orphanage in an unstimulating environment experienced an average decrease of 26.2 points in their intelligence test scores. In follow-up studies three years later, the experimental children had retained their accelerated rate of development in foster homes, while the orphanage children retained their decreased intellectual performance (Skeels 1942). In a follow-up study twenty-one years later, all of the 25 subjects were located. Skeels (1966) found that the thirteen children in the experimental group were all self-supporting. Not one of them was in an institution. Of the twelve in the contrast group, one had died and four were wards of institutions. In terms of education, the experimental group had completed a median of 12th grade; four subjects had a college education. The contrast group completed a median of third grade.

Kirk (1958, 1965) conducted an experiment on effects of preschool education on the mental and social development of young, mentally retarded children. Two preschool groups were organized—one in the community and the other in an institution. Children who received the two years of preschool education increased in both mental and social development and retained the increase to age eight. Those who did not receive preschool education dropped in both their IQ and SQ (social quotient).

An extensive experiment on the effects of preschool education was conducted by Heber, and others (1972). Heber hypothesized that intervention in the Kirk experiment was too late, as it started at the age of four, and that such intervention should begin at birth. Heber selected newborn black children from disadvantaged families whose mothers had IQs of less than 70. At three months of age, the children were taken to a day school for an all-day program. This all-day program continued until the children entered public school at the age of six. A similar group of babies of disadvantaged mothers received no such intervention but were tested periodically. Both groups of children were examined with psychometric tests and rating scales throughout the experiment. There was little difference between the two groups at age twelve months but after that, differences began to appear. The experimental children scored at the superior level during all six years of the study. On the other hand, the IQs of the control children tended to drop as the children's age increased so that by the time they were about six years old, they had a mean IQ of about 92. There were approximately thirty points difference in IQ between those who had received attention and stimulation at an early age and those who had not. Heber gave many other tests and found approximately the same growth curves; namely, that the experimental group was substantially ahead of the control group after age two. Kirk, Kliebhan, and Lerner (1978) concluded from such data that intensive and appropriate education at an early age can account for a twenty to thirty point increase in IQ.

A reanalysis of the Head Start data supports this point of view. Lazar (1979) conducted a study of pupils who had been enrolled in the early Head Start programs after a decade or so to measure the long-term effects of preschool programs. The criteria used to measure effectiveness were (1) Was the person placed in a special education class during schooling or in a regular class? (2) Was the child left back a grade or more? (3) Did the youngster finish high school by age eighteen?

The findings of the follow-up Head Start data showed that a greater percentage of control children were assigned to special education classes than those youngsters who had attended the infant and preschool programs. Moreover, the differences in special education placement and grade retention were so great as to be "cost effective". That is, the data indicated that society saves money by providing preschool education. After analyzing the data in the final report of the follow-up Head Start study, the Comptroller General (Lazar 1979) concluded that early intervention does indeed improve later performance of low-income children and leads to an improvement in the quality of life for their families. Lazar (1979) sums up the analysis: "It is clear that a sensible program of early education can indeed prevent later school failure and reduce the need for remedial programs. All of the early intervention programs studied were effective. More concisely: *'Prevention pays off'* " (Lazar 1979, p. 7).

The belief that interventional strategies can enhance cognitive growth in children provides the common cord binding together the fields of early childhood and special education (Anastasiow 1976).

Two Theories of Cognitive Development

There are two schools of thought regarding how cognitive abilities develop in children. One is a *developmental* perspective; the other is a *behavioral* perspective. These two theories of cognitive development can be contrasted by examining the conceptual frameworks of two eminent psychologists—Piaget, a developmental psychologist, and Gagné, a behavioral psychologist.

The Developmental Theory of Cognitive Maturation: Piaget

Jean Piaget, the famous Swiss psychologist, offers ideas about cognitive development in children which have become the foundation of many early childhood programs. An understanding of some of Piaget's basic contributions is important because it represents a developmental or maturational way of thinking about cognitive growth in children.

Much of the early work in child development concentrated on motor and physical growth. Piaget's primary interest, however, was the child's cognitive growth and the child's thinking processes. Although Piaget had been writing for four decades, his work had little impact on American psychology until the 1960s and 1970s when his writings were translated from French and "rediscovered." Hundreds of studies have been generated from the work of Piaget, and these have largely supported his theoretical position.

Piaget contends that children learn through action. From the moment of birth, the child is the active interpreter of the environment. The child builds what Piaget calls an internal "schemata," or an inner construct of the world. This schemata becomes the basis for further thought. The concepts of *assimilation* and *accommodation* are central to Piaget's theory of cognitive development.

Assimilation and accommodation. *Assimilation* is the process by which children take into their models of thinking the awareness of aspects of the environment. That is, children incorporate new experiences into their already existing schemata or cognitive structures. In *accommodation* children revise their internal schemata to fit their observations when confronted with something they cannot understand. The child focuses on the new features of the situation and changes the internal schemata or cognitive structure accordingly. In other words, the child adapts to the environment and structures knowledge in two complementary ways—assimilation and accommodation. Let us take the example of a young child picking up a ball. The process of assimilation of a grasping technique already mastered will help the child in picking up the ball; the child will also accommodate to the new features of this ball by modifying his or her cognitive structure. In accommodation there is an expansion of the existing internal cognitive structure. Cognitive development results from a succession of these expansions in the internal cognitive structures.

Stages in cognitive growth. Another important feature of Piagetian theory is the concept of sequential stages of cognitive development. Each child progresses through each of these stages in a common sequential manner. While age levels are attached to each stage, these are only approximations of the age at which each stage is reached. Some children master a particular stage earlier; others later. Certain cognitive behaviors are manifested at each stage, and the teacher can determine the child's stage of development by examining the tasks that a child is able to perform consistently.

1. *Sensorimotor period: Birth to two years of age.* During this stage the child learns through sense and movement and by interacting with the physical environment. By moving, touching, hitting, biting, and so on, and by physically manipulating objects, the child learns about the properties of space, time, location, permanence, and causality.

2. *Preconceptual thought period: Ages two to four years.* Speech begins during this period, and the child makes rapid progress in learning the names of objects and using speech to communicate ideas. During this period the child masters an increasingly large set of concepts and further differentiates cognitive processes. The learning is accomplished by imitation, symbolic play, drawings, mental images, and verbal evocation of events. The child's thinking is dominated largely by the world of perception.

3. *Intuitive thought period: Ages four to seven years.* This stage is an extension of the preconceptual thought period. It is characterized by the mastery of more complex forms of language. In addition, laws of physics and chemistry, such as conservation of number, mass, and the like are brought under control.

4. *Concrete operations period: Ages seven to twelve years.* It is in this stage that the child develops the ability to think through relationships, to perceive consequences of acts, and to group entities in a logical fashion. Children are now better able to systematize and organize their thoughts. These thoughts, however, are still shaped in large measure by previous experiences, and they are dependent upon concrete objects that the children have manipulated or understood through the senses. Children can now deal with aspects of logic, including classes, number, relations, and reversibility.

5. *Formal operations period: Ages eleven to fifteen years.* This stage reflects a major transition in the thinking process. At this stage, instead of observations directing thought, thought now directs observations. The individual now has the capacity to work with abstractions, theories, and logical relationships without having to refer to the concrete. The formal operations period provides a generalized orientation toward problem-solving activity.

Some early childhood programs are based on behavioral theories of cognitive learning. Behavioral theorists tend to reject the notion that cognitive learning occurs *only* through the maturational process. Instead, they see children as respondents to the stimulation in the world about them. Cognitive development (like other areas of behavior) depends upon a basic system of reinforcement. When desired cognitive responses are rewarded, the child will tend to repeat that type of behavior. Cognitive learning occurs according to principles of behavioral and reinforcement theory. Mechanisms such as imitation, modeling, operant conditioning, and reinforcement are essential instructional strategies.

Gagné (1970), a behavioral psychologist, is a proponent of the theory that systematic planning is needed for cognitive learning to occur. He proposes eight phases in the process of learning.

1. Presenting the stimulus or information. This is the motivation or incentive to learn.
2. Directing the child's attention to what is to be learned.
3. Providing a model of the performance that is expected.
4. Furnishing external prompts.
5. Guiding the direction of thinking.
6. Inducing transfer of knowledge.
7. Assessing learning attainment.
8. Providing feedback.

The behavioral psychologists believe that it is important for the teacher to carefully plan experiences and structure the learning environment for the child's development of desired cognitive behaviors. The *skill instruction curriculum* described in the next section of this chapter is based on the behavioral view of cognitive development.

Early Childhood Curriculum Approaches to Cognitive Development

Three different types of curriculum approaches to foster the development of cognitive or thinking skills in young children are proposed in the field of early childhood education. They are (1) the enrichment curriculum, (2) the skill instruction curriculum, and (3) the cognitive emphasis curriculum. Each of these perspectives is based upon a different theory of child development. Consequently, each views the role of the child, the teacher, and the school environment in a different way.

Enrichment Curriculum

The enrichment curriculum is based upon a maturational view of child development. The theories of developmental psychology underlying the enrichment perspective presume that there is a natural growth sequence for the young child, including the maturation of cognitive skills and abilities (Gesell 1940; Ames 1968). The role that education should play is to enhance the opportunities for the child to develop these natural growth processes by providing a learning environment that is enriching, encouraging, and nurturing. Under such favorable open circumstances, the child's own inner drive and need to learn will naturally propel those activities and behaviors that will permit cognitive abilities to emerge and develop. This approach is called *child oriented* since it is concerned with the individuality of the child. It is also called *present oriented* because the prime concern is the child's immediate life and needs—not the child's future position and needs in society.

The enrichment perspective is often viewed as the "traditional" program of the nursery school. It is a "whole child" approach, promoting growth of the child's physical, social, emotional, language, and intellectual development. The teacher capitalizes on opportunities for incidental and informal learning.

Skill Instruction Curriculum

The skill instruction curriculum is based upon the principles of behavioral psychology. Proponents of this approach maintain that direct intervention is needed to bring about cognitive learning in young children. The role of the educator is to carefully plan and structure learning experiences to build specific academic skills thought to be needed.

The skill instruction curriculum is *goal oriented*; it is concerned with the child's adaptation into society. It is also *future oriented* in that it advocates teaching specific skills as early as possible—skills the educator believes the child will need at some future time. These skills are essentially observable academic behaviors. The educator first predetermines the kinds of behaviors that are needed to perform in academic areas, such as reading and arithmetic. These behaviors are then directly taught to the child as early as possible. Thus emphasis is placed on teaching specific academic skills of reading and arithmetic during the preschool years. The curriculum intervenes in the child's development, and the educator, in effect, selects those instructional experiences that are thought to lead to successful academic performance. It is assumed that the educator can make sound judgments as to how the child should be trained and instructed. Curriculum plans based on the skill instruction theory are found in many programs.

Compensatory programs for disadvantaged children are often based on this model (Bereiter and Engelmann 1968). The underlying premise is that it is necessary to provide compensation for lower-class children for not having received the kinds of instruction that middle-class children are likely to receive in the home. Middle-class parent teaching is sometimes referred to as the "hidden curriculum" of the middle-class home. For example, middle-class children are more likely to learn the skill of recognizing letters of the alphabet than are lower-class children. The impetus behind the development of "Sesame Street" was to bring the hidden curriculum to the disadvantaged child through television.

Cognitive Emphasis Curriculum

The cognitive emphasis curriculum is based on the ideas and theories of the field of cognitive psychology. Many of the concepts and curriculum programs stem directly from the work of Jean Piaget (1971). The major concern is with the way that children develop cognitive abilities— abilities such as memory, discrimination learning, problem-solving ability, concept formation, verbal learning, and comprehension. One of Piaget's important insights about children is that they do not think like adults, but they go through distinct stages of development which are characterized by particular types of thinking. This approach therefore, requires an "open framework" curriculum (Weikart 1974). The curriculum focus is upon the underlying processes of thinking and cognition, with emphasis upon learning that comes through the child's direct experiences and action. Unlike the skill instruction curriculum, the cognitive approach omits training in specific areas, such as reading or arithmetic.

The cognitive approach organizes the curriculum to accomplish cognitive and language development. Children learn as a result of their active involvement within the environment, as structured by the teacher. Curriculum programs based on cognitive development include those of Gray and Klaus (1968), Karnes (1969), Weikart (1970), Kamii (1973), and Elkind (1973).

In some ways the Montessori-type curriculum might also be

considered within the cognitive emphasis perspective (Montessori 1964; Orem 1969; Miezitis 1973). The Montessori curriculum is based on the idea that mental or cognitive development is a product of the interaction between the structure of the organism (child) and the structure of the environment (classroom). This type of program uses a "prepared environment" consisting of self-instructional classroom materials. The teacher's role is to mediate or assist the child-material interaction. The child's mental development occurs as the child learns to use the material and apparatus in the prepared environment.

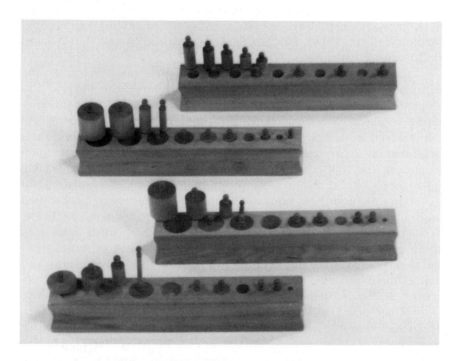

Research on Early Childhood Curriculum Models

Which curriculum model is most effective in improving the thinking skills, intellectual growth, and school performance of the preschool child? The opportunity to provide some answers to this question came with the development of the Head Start programs for preschool disadvantaged children.

Since the various Head Start programs used different curriculum models, they offered an unprecedented opportunity to conduct research on early childhood curriculum models. Head Start is discussed in

Chapter 10 as well as in other sections of this book. Briefly, Head Start, which began in 1964 as part of the War on Poverty, became one of the most influential, massive, federal social experiments in the history of the preschool intervention effort. Funded by the Office of Economic Opportunity, it provided preschool education for three, four, and five year olds from economically deprived homes. It was hoped that it would help children who might otherwise come to school unprepared and unmotivated to learn.

Studies that attempted to compare the relative effects of preschool programs based on several different curriculum models were conducted by Kohlberg (1968), Karnes (1969), DiLorenzo (1969), Westinghouse (1969), Weikart (1970), Hodges, McCandless, and Spicker (1971), and Becker and Engelmann (1976).

Karnes (1969) compared four types of preschool programs: the Karnes ameliorative preschool (cognitive emphasis), the Bereiter-Englemann program (skill instruction), a Montessori-type program (cognitive emphasis), and a traditional preschool program (enrichment). All the children were from the Urbana, Illinois area, from neighborhoods described as depressed. DiLorenzo (1969) compared three preschool programs: the traditional (enrichment), the Bereiter-Engelmann (skill instruction), and a Montessori program (cognitive emphasis). Eight different schools in New York state were used in this study, all classified as disadvantaged as indicated by the father's occupational rating. In the Weikart and others (1970) research conducted in Ypsilanti, Michigan, three programs were compared: a Piagetian cognitive program (cognitive emphasis), a Bereiter-Engelmann program (skill instruction), and a traditional program (enrichment). The population sample was described as disadvantaged.

Miller and Dyer (1975) reported on a study involving fourteen Head Start classes. Two were Montessori programs (cognitive emphasis), four were traditional (enrichment) programs, one a Bereiter-Engelmann (skill instruction) program, and one combined an emphasis on aptitude and attitude.

In general, the findings of these and other early Head Start research projects showed that all the curriculum models had an immediate short-term impact on children who had attended the preschool program. Children from all program models scored better than comparable children who did not receive preschool education. Head Start children improved significantly in intellectual test scores. However, the data in these early studies showed that the gains did not last beyond the first year or two in school. The Head Start children gradually drifted back toward the performance level of their classmates who did not have a preschool experience. These results were very disappointing to supporters of the Head Start movement and to early childhood educators (Moore 1977). Various explanations of the phenomenon of fading score superiority were offered. Among them was the need to extend the early childhood intervention strategies beyond the preschool years into elementary grades and to start it earlier than age three (Bissell 1973; Lillie 1975).

As noted earlier, however, the long-term follow-up studies of Head Start showed more promising results (Lazar 1977). The long-term follow-up study of Head Start effectiveness did not evaluate the effects of different curriculum models. Instead this study evaluated the effects of all types of curriculum models after ten or more years. These data support the idea that Head Start and early intervention are effective, giving children long-lasting consequences in their performance in school (Weinberg 1979; Moore 1978). Lillie makes the following points about the various early childhood curriculum models (Lillie 1975):

1. Planning and organization are essential elements in effective early childhood programs.

2. There is no one best curriculum approach for early childhood education.

3. It is very difficult to replicate a reported curriculum in another learning environment.

4. Research should look at distinct features of various curriculum approaches and their effects on behavior of individual children within groups.

Instructional Strategies for Teaching Cognitive Skills

Principles of the Cognitive Curriculum

Classroom activities should be planned with the child's developmental stage of cognitive growth in mind. Furth and Wachs (1975, pp. 43–47) specify six characteristics of curriculum activities which enhance cognitive growth. They view it as a way to teach thinking.

1. *The activity of thinking is worthwhile in itself.* Thinking skills are not developed in the child as a means to accomplish something else but as an end in itself.

2. *The structured activities are to enhance the child's developing intelligence, not to take away the individual freedom that is a condition of healthy psychological growth.* Both the teacher and the child initiate activities. The teacher plans and prepares the activities for the child, but at the same time the child has the freedom to participate or not participate and has individuality of style and timing in responding to the task.

3. *The activities are developmentally appropriate so as to challenge the child's thinking but not too difficult so as to invite failure.* The teacher's task is to know the general type of activities that are appropriate for the child's cognitive stage. The activities must be difficult enough to challenge the child's thinking. However, if they are too difficult, this leads to failure and a psychologically unhealthy use of low-level thinking.

4. *The child is involved in, and focuses his or her attention on, the activity and not on the teacher as if the teacher were the source of knowledge.* It is the child who initiates intellectual growth. The teacher can only provide the occasion, prompt, facilitate, and encourage.

5. *Activities are performed by each individual child with a group of peers with whom he or she relates socially and cooperatively.* A small group of children provides an effective atmosphere for cognitive learning. Children learn from imitation and are encouraged by successful activities of others.

6. *Teachers provide the model of a thinking person for the child.* The teacher must be free from rigid regulations and take the initiative within the general structure. The teacher can influence a child's developing intelligence by providing occasions and opportunities and by serving as a model of a thinking person to imitate.

Instructional Strategies

There is a common body of preschool activities, regardless of the theoretical basis of that curriculum. They commonly include the pre-academic skills of colors, shapes, numbers, letters, parts of wholes, the function and use of objects, and the use of speech parts. Most of the curriculum approaches recognize that the child must learn to make comparisons, classify and categorize, build vocabulary, reason and make judgments (Hare and Hare 1977). Weikart (1971), suggests the following activities:

1. *Classification activities:* ability to group objects that have similarities. There are three subgroups:
    a. *relational classification:* grouping objects on the basis of function (for example, put all of the things we can drink together).
    b. *descriptive classification:* grouping on the basis of common attributes (for example, put all of the red items or round items together).
    c. *generic classification:* grouping items on the basis of general classes or categories (for example, put all of the furniture or fruit together).
2. *Seriation activities:* putting things or events in order or sequence. There are three subgroups:
    a. *ordinal sizes:* for example, *big, bigger, biggest; small, smaller, smallest; short, shorter, shortest.*
    b. *ordinal positions: first, last, middle, third.*
    c. *ordinal patterning:* copying a sequence of beads.

Time sequences are often included in seriation as well. For example, arranging pictures that tell a story into the correct time sequence.

3. *Spatial relations;* the relationship of the child to the space in the outer world. There are several subgroups:
   a. *body awareness and body concepts:* naming and identifying parts of the body, moving parts of the body.
   b. *position:* developing concepts such as *on, off, into, over, under, next to, on top of.*
   c. *direction:* directional concepts such as *up, down, forward, backward.*
   d. *distance:* concepts such as *near, far, close to, far from.*
4. *Temporal relations.* These activities are related to time. Subgroups are:
   a. *beginning and end of time intervals:* such as *now, start, stop, end.*
   b. *ordering of events:* planning and evaluation concepts such as *first, last, next, again.*
   c. *different time lengths:* such as *a short time, a long time, a longer time.*

Specific Teaching Activities

Teaching concepts.   *Conceptualization* refers to the intellectual process needed to group diverse things according to common properties. The ideas resulting from this process are called *concepts.* While concepts may deal with concrete things, they are in themselves abstractions. For example, the concept of "roundness" develops from many concrete experiences with round objects—plates, balls, oranges, frisbees. Round objects are concrete; they can be touched, seen, and so on. The idea of "round," however, exists only in the mind. The brain creates it. It is an abstraction—not reality.

The concepts of the shape round and the color red are easier than more complex concepts such as "weather" or "time." Still more difficult are concepts such as "fairness" or "loyalty." As the concept gets further away from a basis of concrete experience, it becomes more difficult. Thus the curriculum must give the child many concrete opportunities to develop concepts. The handicapped child may have much more difficulty than the normal child in developing concepts needed for further learning. If there is a physical disability, the child may not have the opportunity to have the primary experience. For example, the blind child would have difficulty developing the concept of color, such as "red." Learning disabled children frequently have difficulty in being able to recall concepts. For handicapped children, therefore, greater direct experience for concept development is needed wherever possible.

Concept of color: red.   Associate the color red with an object the child is familiar with, such as catsup. If the new object is the color of catsup, it is red. Show the child a bottle of catsup. Group objects and drawings that are red together. Start with two objects (later three objects) of various colors. Ask, "Is this red?" Later on, after other colors have been taught, ask the child to identify the color when three colors are presented at one time. Have the child select which objects fit which color.

Teaching spatial relations.   Spatial relationships such as *on, in, between, under, in front of, next to* are often difficult for handicapped children to understand. Use a box and an object to help the child. Place the object (such as a block) *in* the box, and say," The block is *in* the box." The child is then asked to place the object *in* the box. The teacher places the object in the box and asks, "Where is the block?" Similar activities are used to teach other spatial relations. First each is taught in an isolated fashion; later directions can be mixed.

Teaching numbers.   Number concepts such as *more, less, first, last* are important and should be included in the curriculum. To teach "one more," have the child build a tower and then add "one more" block to it. Then *one more* and so on. Using a pasting activity, ask the child to paste *one more* flower. At snack time, ask the child to take *one more* cracker. During a working period, ask the child to add *one more* bead to a chain. In other words, provide many opportunities to have direct experience with the cognitive skill being taught.

Teaching classification skills.   Classification involves grouping or sorting of objects according to some rule or principle. Children can be grouped into boys and girls, or into big and small, or into brunettes, blonds, and redheads. Children often have much difficulty with classification. They confuse the thing with the class. That is, they confuse the physical object with the class to which it belongs. They also have difficulty with the language of classification and with the fact that an object can belong to two or more classes. For example, one child could not see that a plate could be called round, since it was a plate. When children were asked if the moon could be called "cow," they said no because it does not give milk. Handicapped children in particular need many experiences in sorting and classifying.

Matching games.   Have two containers and several objects. Ask the child to put the red items in one container and the blue items in the other. Do the same thing with shapes and textures. Later ask the child to sort objects without the container—on a piece of paper or simply on two sides of a table. Then have the child select his or her own sorting principles.

Sorting games.   Make nine geometrical cutouts: three triangles, three circles, three squares, of three colors: blue, yellow, red. Have children sort them. At first they will classify by color, later by shape. The principle being taught is that the way one classifies is arbitrary. Other objects that can be used are buttons, silverware, pictures, or toys.

Teaching sequencing. This cognitive skill involves recognizing the sequential order of things. The item is correctly placed when it takes into account the neighboring items and the sequence or pattern that the items form within the whole. There can be a sequence to auditory activities, visual activities, and movement activities. There is also a sequence to events.

Bead stringing. One type of sequential activity is copying a bead pattern using different shapes or colors of beads. Bead patterns can be placed on a transparency to use this activity with a group of children.

Auditory pattern games. A series of rhythm patterns can be made by clapping, tapping, or using a drum where the child is asked to copy the pattern.

Story sequence. A child repeats a story by highlighting the sequence of events in the story. Three or four pictures which illustrate the sequence can be used, and the child places these in appropriate order (top to bottom or left to right) and then relates the story. Cartoons or comic strips can be cut apart and used for this purpose. Children need to be taught the relationship from one picture frame to the next.

Flannel board cutouts are also useful in helping the child order the events of the story.

Arranging. The child is given several objects and asked to arrange them in a sequence. For example, four circles or sticks can be arranged from biggest to smallest or longest to shortest.

Guessing or discovery games. Logical thinking involves reasoning and predicting. Some games help the child experience this process. Riddles are an activity children enjoy. "I am thinking of an object that is white, long, breaks easily, and leaves its mark on a chalkboard." When telling or reading a story, ask the child to guess what will happen next. Then check out the event to see if the child was correct. Use an ordered series with a pattern, and have the child tell which one comes next.

Creative thinking. Many of the activities and lessons in education are designed to teach a specific concept or skill. These lessons may be thought of as lessons to teach *convergent* thinking because the child must close in on a particular point established by the teacher. The contrast to this type of lesson are those that teach *divergent* thinking. These are open-ended lessons in which the child is encouraged to expand the thinking process into areas beyond those determined by the teacher. Play and dramatics can encourage this type of activity. They are more self-directed than activities designed for convergent thinking. Nevertheless, this is an important part of the cognitive curriculum and one that should not be neglected.

Toy library. A toy library of games and play ideas and materials is suggested by Johnson (1978). Such a resource would give teachers, aides, parents, grandparents, and others who work with children the opportunity to borrow materials and games for use with children.

Summary

Cognitive skills are a collection of mental abilities related to thinking activities. They include knowing, recognizing, developing concepts, organizing ideas, remembering, problem solving, labeling, relating cause and effect relationships, drawing inferences, and developing rules and generalizations. All curriculum areas require cognitive abilities.

The early years are vital to cognitive development. Research has shown that early intervention and the right environment can improve cognitive abilities.

There are two theories of cognitive development. One is the maturational theory, which is related to the theories of Piaget. The other is the behavioral view of cognitive learning, which is related to the work of Gagné.

There are three different types of curriculum approaches to cognitive development in early childhood education. They are (1) the enrichment curriculum, (2) the skill instruction curriculum, and (3) the cognitive emphasis curriculum. Research attempting to show which of these approaches is the best is still inconclusive.

Instructional strategies for cognitive development include activities to teach concepts, spatial relations, numbers, classification, sequencing, discovery, and creative thinking.

Review Questions

TERMS TO KNOW

a. *cognitive skills*

b. *assimilation*

c. *accommodation*

d. *Piaget*

e. *Gagné*

f. *developmental psychology*

g. *behavioral psychology*

h. *enrichment curriculum*

i. *skill instruction curriculum*

j. *cognitive emphasis curriculum*

1. Compare the heredity and the environment viewpoints of intelligence and cognitive growth.
2. What are Piaget's stages of cognitive growth?
3. Discuss the ways cognitive abilities develop from a developmental theory viewpoint and from a behavioral theory viewpoint. What are the differences?
4. Describe the curriculum models of the enrichment curriculum, the skill instruction curriculum, and the cognitive emphasis curriculum.
5. Plan a teaching lesson in some area for each curriculum model.
6. Which curriculum model do you think is best for the handicapped preschool child? Why?

References

AMES, L. D. Learning Disabilities: The Developmental Point of View. in *Progress in Learning Disabilities*, Vol. I, ed. H. Myklebust. New York: Grune & Stratton, 1968, pp. 39–76.

ANASTASIOW, N. J. Human Development and Process of Education, in *Children with Special Needs: Early Development and Education*, eds. H. Spicker, N. Anastasiow, and W. Hodges. Leadership Training Institute-Special Education. Exceptional Child Program. Bureau of Adult and Occupational

Education, U.S. Office of Education, Department of Health, Education, and Welfare, 1976, pp. 5–14.

BECKER, W. C., AND S. ENGELMANN. Technical report 1976–1. Eugene, Oregon, U. of Oregon, 1976, Cited in N. Haring and B. Bateman, *Teaching the Learning Disabled Child.* Englewood Cliffs, N.J.: Prentice-Hall, Inc., 1977.

BEREITER, C., AND S. ENGELMANN. *Teaching Disadvantaged Children in the Pre-school.* Englewood Cliffs, N.J.: Prentice-Hall, Inc., 1968.

BISSELL, J. The Cognitive Effects of Preschool Programs for Disadvantaged Children, in *Revisiting Early Childhood Education: Readings,* ed. J. Frost. New York: Holt, Rinehart & Winston, 1973, pp. 223–241.

BLOOM, B. S. *Taxonomy of Educational Objectives.* New York: Longmans, Green, 1956.

BLOOM, B. S. *Stability and Change in Human Characteristics.* New York: John Wiley, 1964.

DiLORENZO, L., AND OTHERS. *Prekindergarten Programs for Educationally Disadvantaged Children.* New York: State Education Department, 1969.

ELKIND, D. Preschool Education: Enrichment of Instruction, in *Early Childhood Education,* ed. B. Spodek. Englewood Cliffs, N.J.: Prentice-Hall, Inc., 1973, pp. 108–121.

FURTH, H., AND H. WACHS. *Thinking Goes to School.* New York: Oxford University Press, 1975.

GAGNÉ, R. *Conditions of Learning.* New York: Holt, Rinehart & Winston, 1970.

GESELL, A. *The First Five Years of Life: Guide to the Study of the Preschool Child.* New York: Harper & Row, 1940.

GODDARD, H. *Feeblemindedness: Its Causes and Consequences.* New York: Macmillan, 1916.

GRAY, S., AND R. KLAUSE. The Early Training Project, *Monographs of the Society for Research in Child Development.* 1968, 33.

HARE, B., AND M. HARE. *Teaching Young Handicapped Children.* New York: Grune & Stratton, 1977.

HEBER, R., AND OTHERS. Rehabilitation of Families at RISK for Mental Retardation, *Progress Report.* Madison, Wis.: Rehabilitation Research and Training Center in Mental Retardation, 1972.

HODGES, W. L., B. McCANDLESS, AND H. SPICKER. *Diagnostic Teaching for Preschool Children.* Arlington, Va.: Council for Exceptional Children, 1971.

HUNT, J. *Intelligence and Experience,* New York: Ronald Press, 1961.

JENSEN, A. How Much Can We Boost IQ and Scholastic Achievement? *Harvard Educational Review,* 1969, 39 (1), 1–123.

JENSEN, A. *Bias in Mental Testing.* New York: MacMillan, 1979.

JOHNSON, S. A Toy Library for Developmentally Disabled Children, *Teaching Exceptional Children,* 1978, 11, 22–26.

KAGAN, J. Preschool Enrichment and Learning, in *Revisiting Early Childhood Education: Readings,* ed. J. Frost. New York: Holt, Rinehart, & Winston, 1973, pp. 187–201.

KAMII, C. A Sketch of the Piaget-Derived Preschool Curriculum Developed by the Ypsilanti Early Education Program, in *Early Childhood Education,* ed. B. Spodek. Englewood Cliffs, N.J.: Prentice-Hall, Inc. 1973, pp. 209–229.

KARNES, M. *Research and Development on Preschool Disadvantaged Children.* Washington, D. C.: Office of Education, 1969.

KIRK, S. *Early Education of the Mentally Retarded.* Urbana, Ill.: University of Illinois Press, 1958.

KIRK, S. Diagnostic, Cultural, and Remedial Factors in Mental Retardation, in *Biosocial Basis of Mental Retardation,* eds. S. F. Osler and R. Cooke. Baltimore, Md.: Johns Hopkins Press, 1965.

KIRK, S., J. KLIEBAHN, AND J. LERNER. *Teaching Reading to Slow and Disabled Learners.* Boston: Houghton Mifflin, 1978, Chapter 2.

KOHLBERG, L. Montessori with the Cultural Disadvantaged, in *Early Education,* eds. R. Hess and R. Bear. Chicago: Adline, 1968, pp. 105–118.

LAZAR, I., AND OTHERS. *The Persistence of Preschool Efforts: A Long-term Follow-up of Fourteen Infant and Preschool Experiments.* Summary Report of the Consortium on Developmental Continuity, Education Commission of the States, Grant 18–76–078433. Washington, D. C.: U. S. Department of Health, Education and Welfare, 1977.

LAZAR, I. Does Prevention Pay Off? *The Communicator.* Council for Exceptional Children, Division of Early Childhood. 1979, Fall 1–7.

LILLIE, D. L. *Early Childhood Education.* Chicago: Science Research Assoc., 1975.

MIEZITIS, S. The Montessori Method: Some Recent Research, in *Revisiting Early Childhood Education: Readings,* ed. J. Frost. New York: Holt, Rinehart & Winston, 1973, pp. 123–149.

MILLER, L., AND J. DYER. Four Preschool Programs: Their Dimensions and Effects, *Monograph of the Society for Research on Child Development.* 1975, 56.

MONTESSORI, M. *The Montessori Method.* New York: Bently, 1964.

MOORE, S. The Effects of Head Start Programs with Different Curricular and Teaching Strategies. *Young Children,* 1977, September, 55–61.

MOORE, S. Persistance of Preschool Effects: A National Collaborative Effort. *Young Children,* 1978, March, 65–71.

NEISSER, U. *Cognitive Psychology.* Englewood Cliffs, N.J.: Prentice-Hall, Inc., 1967.

OREM, R. C., ed. *Montessori and the Special Child.* New York: Putnam, 1969.

PIAGET, J. *Biology and Knowledge.* Chicago: University of Chicago Press, 1971.

SKEELS, H. A Study of the Effects of Differential Stimulation on Mentally Retarded Children: A Follow-up Study. *American Journal of Mental Deficiency,* 1942, 46, 340–350.

SKEELS, H. Adult Status of Children with Contrasting Early Life Experiences. *Monographs of the Society for Research in Child Development,* Chicago: University of Chicago Press, 1966, 31.

SKEELS, H., AND H. DYE. A Study of the Effects of Differential Stimulations on Mentally Retarded Children. *Proceedings and Addresses of the Sixty-Third Annual Session of the American Association on Mental Deficiency,* 1939, 44, 114–130.

WEIKART, D. P., AND OTHERS. *Longitudinal Development of Effective Preschool Programs: Results of the High-Scope Ypsilanti Perry Preschool Project.* Ypsilanti, Mich.: High-Scope Educational Research Foundation, 1970.

WEIKART, D., AND OTHERS. *The Cognitively Oriented Curriculum: A Framework for*

Preschool Teachers. Washington, D. C.: National Association for the Education of Young Children, 1971.

WEIKART, D. Curriculum for Early Childhood Special Education. *Focus on Exceptional Children*, 1974, 6, 1–8.

WEINBERG, R. Early Childhood Education and Intervention. *American Psychologist*, October, 1979, 914–917.

WESTINGHOUSE LEARNING CORP. AND OHIO UNIVERSITY. *The Impact of Head Start: An Evaluation of the Effects of Head Start on Children's Cognitive and Affective Development.* Washington, D. C.: Office of Economic Opportunity, 1969.

Teaching Communication Skills

Chapter **Seven**

Language and speech skills are unique. They are learned, rather than instinctive, human characteristics. They separate people from other living creatures. There are other animals (that is, bees, birds, dolphins, chimpanzees) that have developed communication skills, but only homo sapiens possess the species-specific characteristics of language and speech.

Communication is a complex process which serves many functions. It enables us to learn about the past, dream about the future, comprehend abstract concepts, and socialize with others. This chapter discusses the components of communication—language, speech, and nonverbal skills—as well as the conditions which interfere with normal language development. The last section of this chapter provides suggested activities for enhancing the development of all aspects of communication skills.

What Communication Skills Are

A distinction is usually made between language and speech as the two primary verbal components of communication. *Language* is a structured system of signs, sounds, and symbols which have commonly understood meanings. *Speech,* on the other hand, is the tool for conveying this system orally. Cazden (1972, p. 2) elaborates the difference between language and speech more eloquently:

Language is knowledge in our heads; speech is the realization of that knowledge in behavior. Language consists of all the words in a person's mental dictionary, and all the rules at his (usually nonconscious) command for combining those words into an infinite number of novel sentences that he hears. Speech, by contrast, consists of his actual utterance spoken to particular people in particular situations. Language exists even in moments of silence and sleep; speech exists only in moments of actual speaking or listening, the silent activation of language in thought.[1]

[1] From Courtney B. Cazden, Child Language and Education. Copyright (c) 1972 by Holt, Rinehart and Winston, Inc. Reprinted by permission of Holt, Rinehart and Winston.

Language and speech skills are those abilities which enable one to communicate with others and with oneself. There is little doubt that there is a strong interdependency between these skills and thought; at times, it is difficult to distinguish between them. Whorf (1956) even hypothesizes that the language one uses determines how one thinks. Many theorists (Luria 1961; Myklebust 1960; Piaget 1952; Vygotsky 1962) claim that thinking, or *inner language,* is the foundation for higher-level communication skills. Inner language relates to the integration and organization of sensory and perceptual experiences the individual is continuously encountering. Vygotsky refers to this process as "inner speech" while Piaget labels this stage "preoperational thought." This level of development enables the child to associate the spoon with food, the ringing of the telephone with the phone itself, or to "drive" the toy car along the floor.

Receptive language refers to the ability to listen (receive) and to comprehend what others are speaking. It is generally thought to develop simultaneously or in conjunction with inner language, supplying the child with the necessary words with which to think, associate, and assimilate impinging experiences. Receptive language appears intact when the child attends to noises and voices or shows awareness of sound (for example, turns the head to localize sound), discriminates between sounds (for example, fetches the socks rather than the box), and shows understanding by responding appropriately to a request. It is usually obvious that the average child acquires the meaning of words between the age of six to ten months.

Expressive language (other than mimicking) can develop only after receptive language because input must precede output. One must understand a word before it can be produced in a meaningful manner. Expressive language is the process of producing meaningful linguistic sounds. The average child generally begins to say words meaningfully at the age of ten to eighteen months.

Reading and writing are the highest levels of verbal symbolic behavior. They are both dependent on visual processes and generally do not develop without formal teaching. They are beyond the scope of this book since they usually do not concern the education of the preschool child, particularly one with special needs, unless the child is gifted.

The relationship between all of these developmental levels of verbal communication is illustrated in Figure 7–1.

However, a more pertinent conceptual model of language development is illustrated in Figure 7–2. It shows that inner language and receptive language might develop simultaneously and that both contribute to auditory expressive language.

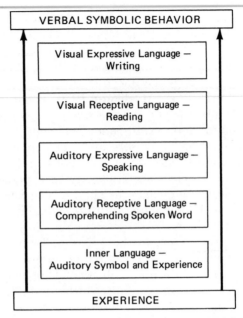

Figure 7–1 **The Developmental Hierarchy of Verbal Communication** *From H. Myk lebust, Psychology of Deafness. New York: Grune & Stratton, 1960, p. 232.*

Prior to the advent of expressive language, the child goes through several processes:

1. *cooing-crying:* response to internal stimulation (zero to four months)
2. *babbling:* repetition of sounds for their own sake: a manifestation of identification with humans (three to six months)
3. *jargon:* babbling with intonation and stress (six to eight months)
4. *approximation or echolalia:* words without meaning (six to twelve months)
5. *holophrasing:* use of one word for larger thoughts (nine to fourteen months)

These are stages of normal language development.

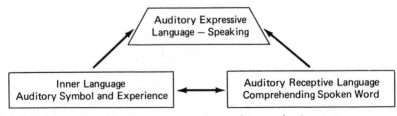

Figure 7–2 **Relationship of Inner, Receptive, and Expressive Language**

Communication Skills in the Early Years

The acquisition of language begins long before the first word is spoken—at birth or possibly even in utero. Interactions and adaptations to the environment take the form of reflexes, such as grasping, sucking, and eye movements. However, according to Bruner (1976), the baby is sociocentric from the beginning because it is stressful to be in a noncommunicative situation. Within a few months, a baby's cry shows signs of patterns, a cry followed by a pause to listen for reactions before another cry. By two months, the infant can make a cry that demands or one that awaits a response from the caregiver. In a few months a baby will even communicate nonvocally, for example, by extending arms to be picked up. While the young child is trying to communicate, both verbally and nonverbally, with others, the thinking processes tend to be egocentric or self-centered. Children view life only from their own perspective. This can be most easily documented when a child uses egocentric speech, that is, talks aloud to oneself (Piaget 1957). The child does not try to communicate with others, expects no answers, often does not care whether anyone listens. Children are merely thinking aloud. Vygotsky (1962) believes this private speech, besides being a means of expression and releasing tension, becomes the vehicle for thoughts in solving a problem. He believes egocentric speech is the transition from vocal to inner speech (thinking). While egocentric speech is very prevalent among preschoolers, most research shows a decline after age five with a disappearance between seven and ten years of age.

Language development has been extensively researched and reviewed (Bellugi and Brown 1964; Bloom 1978; Ervin-Tripp 1966; McCarthy 1954). The earlier longitudinal diary studies of individual children and cross-sectional studies of large numbers of children resulted in the specification of milestones in the development of language ability in young children. Table 7–1 lists these milestones from infancy to five years according to age and typical behavior. These milestones are only gross, general indices of development and should be utilized as such. Research (Berko 1958; Brown 1957) has demonstrated that children learn an underlying linguistic system rather than all sounds and possible words and sentences in a language. Rather than unitary stages of development, the milestones thus overlap and change appears to be continuous.

Linguistics

Language skills can be viewed in terms of four linguistic systems: phonological, semantical, syntactical, and pragmatical. *Phonology* refers to the acoustic or sound characteristics of speech. *Phonemes* are the

TABLE 7–1 **Milestones in the Development of Language Ability in Young Children***

Average Age	Question	Average Behavior
3–6 months	What does he do when you talk to him? Does he react to your voice even when he cannot see you?	He awakens or quiets to the sound of his mother's voice. He typically turns eyes and head in the direction of the source of sound.
7–10 months	When he can't *see* what is happening, what does he do when he hears familiar footsteps . . . the dog barking . . . the telephone ringing . . . candy paper rattling . . . someone's voice . . . his own name?	He turns his head and shoulders toward familiar sounds, even when he cannot see what is happening. Such sounds do not have to be loud to cause him to respond.
11–15 months	Can he point to or find familiar objects or people when he is asked to? *Example:* "Where is Jimmy?" "Find the ball."	He shows his understanding of some words by appropriate behavior; for example, he points to or looks at familiar objects or people, on request.
	Does he respond differently to different sounds?	He jabbers in response to a human voice, is apt to cry when there is thunder, or may frown when he is scolded.
	Does he enjoy listening to some sounds and imitating them?	Imitation indicates that he can hear the sounds and match them with his own sound production.
1½ years	Can he point to parts of his body when you ask him to? *Example:* "Show me your eyes." "Show me your nose."	Some children begin to identify parts of the body. He should be able to show his nose or eyes.
	How many understandable words does he use—words you are sure *really* mean something?	He should be using a few single words. They are not complete or pronounced perfectly but are clearly meaningful.
2 years	Can he follow simple verbal commands when you are careful not to give him any help, such as looking at the object or pointing in the right direction? *Example:* "Johnny, get your hat and give it to Daddy." "Debby, bring me your ball."	He should be able to follow a few simple commands without visual clues.
	Does he enjoy being read to? Does he point out pictures of familiar objects in a book when asked to? *Example:* "Show me the baby." "Where's the rabbit?"	Most two-year-olds enjoy being "read to" and shown simple pictures in a book or magazine, and will point out pictures when you ask them to.
	Does he use the names of familiar people and things such as *Mommy, milk, ball,* and *hat?*	He should be using a variety of everyday words heard in his home and neighborhood.

Age		
	What does he call himself? Is he beginning to show interest in the sound of radio or TV commercials? Is he putting a few words together to make little "sentences"? *Example:* "Go bye-bye car." "Milk all gone."	He refers to himself by name. Many two-year-olds do show such interest, by word or action. These "sentences" are not usually complete or grammatically correct.
2½ years	Does he know a few rhymes or songs? Does he enjoy hearing them? What does he do when the ice cream man's bell rings out of his sight, or when a car door or house door closes at a time when someone in the family usually comes home?	Many children can say or sing short rhymes or songs and enjoy listening to records or to mother singing. If a child has good hearing, and these are events that bring him pleasure, he usually reacts to the sound by running to look or telling someone what he hears.
3 years	Can he show that he understands the meaning of some words besides the names of things? *Example:* "Make the car go." "Give me your ball." "Put the block in your pocket." "Find the big doll." Can he find you when you call him from another room? Does he sometimes use complete sentences?	He should be able to understand and use some simple verbs, pronouns, prepositions, and adjectives, such as *go, me, in,* and *big.* He should be able to locate the source of a sound. He should be using complete sentences some of the time.
4 years	Can he tell about events that have happened recently? Can he carry out two directions, one after the other? *Example:* "Bobby, find Susie and tell her dinner's ready."	He should be able to give a connected account of some recent experiences. He should be able to carry out a sequence of two simple directions.
5 years	Do neighbors and others outside the family understand most of what he says? Can he carry on a conversation with other children or familiar grown-ups? Does he begin a sentence with "I" instead of "me"; "he" instead of "him"? Is his grammar almost as good as his parents'?	His speech should be intelligible, although some sounds may still be mispronounced. Most children of this age can carry on a conversation if the vocabulary is within their experience. He should use some pronouns correctly. Most of the time, it should match the patterns of grammar used by the adults of his family and neighborhood.

*From the National Institute of Neurological Diseases and Stroke. *Learning to Talk: Speech, Hearing and Language Problems in the Pre-School Child.* Washington, D.C.: U.S. Department of Health, Education, and Welfare. 1969.

individual elements within a group of sounds, the units of sound such as /m/ or /ch/. *Semantics* refers to meanings between the signs (the word "bed") and its referent (the actual bed). Unlike the other linguistic systems, semantics continues to grow and develop throughout a person's life as vocabulary increases. *Syntactics* refers to the order in which words are strung together in the formation of a phrase or sentence. It is the rules of grammar construction and the organization of language, known as morphology. Whereas a phoneme is the smallest unit of sound, a *morpheme* is the smallest unit of meaning. For example, although the word bread has five letters, it has only three phonemes: br/e/d and one morpheme. *Pragmatics* refers to the way in which language is used in the environment. It is concerned with the purposes or functions served by language, how these purposes are related to wider interpersonal and sociocultural factors, and the effects these factors have on the use of language.

FUNKY WINKERBEAN By Tom Batiuk

Funky Winkerbean *by Tom Batiuk, (c) 1980 Field Enterprises. Courtesy Field Newspaper Syndicate.*

Speech Skills

Speech skills are dependent on several components: auditory perception, articulation, and voice (Bangs 1968). These components work together in an integrated manner to receive and produce word symbols.

Auditory perception is the integration of the hearing sensation with the act of listening. It is dependent on the child's ability to hear and organize the incoming stimuli into patterns, to attach significance to the sensation.

Articulation is dependent on auditory perception and a neuromuscular system capable of producing the various vowel and consonant sounds. Table 7–2 indicates the average age at which the motor system is capable of handling various sounds in English. *Voice* is the actual sound and includes pitch, quality, timing, and loudness.

TABLE 7–2   Order of Phonemic Development by Age

Chronological Age (C.A.)	Phoneme
3½ years	all 14 vowels, p, b, m
4½ years	n, ng, w, h, t, d, k, g, all dipthongs (vowel blend)
5½ years	f, v, y, th (voiced and voculars), l, wh
6½ years	r, s, z, ch, j, sh, zh
7 years	consonant blends (cl, dr, st, and so on)

From C. Weiss and H. Lillywhite. *Communicative Disorders: A Handbook for Prevention and Early Intervention.* St. Louis, Mo.: C. V. Mosby, 1976, p. 51.

The degree to which a child's language can be understood is also developmental, progressing from babbling and approximations to normal speech. Along the way, understandability or intelligibility may be affected by omissions, substitutions, and/or distortions. Table 7–3 indicates the development of intelligibility according to chronological age.

Nonverbal Communication

Another component of communication is nonverbal—conveying meaning without words. Egolf and Chester (1973) estimate that up to 93 percent of all communication is nonverbal. This includes such factors as gestures, facial expressions, body posture, tone of voice, physical attributes, and many others. Just as other aspects of communication, it is learned and may prove to be a stumbling block for some children.

All aspects of communication skills develop through imitation, practice, and the interaction of cognitive and linguistic processes. These cognitive and linguistic processes of perception, imagery, motivation,

TABLE 7–3   Development of Intelligibility

Chronological Age (C.A.)	Percent of Intelligible Speech
18 months	25
24 months	60
30 months	75
36 months	85
42 months	95
48 months	100*

From C. Weiss and H. Lillywhite. *Communicative Disorders: A Handbook for Prevention and Early Intervention.* St. Louis, Mo.: C. V. Mosby, 1976, p. 51.

* Does not mean perfectly normal speech; it means understandable speech.

and symbolization modify both the reception and expression of language and the intermediate organizing process which must sort, code, store, and retrieve the various components of information, a very complex endeavor. In addition, researchers have yet to resolve the following issues:

1. How much difference does the presence or absence of language make?
2. Are people's thoughts affected by the particular speech patterns or language forms with which they are familiar?
3. Which develops first, the nonverbal idea or the words to express it?

Whether thinking and language are related or just good friends is immaterial to recognizing that many conditions may impede language development.

Conditions Which Impede Normal Language Development

The learning of language may be disrupted for a variety of reasons. McGrady (1968) hypothesizes four major causes for the disruption of the language-learning process. These causes and their corresponding conditions are listed in Table 7–4.

Sensory Deprivation

Children who are deaf from birth tend to develop certain characteristics which differentiate them from others having difficulty learning language (Myklebust 1954). These children do not babble for long because they cannot hear their own voices. Their voices have a characteristic nonmelodious quality. Gestures are frequently used and understood. They attend to facial expressions, movements, and other visual cues and usually are also sensitive to tactile sensations and impressions. The hard-of-hearing child should be seen on a continuum between the deaf child and the hearing child. The degree of loss varies in both *frequency* and *intensity*. To hear human speech, one must be able to respond to frequencies between 500 and 2,000 vibrations per second. The degrees of sound intensity, or loudness, are measured in decibels (dB) and are the second dimension of hearing acuity. Not only is input affected by hearing impairment, output of speech sounds becomes a laborious, if not impossible, task, depending on the degree of loss.

TABLE 7–4   Disruption of Language Learning

Cause	Conditions
Sensory deprivation	Hearing impairment
	Visual impairment
Experiential deprivation	Cultural deprivation, lack of opportunity
	Cultural difference
Emotional disorganization	Personality disorder
	Autism, psychosis, neurosis
Neurological dysfunction	Mental retardation
	Neuromotor disorders
	Organic impairments
	Childhood aphasia
	Specific learning disabilities

Vision also plays an important role in the development of verbal communication. The eyes are used to verify what is heard, relate objects with their verbal symbols, study faces, get feedback, and develop a sense of space, distance, and proportion (Weiss & Lillywhite 1976). A surprisingly large percentage of blind and visually impaired children have deficient speech and language, primarily in the acquisition of word concepts which are based on reference to visual experiences, abstractions, or images. For example, a blind child would have difficulty fully understanding the phrase "blowing smoke rings." This is referred to as "verbalism" (Cutsforth 1951).

Experiential Deprivation

If one is to learn language, one must have certain types of experiences. Hearing-impaired and visually impaired children lack certain experiences, but young children with normal hearing and vision may not learn language because of social, cultural, and/or economic limitations. This is generally based on a lack of opportunities which characterize the early home environment and even educational conditions. Environmental factors known to adversely affect language development include multiple, closely spaced births, crowded living conditions, disruptions in consistent care giving (too many different people caring for the child after six months of age), institutionalization (that is, orphanages), inadequate food and health care, and bilingualism (two languages spoken to the child). The interaction between experiential deprivation and language has been summarized by Bloom, and others (1965) as it affects children from low-income environments. The language generally used in these homes uses vocabulary, grammar, and language patterns that differ from standard English. Thus it affords the child inadequate models and insufficient opportunity to practice speaking. Experiential deprivation can create differences in language development for the preschool child. Moreover, these differences in language development tend to widen as the child gets older (Deutsch, and others 1964). One purpose of Head Start was to overcome the detrimental effects of experiential deprivation.

Language deficiencies due to experiential deprivation should not be confused with cultural and language differences. Language differences are not synonymous with language deficiencies. Language differences are known as dialects. There are many English dialects prevalent in the United States today, each from a different subculture. Dialects exhibit syntactical, semantical, and phonological variability. That is, the structure of the sentence may be different, the label given to familiar objects may change, or the pronunciation or speech inflection may differ. The dialect heard on radio and television is known as Standard American English. Nonstandard English should be viewed as a different but equal language system (Lerner 1981). For instance, some inner-city children use a dialect which is structurally systematic and functionally adequate (Carroll 1973). Other inner-city children have a "restricted linguistic code" (Bernstein 1964). When children are placed in a daycare center, nursery school, or other early childhood setting where the adults have significantly different language backgrounds, it is important that continuous efforts be made to separate language deficiencies from language differences before remedial programs are instituted.

Emotional Disorganization

Language deficits due to emotional disorganization are perhaps the most difficult and uncharted types of language disturbance (McGrady 1968), possibly due to their low prevalence and unique combinations of characteristics. Children with severe emotional disorganization, such as those with infantile autism or childhood schizophrenia (Churchill 1972; DeMeyer, and others 1971; Goldfarb 1961; Kanner and Eisenberg 1956; Myklebust 1954; Rimland 1964; Wing 1976), are likely to have one or more of the following traits in language, speech, and communication:

1. *Mutism or elective mutism* (functionally equivalent); child does not talk at all.
2. *Nonfunctional expressive language;* child uses ecolalia or gibberish.

3. *Pronoun reversals;* child uses expression "me want cookie" beyond the normal stage of such usage.

4. *Lack of verbal requests;* child does not use phrases such as "I want" or "give me."

5. *Articulation problems* in conjunction with above traits.

6. *Severe receptive language dysfunction;* child does not respond to own name, follow simple directions, understand multiple meanings of words.

7. *Exclusive use of egocentric speech;* child does not use words for interpersonal communications.

These traits must be accompanied by other behavioral characteristics, (for example, perceptual impairments, social withdrawal, self-stimulating behavior, such as head banging or rocking, proprioceptive or vestibular stimulation, such as whirling or swinging), which may vary in severity, before a child is diagnosed as schizophrenic or autistic (Gardner 1977). Nevertheless, deviations in language development are a primary consideration in making a differential diagnosis. When such behavioral characteristics are present, the child is almost always significantly impaired in *all* aspects of the developmental process. Thus, language training alone is ineffective. Chapter 8, Teaching Social and Affective Skills, suggests activities for dealing with the affective (psychosocial) domain in preschool children.

Neurological Dysfunction

Language deficits not due to sensory deprivation, experiential deprivation, or emotional disorganization may be due to some degree of neurological dysfunction. Several handicapping conditions are discussed under neurological dysfunctions as separate entities. In reality, they may overlap.

Mental retardation was previously discussed in Chapters 1 and 2. Due to the relationship between language and thinking, communication skills are generally delayed in various degrees with this group of children. The greater the degree of mental retardation is, the greater the degree of language and speech disability (Dunn 1973; Fallen 1978). Oral language stimulation at an early age may minimize later language disabilities and avoid social and emotional problems as well.

Neuromotor disorders, such as cerebral palsy, have a strong relationship with language deficits. It has been estimated that about 50 percent of children with such disorders have speech and language problems due to a number of related conditions: difficulty in use of the speech apparatus itself, associated perceptual problems, and limited ability to move about which affects the experiences necessary for language development.

Organic impairments of the speech mechanism, such as cleft palate and lip, deformity of the jaw, tongue, or larynx (voice box) may all cause temporary or permanent language and speech problems which need to be recognized and dealt with by the speech and language clinician.

Childhood aphasia is another central nervous system dysfunction that interferes with the association between the spoken symbol or word and the corresponding element of experience. It may be an input, processing, and/or output problem. That is, the child may not be able to understand speech (receptive aphasia), use speech (expressive aphasia), or use language for any purpose (central aphasia) (Myklebust 1954). Eisenson and Ingram (1978) report that aphasic children have perceptual problems which cause faulty discriminations and categorizations. These children learn grammatical rules more slowly, thus they need a vocabulary of almost 200 words before they can produce a two-word utterance, whereas a normal child combines two words with a vocabulary of only about 50 words. Moreover, aphasic children's language and speech skills develop differently than do normal children. There is a qualitative distinction.

Specific learning disabilities often involve language deficits of various types. Some educators tend to avoid this term with preschool children, preferring "developmental delay" as a noncategorical term to encompass children with problems which may be attributable to more than one condition or cannot be "pigeonholed" neatly.

A Classification System for Speech and Language Disorders

Classifying language and speech problems according to the cause or etiology of the condition has several hazards (Nation and Aram 1977). First, it is a management problem. If a child is retarded, as opposed to having a sensory deficit, who is responsible for evaluating and working with that child's communication problems? Second, when the cause is seen as the disorder, the child is categorized with children who may have no resemblance to the child in regard to severity of the problem. Grouping severe and profound children with borderline children or deaf with mildly hearing impaired serves little educational purpose. Third, using etiologies (causes) makes professionals assume that there is a simple cause-effect relationship to explain language and speech deficits. One must keep in mind that there is rarely a clear-cut, uncomplicated case in special education. Many factors are involved. A description, based on the degree of the problem, seems a more useful way to look at young children's language deficits. McLean (1974) proposes three groupings of children with communication disorders: nonverbal children, language-disordered children, and speech-impaired children. This cuts across causes or etiologies.

The smallest group, *nonverbal children*, would include any children with no language at all—some autistic children, some severely and profoundly hearing impaired, some with physical handicaps, and some with multiple handicaps and/or profound retardation. PL 94–142 provides for all handicapped children; thus, none can be excluded because of the severity of the problem.

A *language disorder* is the inability to relate linguistic symbols to experience because of a central nervous system dysfunction (McGrady 1968). It would include the aphasic child, the child with specific learning disabilities, and those with mild language problems. The language disorder may take several forms (Bangs 1968):

> 1. Disorders of semantics—reduced vocabulary comprehension (receptive) and/or reduced vocabulary usage (expressive).
> 2. Disorders of syntax and morphology—inability to comprehend connected discourse, awkward sentence construction, improper sequencing of words, omissions of words, and incorrect use of morphological rules.

Many of these children do not follow an orderly pattern when learning the language code; others follow the normal pattern but more slowly and thus may be referred to as language delayed. Figure 7–3 lists possible signs of receptive language problems followed by possible signs of expressive language problems.

The last group of children—*speech impaired*—is the largest of all. It includes children who have voice disorders, stutter, or have articulation problems. Speech impairments do not involve the central nervous system. They are problems in the formation of the sounds needed for the expressive use of oral language. Possible signs of speech impairment are listed in Figure 7–4.

Voice disorders, such as inappropriate intensity, pitch, or quality may be related to a malformation of the vocal or auditory mechanism. If so, surgical or prosthetic intervention and speech therapy may be successfully used (Safford 1978). If not, the speech therapist might employ a learning method where the child hears the voice as feedback to modify the voice disorder.

Stuttering is noticed so frequently during the preschool years that it is generally considered a normal speech characteristic. It is advisable to ignore this behavior and recommend to parents that they not ask the child to slow down or begin again. Only if the stuttering persists for an

Figure 7–3   Possible Signs of Language Problems

Receptive

1. By 6 months, child does not quiet to the sound of the caregiver's voice.

2. By 11 months, child does not turn head and shoulders towards familiar sounds (that is, phone ringing, footstep) even when there is nothing to be seen.

"3. By 15 months the child does not understand and respond to name, 'no-no,' 'bye-bye,' and 'bottle.'

4. By 21 months the child does not respond correctly to 'Give me that,' 'Sit down,' 'Stand up.'

5. By 24 months the child does not understand and point to, on command, mouth, nose, hair, and ears.

6. By 30 months the child does not understand and demonstrate, on command, in, on, under, front, and back.

7. By 48 months the child cannot answer correctly the questions: What do we sleep on?' 'What do we sit on?' 'What do we cook on?' 'What is your name?' 'What do you do when you are hungry?' 'What do you do when your thirsty?' [by pointing or gestures].

8. By 48 months the child cannot distinguish boy from girl, big from little, one object from two or more objects.

9. By 60 months the child cannot tell the use of book, stove, house, and key.

10. By 60 months the child cannot distinguish soft from hard, smooth from rough, and tell why we have a chair, house, dress, and window.

Expressive

1. By 18 months the child is not saying at least six words with appropriate meaning.

2. By 24 months the child is not combining words into phrases, such as 'Go bye-bye,' 'Want cookie.'

3. By 30 months the child is not using short sentences, such as, 'Mommy see dolly,' 'Daddy go bye-bye.'

4. By 36 months the child has not begun asking simple questions.

5. By 48 months the child's sentences are telegraphic, reversed, or confused, such as, 'Me car go.' 'Baby loud crying,' 'Candy me want.'

6. By 48 months the child is not using auxiliary verbs, such as, 'is,' 'have,' and 'can.'

7. By 60 months the child is not using the personal pronoun 'I' such as 'Me (instead of I) want a cookie,' or uses name instead of pronoun, such as 'Bobby (instead of I) want a drink.'

8. By 60 months the child consistently uses incorrectly past tenses, plurals, and pronouns, such as 'Them threw a balls.'

9. By 60 months, the child's expressive vocabulary is limited and shallow, fewer than 200 to 300 simple words.

10. The child's language has not improved in sentence length, complexity, and accuracy within any 6-month period after age 2.

11. The child has difficulty in self-expression, according to the age level, or is concerned or teased about the language used."

From C. Weiss and H. Lillywhite. Communicative Disorders: A Handbook for Prevention and Early Intervention. St. Louis, Mo.: C. V. Mosby, 1976, p. 176–178.

Figure 7–4 Possible Signs of Speech Problems

"1. The child uses mainly vowels in babbling or speech after twelve months of age.

2. The speech is not more than 50% understandable by age 24 months.

3. There are many consonant omissions by 36 months . . .

4. There is a predominance of vowels in the speech after age 36 months.

5. The speech is not 100% understandable by 48 months; this does not mean all phonemes are used correctly, just understandably.

6. The child omits most initial consonants after age 3.

7. The child omits, substitutes, or distorts any phonemes after age 7.

8. Phonemes are more than 6 months late in appearing, according to normal developmental sequence . . .

9. The speech has not become noticeably more understandable and more fluent in the last 6 months, up to the age of 7.

10. The child is concerned or teased about the speech at any age.

11. The child repeats, hesitates, stops, and starts over frequently.

12. The child has been dysfluent . . . for more than 6 months.

13. The child appears to be struggling to say words, blinks eyes, and grimaces when speaking.

14. The dysfluency becomes noticeably more severe at any time.

15. The child fears speaking situations at any age.

16. The rate of speaking is too fast, too slow, jumbled, or telescoped.

17. The voice quality is nasal (talks through the nose).

18. The voice quality, pitch, or loudness is abnormal (conspicuous).

19. The voice is monotone, dysphonic, or whiney most of the time.

20. The child has persistent, recurring hoarseness or breathiness."

From C. Weiss and H. Lillywhite. Communicative Disorders: A Handbook for Prevention and Early Intervention. St. Louis, Mo.: C. V. Mosby, 1976, p. 172.

extended period of months need the child be seen by a speech therapist or psychologist.

An estimated 60 percent of all instances of defective speech are articulation problems (Safford 1978). They are usually the least serious and most receptive to treatment. Further, they have a tendency to disappear as children develop. However, a speech therapist may help many children learn to develop more mature speech patterns earlier than they otherwise might to avoid omissions, substitutions, or distortions of sounds.

Instructional Strategies for Teaching Communication Skills

There are two competing explanations of language learning. The first is a behavioral explanation wherein speech and language are learned through imitation or *modeling* and *reinforcement* (Hendrick 1975; Safford 1978). According to this view, children learn communication skills partly by imitating the specific speech characteristics in their environment which serve as speech and language models. In addition, if a child's gestures, sounds, and utterances are responded to in terms of adult attention and reaction, reinforcement occurs, and the behavior is maintained. The goals of the teacher are to provide a good model, encourage and reinforce desirable speech and language skills, and provide a secure atmosphere that will promote the learning of these skills.

The second explanation is a psycholinguistic view of language learning (Chomsky 1957). In this perspective, the child is predisposed biologically to learn and use language. Human beings are thought to have an innate capacity for dealing with the linguistic elements common to all languages. What is learned is not a string of words through imitation but rather a set of transformational rules. These rules enable the speaker to generate an infinite variety of novel sentences and enable a listener to understand an infinite variety of sentences heard. Children are born with this internal mechanism for producing and understanding language.

For children with severe communication problems, the internal mechanism for producing language is not intact. Therefore, they are not capable of developing and using language in the normal fashion. What is needed is direct teaching of language and instructional use of the behavioral approach; specifically modeling and reinforcement. Such children usually require the assistance of a variety of professionals; yet they should be included in regular preschool classroom activities as often as possible. Children with no language skills, such as autistic children, seem to benefit from a substitute communication method, such as some type of signing, or rebus symbols, using a visual system to communicate in lieu of an auditory system. Research has shown both strategies to be very effective with nonverbal children.

Children with more subtle communication problems may need to be identified by the classroom teacher through screening techniques and/or systematic observation in a variety of situations over a period of time. The child who is unusually quiet may never be a discipline problem and thus become the one who is most easily overlooked as a potential language disordered child.

Since the normal sequence of language skills necessitates input (reception or listening) prior to output (expression or speaking), the teaching of these skills will be discussed in that order, followed by nonverbal communication skills.

Receptive Language Skills

Listening, a skill that is essential for acquiring verbal communication abilities, is a learned skill. It differs from hearing, the process by which sound waves are received, because it is an active process requiring concentration and thinking. Listening requires a person to deliberately become aware of the sounds so that the brain can translate, interpret, and store them for later use. Figure 7–5 illustrates the relationship of listening with other aspects of the receptive and organizing processes.

To encourage good listening habits, the classroom teacher should keep in mind the following guidelines:

> *Give instructions only once* so that children become trained to tune in the first time. Try not to repeat instructions.
>
> *Use a quiet, normal voice* which provides a good model and requires closer listening than a loud demanding tone.
>
> *Give short, concise, clearly stated instructions* or explanations. Children (and adults) tend to tune out long, rambling, unclear ones.
>
> *Use a moderate rate of speech* which is easier to follow than when a person speaks too quickly—or too slowly.
>
> *Listen attentively* when a child speaks to you. Again, this serves as a good model for what the child is to do.
>
> *Be certain you have the child(ren)'s attention* before you begin your directions. Use eye contact to verify attention. If necessary, block out visual distractions from the child(ren)'s view when speaking.
>
> *Create quiet, calm surroundings* which provide the most conducive environment for the development of listening skills.
>
> *Use a sound clue* or carrier phrase such as "ready" or snap your fingers to alert the child to "tune in." Be consistent with this clue and gradually fade it out.

Wilt (1964) has categorized listening skills into a succession of levels that require progressively more complex abilities. Figure 7–6 illustrates this hierarchy which can be used as a criterion-referenced measure for assessing where the child is currently functioning and what to teach next.

Lerner (1981) suggests strategies for each of these levels of listening. Hatten and Hatten (1975) have devoted an entire booklet to describing a concrete program for language-impaired children. Weiss and Lillywhite (1976) have developed a list with "101 ways to help the

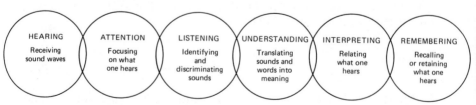

Figure 7–5 The Links of Receptive and Organizing Processes

e.) inferences and conclusions
d.) main idea
c.) details
b.) a sequence of events
a.) directions

6. Comprehends
5. Develops auditory memory of increasing length
4. Understands sentences
3. Develops listening vocabulary of words and concepts
2. Perceives and discriminates isolated single language sounds
1. Perceives and discriminates nonlanguage sounds

Figure 7–6 Hierarchy of Listening Skills

child learn to talk." The teacher needs to be flexible so that the different needs of individual children are met for the promotion of listening skills. Attending for very short periods of time should be the beginning objective. The auditory environment should be kept as structured as possible during listening activities to avoid distractibility and the child's inability to pick out the teacher's voice from the general background of other sounds which causes auditory figure-ground confusion.

Expressive Language Skills

Listening skills are the "readiness" stage of communication skills. They lead to the expressive, speech skills using vocabulary as the bridge. Step-by-step sequential instruction is needed to help the child progress to more complex language structures. However, this must be a slow procedure for the child who has language deficits. It is necessary to control language stimuli so the child is not continuously overwhelmed. All adults caring for a given child—teacher, aide, parents, therapist— should work on the same specific language goals to achieve continuity. Isolate small elements of language to build on. The training must be concrete and experientially based, using real objects rather than pictures, so that meaning is always conveyed. Encourage approximations, rein-forcing any response at first, but gradually switch to an intermittent schedule. Eventually, move to pictures and more abstract concepts. Vocabulary training should proceed from nouns to verbs, followed by adjectives and then adverbs. There are several crucial guidelines for teaching vocabulary (Hatten and Hatten 1975):

> 1. The word and object (or experience) must be presented simulta-neously so the association between the sound and what it refers to becomes clear.
> 2. A new word must be experienced in a variety of ways before it can be meaningful.
> 3. Repetition is mandatory.
> 4. Seeing and hearing what the word is *not* is also important.

For example, the child is handed an orange and the word is said. The child holds it, smells it, and even tastes it after it is peeled and sectioned. At another time, possibly the regular snack time, it is squeezed for juice. The child learns to select it from other entities: first from nonfoods, then from other foods, and finally from other fruits. The teacher then moves from the real object to a flannel cut-out and realistic looking pictures. Additional guidelines for encouraging expressive language include:

Give children enough time to express a thought.

Let children make their needs known; do not anticipate for the child.

Ask open-ended questions rather than those which require only a "yes" or "no" response.

Find interesting things to talk about.

Provide opportunities for repetition and practice.

Use praise and/or tangible rewards very frequently.

The teacher needs to remember that children normally develop syntax in language through a process of interaction between caregiver and child, which is called *expansion.* When the child utters a phrase such as "Bobby, orange," the adult responds by repeating the statement in syntactically expanded form, such as "Oh, Bobby wants an orange." For language-impaired children, it is important to expand the child's statements by only one word or two to give a model which can be understood and imitated.

Expatiation (Spodek 1972) is a form of expansion which requires the adult to react to the child's utterance by expanding it conceptually rather than linguistically. For example, if the child said "Bobby, orange," the adult might respond "I'm sorry, it's almost lunchtime." This form of expansion is more significant for the child who can mimic but has expressive delays due to concept formation, rather than vocabulary or syntactical, problems.

Another language approach, *Distar Language* (Engelmann and Bruner 1967), based on behavior modification principles, rejects these naturalistic strategies and advocates instead a structured patterned drill. This approach does not emphasize meaning primarily but may be successful for some children with emotional disturbances or environmental deprivation.

Expressive language skills can be further developed during many activities in an early childhood setting such as show and tell, dramatic play, group discussion, story sharing and telling, and puppetry. This latter activity is particularly useful for the child who is reluctant to speak, even though the receptive skills are intact. Puppets become the center of attention instead of the child, often enabling the child to express feelings as well as concepts.

Music, with its form, rhythm, and tonal sequences of melody, can also be used in developing communication skills (Thursby 1977). For instance, children can tap out rhythms using contrasting words fast or slow, soft or loud. They can learn verbs such as run, jump, walk, or crawl by responding to music. In still another activity, music can set the mood for a creative story.

Thus, a model for a verbal communication skills program for language-impaired children would contain the following components (Figure 7–7).

Nonverbal Communication Skills

Nonverbal communication skills may also have to be taught. If the child has intact receptive skills, a verbal explanation of gestures, laughter,

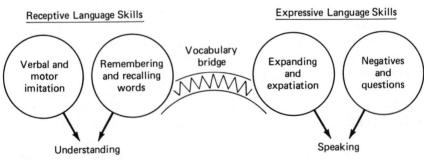

Figure 7–7 Verbal Communication Skills Program

and other nonverbal symbols should be presented to the child simultaneously.

Some children will never develop speech as an effective way of communicating; others may need temporary assistance until their expressive skills are adequate enough to avoid frustration in conveying their needs and expressing their ideas. A communication board (Von Bruns-Connally and Shane 1978) may provide help for both groups. Such a device ranges from relatively simple to sophisticated electric models. For young children, it utilizes pictures and symbols to enable two-way communication dependent on the physical abilities of the child. It is usually designed for the particular needs and abilities of a child and can be modified as the child's needs and abilities change.

Materials for Teaching Communication Skills

There are commercially available language kits (for example, *Peabody Language Kits*) which are designed to stimulate receptive, associative, and expressive linguistic and cognitive processes of preschool children. They contain many concrete objects for teaching meaning more readily as well as chips which can be used in a reinforcement system.

Some materials have been developed with the language-impaired and language-delayed child in mind. When comparing two of these materials, the *MWM Program* and the *GOAL Program* which are both based on the ITPA model, Logan and Colarusso (1978) found that both programs, as supplements, are superior for training expressive skills, but neither is more effective than a regular program for auditory reception. This issue is still open to further investigation.

Some materials are designed primarily for use by parents at home (for example, *Learning Language at Home* [Karnes 1977], books by Hatten and Hatten (1975), and Weiss and Lillywhite (1976). Other communication skills materials for both teachers and parents are listed in Appendix B.

Summary

The importance of verbal and nonverbal communication skills cannot be overemphasized. Not only do these skills affect how one functions in society and interacts with others but they also affect how one thinks and develops cognitive skills. Although these various interrelationships are still not fully understood, a developmental hierarchy of skills has been recognized. Inner, receptive, and expressive language are components of verbal communications.

Normal language development milestones have been documented by many studies of individual children and groups of children. In addition, language skills can be differentiated from speech skills just as language and speech, although closely related, can be distinguished from each other.

There are many conditions which impede normal language development. They can be divided into four general etiological groupings—sensory deprivation, experiential deprivation, emotional disturbance, and neurological dysfunction—or they can be regrouped into classes of severity with nonverbal children as the most severe but smallest class, language-disordered children as the moderate class, and speech-impaired children as the mildest but largest class.

Teaching communication skills necessitates general knowledge of normal language development and specifics for the particular needs of the individual child. Guidelines for group and individual sessions by the teacher, aide, therapist, and/or parent are available along with materials useful for teaching communication skills.

Review Questions

TERMS TO KNOW

a. *inner language*   g. *pragmatics*
b. *receptive language*   h. *sensory deprivation*
c. *expressive language*   i. *experiential deprivation*
d. *phonology*   j. *emotional disorganization*
e. *semantics*   k. *neurological dysfunction*
f. *syntactics*   l. *childhood aphasia*

1. What is the distinction between language and speech?
2. Describe the relationship of inner, receptive, and expressive language. Why is this relationship important to know for a teacher of language-impaired children?
3. Define the three components of speech skills: auditory perception, articulation, and voice.
4. Complete this chart:

Conditions Which Impede Normal Language Development

Sensory Deprivation	Experiential Deprivation	Emotional Disorganization	Neurological Dysfunction
1.	1.	1.	1.
2.	2.	2.	2.

5. Compare and contrast classifying language and speech problems according to etiology with classifying language and speech problems according to degree of the problem.
6. Complete this chart:

Possible Signs of Problems

Receptive Language	Expressive Language	Speech
1.	1.	1.
2.	2.	2.
3.	3.	3.
4.	4.	4.
5.	5.	5.

7. Johnny, age 3–5, is placed in your room on a trial basis for one week. The major presenting problem is that he is nonverbal. List five hypotheses you could check out informally. Explain how you would do each.

References

BANGS, T. *Language and Learning Disorders of the Pre-Academic Child,* Englewood Cliffs, N.J.: Prentice-Hall, Inc., 1968.

BELLUGI, U., and R. BROWN. *The Acquisition of Language.* Monograph of the Society for Research in Child Development, 1964, 29, 2.

BERKO, J. The Child's Learning of English Morphology. *Word,* 1958, 14, 150–177.

BERNSTEIN, B. Elaborated and Restricted Codes: Their Social Origins and Some Consequences. *American Anthropologist,* 1964, 66, Part 2, 55–69.

BLOOM, B., A. DAVIS, and R. HESS. *Compensatory Education for Cultural Deprivation.* New York: Holt, Rinehart, & Winston, 1965.

BLOOM, L., ed. *Readings in Language Development.* New York: John Wiley, 1978.

BROWN, R. Linguistics Determinism and the Part of Speech. *Journal of Abnormal Social Psychology,* 1957, 55, 1–5.

BRUNER, J. Interpreting Baby Talk. *Time,* August 23, 1976.

CARROLL, J. Language and Cognition: Current Perspectives from Linguistics and Psychology, in *Language Differences: Do They Interfere?,* eds. J. Laffey and R. Shuy. Newark, Del.: International Reading Association, 1973, pp. 173–185.

CAZDEN, C. *Child Language and Education.* New York: Holt, Rinehart & Winston, 1972.

CHOMSKY, N. *Syntactic Structures.* The Hague: Mouton, 1957.

CHURCHILL, D. The Relation of Infantile Autism and Early Childhood Schizophrenia to Developmental Language Disorders of Childhood. *Journal of Autism and Childhood Schizophrenia,* 1972, 2, 182–197.

CUTSFORTH, T. *The Blind in School and Society.* New York: American Federation for the Blind, 1951.

DEMEYER, M., and others. A Comparison of Five Diagnostic Systems for Childhood Schizophrenia and Infantile Autism. *Journal of Autism and Childhood Schizophrenia*, 1971, 1, 175–189.

DEUTSCH, M., and others. *Communication of Information in the Elementary School Classroom.* U.S. Office of Education and Cooperative Research Project No. 908, 1964.

DUNN, L., ed. *Exceptional Children in the Schools.* New York: Holt, Rinehart & Winston, 1973.

EGOLF, D. and S. CHESTER. Nonverbal Communication and the Disorders of Speech and Language. *ASHA*, 1973, 15, 511–518.

EISENSON, J., and D. INGRAM. Childhood Aphasia—An Updated Concept Based on Recent Research, in *Readings in Childhood Language Disorders*, ed. M. Lakey. New York: John Wiley, 1978.

ENGELMANN, S., and E. BRUNER. *Distar Language I & II.* Chicago: Science Research Associates, 1967.

ERVIN-TRIPP, S. Language Development, in *Review of Child Development Research*, Vol. 2, eds. L. Hoffman and M. Hoffman. New York: Russell Sage Foundation, 1966, pp. 55–106.

FALLEN, N., and J. MCGOVERN. *Young Children with Special Needs.* Columbus, Ohio: Chas. E. Merrill, 1978.

GARDNER, W. *Learning and Behavior Characteristics of Exceptional Children and Youth.* Boston: Allyn & Bacon, 1977.

GOLDFARB, W. *Childhood Schizophrenia.* Cambridge, Mass.: Harvard University Press, 1961.

HATTEN, J., and P. HATTEN. *Natural Language.* Tucson, Ariz.: Communication Skill Builders, 1975.

HENDRICK, J. *The Whole Child; New Trends in Early Education.* St. Louis, Mo.: C. V. Mosby, 1975.

KANNER, L., and L. EISENBERG. Early Infantile Autism-Childhood Schizophrenia Symposium. *American Journal of Orthopsychiatry*, 1956, 26, 556–564.

KARNES, M. *Learning Language at Home.* Reston, Va.: Council for Exceptional Children, 1977.

LERNER, J. *Learning Disabilities.* 3rd ed. Boston: Houghton Mifflin, 1981.

LOGAN, R., and R. COLARUSSO. The Effectiveness of the MWM and GOAL Programs in Developing General Language Abilities, *Learning Disabilities Quarterly*, 1978, 1, 32–38.

LURIA, A. *Speech and the Regulation of Behavior.* New York: Liveright, 1961.

MCCARTHY, D. Language Development in Children, in *Manual of Child Psychology*, ed. L. Carmichael. New York: John Wiley, 1954, pp. 492–630.

MCGRADY, H. Language Pathology and Learning Disabilities, in *Progress in Learning Disabilities*, Vol. I, ed. H. Myklebust. New York: Grune & Stratton, 1968.

MCLEAN, J. Language Development and Communication Disorders, in *Behavior of Exceptional Children: An Introduction to Special Education*, ed. N. Haring. Columbus, Ohio: Chas. E. Merrill, 1974.

MYKLEBUST, H. *Auditory Disorders in Children.* New York: Grune & Stratton, 1954.

MYKLEBUST, H. *The Psychology of Deafness.* New York: Grune & Stratton, 1960.

NATION, J., and D. ARAM. *Diagnosis of Speech and Language Disorders.* St. Louis, Mo.: C. V. Mosby, 1977.

NATIONAL INSTITUTE OF NEUROLOGICAL DISEASES AND STROKE. *Learning to Talk: Speech, Hearing and Language Problems in the Pre-school Child.* Washington, D.C.: U. S. Department of Health, Education, and Welfare, 1969.

PARENT-CHILD EARLY EDUCATION PROGRAM, *Listening.* Ferguson, Mo.: Ferguson-Floriuant School District, date unknown.

PIAGET, J. *The Origins of Intelligence in Children.* New York: International University Press, 1952.

PIAGET, J. *Language and Thought of the Child.* New York: Meridian Books, 1957.

RIMLAND, B. *Infantile Autism.* Englewood Cliffs, N.J.: Prentice-Hall, Inc., 1964.

SAFFORD, P. *Teaching Young Children with Special Needs.* St. Louis, Mo.; C. V. Mosby, 1978.

SPODEK, B. *Teaching in the Early Years.* Englewood Cliffs, N.J.: Prentice-Hall, Inc. 1972.

THURSBY, D. Music Therapy for Young Handicapped Children. *Teaching Exceptional Children,* 1977, Spring, 77–78.

VON BRUNS-CONNALLY, S., and H. SHANE. Communication Boards: Help for the Child Unable to Talk. *The Exceptional Parent,* 1978, 2(2), 19–22.

VYGOTSKY, L. *Thought and Language.* Cambridge, Mass.: MIT Press, 1962.

WEISS, C., and H. LILLYWHITE. *Communicative Disorders: A Handbook for Prevention and Early Intervention.* St. Louis, Mo.: C. V. Mosby, 1976.

WHORF, B. *Language, Thought and Reality.* Cambridge, Mass.: John Wiley, 1956.

WILT, M. The Teaching of Listening and Why, in *Readings in the Language Arts,* eds. V. Anderson and others. New York: MacMillan, 1964.

WING, L., ed. *Early Childhood Autism.* 2nd Ed. Oxford: Pergamon Press, 1976.

Teaching Social
and Affective Skills

Chapter **Eight**

This chapter discusses the emotional and social development of young children as well as the types of difficulties that handicapped children are likely to have in the affective domain. Suggested activities for enhancing the child's affective growth are provided in the last section.

Children are whole beings. That is, a child is not comprised of separate and discrete components to be identified as language abilities, cognitive abilities, emotional development, or social skills. Rather, these components are all interrelated and interact with each other. The term "whole child" is often used to emphasize this completeness.

Although it is somewhat arbitrary, human behavior is often divided into the cognitive domain and the affective domain. Such a division is useful for purposes of discussion, research, curriculum development, and teaching. The cognitive domain includes the intellectual, academic and thinking skills. It is these skills that are typically stressed in education and take most of our time, effort, and financial support. However, it may be the affective domain—the emotional, social, and psychological status—that can be the most debilitating for the child and the most painful for the parent.

A comprehensive classification of affective objectives was set forth in a study entitled *A Taxonomy of Educational Objectives: Handbook II, Affective Domain* (Krathwohl, Bloom, and Masia 1964). In this work, the affective domain of human development was clearly differentiated from the cognitive domain. The affective domain includes areas such as social skills, emotional status, and the development of values and attitudes.

Not all handicapped young children display problems of a psychosocial nature. Many have a specific disorder related to a single academic area, and they do well in social situations. Some children evidence problems in both academic and psychosocial areas. For other youngsters difficulties are found only in the affective domain, with little or no academic or cognitive problems.

Much of our programming and literature is devoted to academic, intellectual, and cognitive types of learning. However, when intervention programs are restricted to cognitive stimulation, there may be only limited effects and for a relatively short period of time. Programs also need to help children develop motivation, to explore, to learn about their environment, to solve problems, and to offer feedback (Yarrow 1979). Moreover, research shows that handicapped children suffer from many psychological, social, and emotional difficulties. There is an increasing body of information, for example, showing that many learning disabled children present primary interactional learning disabilities (Kronick 1978). In a review of the research on the behavior of learning disabled children, Bryan and Bryan (1978, p. 128) conclude:

There seems to be little question that the learning-disabled child is likely to be rejected by parents, peers and teachers. If you ask either adults or peers, by and large, they will tell you so. Moreover, analysis of the classroom situation suggests that the learning-disabled child's social life is rather different from that of other children. Apparently, he is more often ignored when attempting to initiate a social interaction, is less likely to be interacted with by the teacher for matters not essentially academic, and gets more negative and less positive reinforcement from teachers than his nondisabled counterparts. In short, people do act as if they dislike the learning-disabled child. Whatever distinguishes the learning disabled from the nondisabled in peer interactions, is manifested very quickly. Strangers to children can reliably detect differences between learning-disabled and nondisabled children, and after viewing such interactions only a few minutes.

The research also shows that these children are poor in detecting or perceiving the subtle social cues given by others. This insensitivity may be a source of the handicapped child's difficulty with peers and parents. In general, such children are not liked by others (Bryan and Bryan 1978).

In terms of total life functioning, the psychosocial problems may be far more disabling than academic dysfunction. One school of thought is that the psychosocial disability is a primary, separate and discrete disability, apart from the academic and learning problem. In addition, of course, the failure to learn creates secondary emotional and social problems. It is important, therefore, to closely examine the nature of these affective problems and to look at ways to help such a child.

What Social and Affective Problems Are

What are the characteristics of a psychosocial problem? What behaviors do children with difficulties in the affective domain exhibit? Kronick (1978) provides a comprehensive review of these behaviors and characteristics.

Lack of Schematic and Organizational Judgment

Through a developmental process, the individual learns to organize experiences. The development of social perception is similar to the development of cognitive skills or academic skills, such as reading, language, or mathematics. The individual learns to anticipate processes and then confirms to check whether or not the confirmation is congruent with the expected result. The individual's behavior is then maintained or shifted based upon personal experience, cognitive factors, and feedback. The child with psychosocial problems, however, may have difficulty in several of these steps. Such children may not be able to anticipate the events, they may not be able to confirm whether the action matches what is anticipated, or they may not be able to adjust their behavior when it does not.

Children with psychosocial difficulties may not be able to play with dolls or other toys in social contexts. They may not be able to make judgments about family members vs. strangers. They have difficulty in predicting expected behaviors. For example, they may share a family secret with a casual acquaintance, or they may contribute too extensively to a casual interaction. On the other hand, such children may display a shallowness of interactions by not knowing how to make the appropriate investment in more intimate relations.

Difficulties in Perceiving the Affective Status of Others

One difficulty that children with psychosocial problems have is in the relationship of their own emotional status to that of others. These children are less attuned to the affective state of others, they are more egocentric, and they are less able than their peers to perceive how others feel. Their inappropriate behavior or language is due to the fact that they do not know if the person they are reacting with is sad or happy, approving or disapproving, accepting or rejecting. Since they are so poor in judging the moods and attitudes of other people, they are frequently insensitive to the general atmosphere of a social situation (Moore 1979).

Problems in Socializing and Making Friends

Parents are well aware of the socialization problems of handicapped children. Making friends and having playmates becomes a trying issue—one that is not typically addressed by the school. In fact, for older children and as the preschooler matures, it is afterschool hours and on weekends and holidays that this problem becomes most acute. In a study of the peer popularity of learning-disabled children, Bryan (1976) found that such children suffered significantly more social rejection by their classmates than those without learning problems. A study by Bryan and others (1976) showed that learning disabled children were more likely than controls to emit competitive statements, to make fewer helpful or considerate statements, and to receive more rejection statements. Learning-disabled children were less popular with peers and adults than were controls.

An example of a young child with a social disability is five-year-old Elaine. She was judged to have an IQ score in the high superior range and was able to read simple stories. However, the kindergarten teacher frequently called Elaine's mother to school for conferences about Elaine's disruptive social behavior. She was bossy, did not seem to understand the word "no," cried frequently, pushed others to be first in line, and then kissed and hugged the children to gain affection. Her mother in desperation tried to arrange social situations by inviting a friend to her house to play with her daughter. Elaine would become so excited that she would run around without direction. Within a short time the friend would tearfully beg to go home, while Elaine was in tears because she did not know what went wrong. On one occasion when she was invited to a birthday party, her behavior was so disturbing that Elaine's mother was phoned by the mother of the birthday girl to request that Elaine be taken home.

Problems in Establishing Family Relationships

In addition to problems in establishing successful social relationships with other children, the child's social behavior, and language, motor, and temperamental difficulties lead to problems in acquiring status as a family member. For the young child, of course, the family is the core of the child's life. The child should receive satisfaction and assurance in the relationships of the primary family. The child's immediate family—sisters, brothers, mother, father, grandparents—are often unable to establish these essential relationships, and so the child does not receive satisfaction even within the family sphere.

Poor Self Concept

Ego development and psychodynamic factors have important implications for understanding the child with psychosocial impairments. The normal child, who is intact and is maturing in an even and normal manner, has the opportunity to develop important basic ego functions. The normally developing child has hundreds of opportunities for self-satisfaction, as well as the satisfaction of pleasing others. The parent-child relationship is mutually satisfying because normal accomplishments stimulate the parental response of approval and encouragement.

In contrast, the personality development of a handicapped child does not follow such a pattern. Ego functions are adversely affected if the central nervous system is not intact and is not maturing in a normal and even manner. A disturbance in such functions as mobility and perception leads to an inadequate development of ego functions. Attempts at the mastery of tasks lead to feelings of frustration, rather than feelings of accomplishment. Instead of building up self-esteem, the child's activities produce an attitude of self-derision and do not stimulate the parents' normal response of pride. Instead, they cause the parents to experience feelings of anxiety and frustration, which finally result in rejection or overprotection.

For some handicapped children, the feelings within themselves and the feedback from the outside environment mold a concept of an insecure and threatening world and a concept of themselves as inept

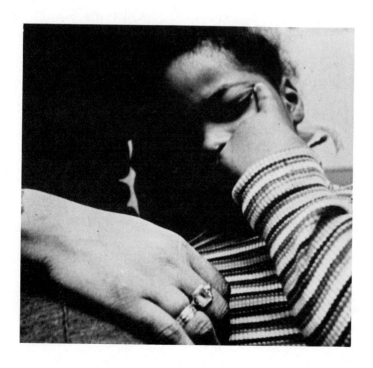

persons without identity. Such children do not receive the normal satisfaction of recognition, achievement, or affection.

Multiple Psychosocial Problems

Some children experience difficulty in more than one area of psychosocial disturbance. In such cases there may be a cluster of problems. Three such clusters are

1. *Fearful or anxious behavior.* These children usually cannot separate from their parents. The children appear to be nervous and have atypical fears and frequent daydreams. The parents report that they cry frequently and have difficulty sleeping.

2. *Immature and dependent behavior.* These children have difficulty taking any initiative or responsibility. Their problems include thumbsucking and wetting, as well as speaking and eating difficulties. They are likely to cling to their mothers.

3. *Lack of self-control.* These children exhibit overactivity, temper tantrums, and attentional disorders. They are often described as negative.

Severe Social and Affective Problems: Autism and Schizophrenia

Severe social and affective problems are known as *childhood psychoses.* Although there is an overlap of symptoms among the childhood psychoses, child psychiatrists have recently agreed on the necessary and sufficient symptoms to distinguish between infantile autism and schizophrenia (DSM–III 1980). Symptoms of *infantile autism* are

1. *Severe withdrawal.*

2. *Severe impairment in verbal and nonverbal comunication;* the child may be mute, use jargon or words, with or without echolalia.

3. *Bizarre responses to the environment;* this includes either abnormal stereotyped preoccupations and/or complex ritualistic behaviors.

All of these symptoms must have developed prior to thirty months of age.

Schizophrenia, on the other hand, is distinguished by the presence of a formal thought disorder. Since this can be documented usually by language, it is often not diagnosable until after thirty months of age.

Psychosocial Development: Erik Erikson

The ideas of Erik Erikson (1963) provide the basis for one widely used model of preschool education that emphasizes the child's psychosocial development. Erikson's theories of psychosocial development are based on Freud's psychoanalytic theory, but they go further and take into account the social and cultural factors that influence the child's behavior.

Erikson sees the personality of the individual developing through a series of interrelated stages. Each stage of personality growth has a critical period of development. These critical stages become a series of turning points which contain both desirable qualities and dangers. The positive and negative features result in a conflict which must be resolved in a positive way if further conflicts are also to be resolved. A brief review of Erikson's stages of psychosocial development follows. The first three stages can take place during the preschool years.

Trust vs. Mistrust Stage: Birth to One Year

It is during this early period that the infant learns to trust the world. Trust is learned when the infant experiences consistency, continuity, and sameness of experience. In this way, the needs of the infant are met, and the child learns to think of the world as a safe and dependable place. The danger of this stage is that suspicion and fear is learned if these early experiences are undependable, inconsistent, unsafe, and if the early care is inadequate. Then the child learns to approach the world with fear and suspicion.

Autonomy vs. Shame and Doubt Stage: Two to Three Years of Age

In the next psychosocial stage of the Erikson theory, the child gains some degree of independence. This autonomy develops when parents and teachers permit children to do what they are capable of—to do it at their own pace and in their own way. Of course, the child still needs careful supervision, but the freedom to perform independently enhances the child's sense of autonomy. The danger in this stage occurs when the parents and teachers do not permit children to do things by themselves. The adults become impatient or they are overly critical, reprimanding or shaming the child for unacceptable behavior. Rather than developing autonomy, then, the child learns self-doubt and shame.

Teachers and parents must tread the fence between too little and too much control.

Initiative vs. Guilt Stage: Four to Five Years of Age

The child now has the physical and language abilities for initiating activity and for exploring the physical world, for being active and on the move. Children need the freedom to explore and experiment and to have questions answered in order to foster the quality of initiative. The danger in this stage lies in the restricting of the initiative, in an attitude that the child's activities are pointless or a nuisance. At this period, also, the child develops a concept of right and wrong. The punishment or disapproval of actions may lead to an oppressive feeling of guilt—which can continue throughout life.

Industry and Inferiority Stage: Six to Eleven Years of Age

This and the following stages of psychosocial development in Erikson's theory go beyond the preschool years. Nevertheless they are briefly described here.

During this critical stage, the child now interacts with a broad spectrum of society, friends, classmates, teachers, and others in his or her social world. The child now develops a sense of industry. Recognition is won by doing, accomplishing, and producing. The danger lies in failure, a sense of inadequacy and inferiority. If children are encouraged to make and do things on their own, are allowed to finish tasks, are given praise for the accomplishments, then they develop the quality of industry. However, if failure is chronic and reinforced, then inferiority develops.

Identity vs. Role Confusion Stage: Twelve to Eighteen Years of Age

This stage is involved with becoming young adults and independent from parents. The danger is role confusion, particularly about sexual and occupational identity.

Erikson's other stages refer to young adulthood, middle age, and old age. Of greatest concern here, however, are the first three stages since they are the years of early childhood.

Implications of the Stages for Instruction

Each stage of psychosocial growth is characterized by a particular conflict which must be resolved in a positive way if future conflicts are to be resolved in a satisfactory manner. The teacher must be aware of the child's stage and the crisis being faced at that time so that the child can be helped to positively overcome the critical elements of the stage.

Behavior Modification

The ideas developed in behavioral psychology and the field of applied behavior analysis are employed in many preschool and special education programs. Among the techniques developed from these fields are those known as behavior modification. *Behavior modification* can be described as a systematic arrangement of environmental events to produce a specific change in observable behavior (Krasner and Ullman 1965; Allen 1980).

Behavior modification requires the teacher to

1. Carefully and systematically observe and tabulate the occurrence of behaviors of concern.
2. Alter the environment so that there is a desired change in the child's behavior.

There are several specific strategies that are used in behavior modification: reinforcement, modeling, shaping, and methods of behavior recording and monitoring.

Reinforcement

An event that follows a behavior and has the effect of controlling that behavior is considered a *reinforcer*. It helps the teacher shape behavior toward the desired responses by rewarding correct behaviors and purposefully ignoring incorrect or irrelevant behaviors. Harlan and Leyser (1980) found that Head Start teachers gave more criticism and less encouragement to emotionally disturbed children than they gave to all other handicapped children. Thus, an intensive effort to change teacher attitudes and help them employ positive reinforcement techniques was essential. Commonly used reinforcers include candy, gummed stars, verbal praise, and smiling faces.

For example, if Jason puts away his art materials with the other children at the end of the free play period, the teacher can reinforce him verbally by saying, "Good work, Jason," or nonverbally, by giving him a hug. If Jason does not clean up, the teacher ignores his behavior.

Modeling

The term *modeling* is used in behavior modification to show an example of the behavior that the teacher wishes the child to acquire. The hope is that the child will observe and imitate this desired behavior. The model could be an adult, teacher, parent, or another child. For example, if Sarah watches another child playing with a new toy that makes pleasant sounds, she will imitate that play behavior when given that same toy. Several researchers have reported that the modeling tactic has been successful in improving psychosocial skills. Children learned to share toys with classmates, engage in appropriate physical contact, and make complimentary remarks to each other (Cooke and Apolloni 1976; O'Leary and O'Leary 1977; Strain, Gable, and Hendrickson 1978).

Shaping Behavior

Shaping behavior means the reinforcement of successful approximations of a desired act. It can be used when the child simply does not respond or when the child begins to make a mistake.

For example, if Pam refuses to hang up her coat, the teacher thinks through the successive steps needed for Pam to hang up her coat. The teacher starts with the first step and rewards Pam if she performs that act. Then each step along the way is rewarded. For example, walking to the coat hook, picking up the coat, finding the loop, and so on.

Methods of Behavior Recording and Monitoring

Behavior modification stresses the importance of objective recording of the child's behavior as the basis for judging whether or not the desired change has occurred. The teacher could use a checklist, a graph, a chart, simple counting, and the like. There are two general ways of measuring observations. One is by *frequency*. For example, the teacher measures how often Jenifer has a temper tantrum. The other is by *duration*. The teacher measures how long Scott remains isolated from the other children in his group.

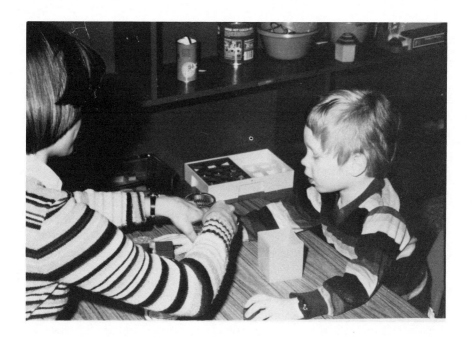

It is important for teachers to keep accurate, objective records in order to establish a baseline. The *baseline* is a frequency or duration measure prior to the implementation of behavior modification.

Once a system of behavior modification is put into operation, the teacher should record changes in the events. Specific target behaviors can be identified and recorded as they occur. Intervention then is based on a systematic analysis of what the teacher sees the child doing. Behavior modification procedures are especially useful in eliminating undesirable psychosocial behaviors and establishing desirable behaviors.

Play: A Learning Activity

Play is a natural activity of children. Children need to play, and play serves an essential role in the young child's development.

The Role of Play in Child Growth

The spontaneous and creative activities of play make invaluable contributions toward the child's learning of cognitive, language, motor, and social skills. The child learns in a natural way about colors, shapes, textures, forms, sizes, rules, and people through play. An endless variety of materials, blocks, paints, sand, toys, clay, boxes, balls, and the like, can be used. The child learns motor skills by playing with balls, skates, ropes, tricycles, wagons, playground equipment, and sewing. Cognitive skills are developed through games, dolls, and creative activities. Social and communications skills are nurtured through group activities with another child, or group games, like playing house, or playing Superman. The essence of play is that it is child-originated and child-oriented and that the child's own intrinsic absorption in mastery provides the energy for the learning experience (Hartley 1971).

Early childhood educators understand the value of play for the young child and the need to provide play opportunities, including uninterrupted time. In fact, the right to play richly, joyously, and freely has been called the precious right and necessity of early childhood—one that must be carefully guarded (Hartley 1971).

Play can be classified into two general types—*spontaneous play* and *directed play*. *Spontaneous play* is initiated by the child. It is not consciously influenced by the desire of adults. It is free and without adult-set goals or objectives. The children solve their problems to their own satisifaction. This free, child-oriented, spontaneous type of play can provide the key for intellectual development (Almy 1967).

Directed play is structured, initiated, or planned by others, such as adults, parents, or teachers. The tendency in education today is for more controlled educational or directed play. We have turned the child's instinctive need for spontaneous play into planned and directed educational play. The aim or goal of this directed play is determined by the adult, and the value of the play activity is assessed by what is learned. Many early childhood educators decry this trend, fearing that it has resulted in an overcapitalization of the child's innate desire for play. They fear an exploitation of the child's natural instinct for play. There is at present a tug-or-war between those who feel that children would benefit from more spontaneous play and those who believe that learning is enhanced by more directed and structured play.

Play and the Handicapped Child

Play activities are as essential for the young handicapped child as for the nonhandicapped. However, its importance and role in the curriculum are often neglected. The handicapped child needs play activities. The teacher must plan for appropriate opportunities and an environment appropriate to the handicapped child. Handicapped children do not appear to learn as easily as the nonhandicapped through spontaneous play and, therefore, need more directed and structured play.

Functions of Play for the Handicapped

Wehman (1978) sees play as having four major functions for the young handicapped child.

1. *To facilitate growth of desirable behaviors in motor, language, cognitive, and social skills.* The play activities can help the child develop gross and fine motor skills through physical activities. Language skills can be developed through communication and expressive activities in group games. Social skills are developed through cooperative group work. Cognitive skills, problem solving, concepts, creative activities are developed through games and thinking play.

2. *To reinforce instructional activity.* Once a skill is learned, play provides a means for practicing and reinforcing that skill in a way that provides pleasure and fun for the child. Children enjoy the practicing and perfecting of a skill when it is viewed as play.

3. *To inhibit socially inappropriate behavior.* When children are actively involved in a play activity, they inhibit behaviors which are considered socially unacceptable. Research shows that there is a significant reduction

in self-stimulating behaviors through the acquisition of play skills. Behaviors such as self-inflicting aggression, stereotypical rocking behavior, and bizarre vocal sounds are decreased or eliminated through play (Wehman 1978).

4. *To provide pleasure or joy.* Play provides pleasure, joy, fun, and a diversion from daily routines for people of all ages. Handicapped children are no exception and are even more in need of the pleasures of playing with toys and games. Severely handicapped children may need direct instruction in how to play or to use free time. Mildly handicapped children will be able to enjoy many leisure activities without precise training and direction.

Play Problems of Young Handicapped Children

The value of spontaneous play in learning and child growth has been extolled by early childhood educators. The problem is that many handicapped children fail to develop play activities by themselves in a spontaneous manner. The more severe the handicapping condition, the less likely the child is to develop play behavior without external stimulation and direction. Many handicapped children must be taught to play; they need external cues, direct instruction, and careful supervision. Strategic arrangements of play materials may also be needed.

Handicapped children need special toys and play materials. Their toys must be more durable than those needed by the nonhandicapped because with slowly emerging skills, the child will use the toy over a longer period of time than the normal child. Also, the child may be stronger and larger than the nonhandicapped child when the toy is used.

Many recreation specialists are not trained to understand the unique behaviors and needs of handicapped children. For example, they may not understand the lack of spontaneity with toys that is characteristic of many handicapped young children. Wehman (1978) points out that what frequently occurs when young handicapped children are introduced to a roomful of toys is repetitive and nonfunctional actions with playthings. In such a situation, the nonhandicapped child would play with the toys by beating the drum, blowing the horn, and bouncing the ball. The developmentally delayed child, however, may hit the horn repetitively on the floor until it breaks. Therefore, teachers in early childhood special education must have a specialized set of skills combining competencies in recreational therapy with competencies in early childhood and special education and behavioral management techniques. This includes a thorough understanding and working knowledge of reinforcement theory, modeling, shaping behavior, and methods of behavior recording and monitoring. These techniques were discussed earlier in this chapter.

Kinds of Play

Four categories of play for the young handicapped child are specified by Wehman (1978): (a) *exploratory play*, (b) *toy play*, (c) *social play*, and (d) *structured game play*. These four types are somewhat hierarchical in nature, although they may be overlapping as well. The four categories are useful in assessing the child's present level of play behavior and in planning a play curriculum.

   1. *Exploratory play.* In this kind of play, the child explores the environment by engaging in motor, sensory, and searching behavior.

   2. *Toy play.* In this type of play, the child interacts with toys and other play material. The child pushes, pulls, puts together, takes apart, throws, or pounds a toy.
   3. *Social play.* In this type of play, the child interacts with other individuals—an adult, parent, teacher, or another child. The child learns to cooperate and communicate. The child also learns psychosocial skills by sharing, taking turns, planning, and interacting. This type of play may be a way of integrating nonhandicapped and handicapped preschoolers. Guralnick (1980) found that nonhandicapped and mildly handicapped children interacted with each other during free play more frequently than expected.

4. *Game play.* This type of play is considered the highest and most complex level of the play skills sequence. Rules are set forth in games that must be followed. Playing a game requires cooperation and communication. The child must learn to both win and lose. Care should be taken that the rules are simple enough for the child to understand.

One of the best examples of the success of play for the handicapped is the annual *Olympics for the Handicapped* events. In these events, handicapped youngsters have the chance to participate at a local, state, and national level in athletic events which are limited to handicapped children. The "Olympic" events gain in popularity each year and are enjoyed by all participants.

Instructional Strategies for Teaching Psychosocial Skills

While the normal child is able to learn social skills through daily living and observation, the child with difficulties in the affective realm needs specific teaching to learn about the social world. This child must be helped to understand the nuances of the social world and the meaning of silent language in interactions with people. Just as children must be taught academic skills—reading, writing, spelling, arithmetic—they must also be taught to learn to live with and around other people. Just as we must use different methods to teach school subjects, so we have to use different methods to teach children how to get along with others.

The term *values clarification* has been used by Simon (1972) to discuss this very personal aspect of human existence. Values clarification deals with the humanistic part of living—feeling, emotions, love, self-esteem, dreams, awareness, sharing. A small volume designed to help teachers develop values with exceptional children by Simon and O'Rourke (1977) has many excellent suggestions that can be adapted for the handicapped preschooler. Some of these ideas are reported in this section.

Simon and O'Rourke (1977) write about developing values in exceptional children. They see helping children learn about themselves and their identity as an essential part of education, particularly the need for developing a stable, firmly based, high evaluation of self, for self-respect, and for the esteem of others. Strategies designed for building psychosocial skills should help children grow, become more human, build self-esteem, and learn to be in tune with the world and themselves.

Show and tell. A well-known activity with preschool and primary teachers is the activity of Show and Tell (sometimes cynically referred to as "Bring and Brag"). The child is simply asked to bring something to show or share with the group. The activity puts the child in the limelight, and the child has a few minutes to experience being the focus of the group. The child could bring a new toy, a Mickey Mouse hat, talk about a trip, show a tooth that fell out, or show something for a pet. Children like to bring their "show-and-tell" item in a paper bag to deepen the suspense or surprise. Behind each article is something very personal, of value to the self. For the child who is too shy or frightened to speak before a group, merely showing the article would be a first step. Later the child might be asked to talk about the item in one sentence. The show-and-tell activity can be developmental with children learning to express more of themselves over time.

About me. In this activity children have the opportunity to reveal themselves to others—their likes, dislikes, fears, hopes, and dreams. The children sit in a comfortable group—possibly a circle—and take turns telling something about themselves. They might tell about their favorite television show, book, color, food, toy, or pet. Another discussion could concern things they dislike, or what they would like to do, or the dreams they have had.

Building self-worth with pictures. Take Polaroid pictures of children or have them take pictures of each other. Make posters or pages of a book with each child's picture. Have the child sit in the center of the group, with his or her picture. The other children can dictate a sentence about the child to put with the picture. For example,

- Jean shares toys with others.
- Tom listens at story time.
- George told us about his trip to the circus.
- Mary watered all the plants today.

Another way of using pictures is to take slides of the children engaged in activities at school. Show the slides and discuss the activities.

The outerspace man. Have the children pretend that a space ship from another planet landed in the school yard. Have the children discuss what the space man will look like. Then have the children draw a large picture of this person and give him a name. Ask one child or the teacher to sit behind the poster and become the voice of the outerspace man. Ask questions such as: "The people from the planet Crypton want to know what you enjoy about living on Earth. What do you think the Crypton people would enjoy about living on Earth. What do you think the Crypton people would enjoy doing or seeing? What should people from Crypton be careful about here on Earth?" This activity might be too advanced for those children with language or cognitive handicaps.

Pictures and feelings.   Give each child a magazine and ask them to cut out one picture of a person that shows emotions. The picture should show how a person feels—happy, sad, angry, thoughtful, worried, frightened. Paste the picture on a separate piece of paper. Discuss each picture. How does this person feel? What do you think might have made the person feel that way? How should you treat a person who feels this way? This activity gives the children the opportunity to discuss the feelings and emotions of others and ways to detect these feelings as well as how to react to them in an objective way.

Relax and remember.   In this activity, the children are asked to relax their bodies, to close their eyes, and to see things in their mind's eye. They are asked to conjure up memories of places, things, and feelings. They are asked to see, taste, hear, and feel. Some items could be

- a peanut butter sandwich
- splashing in a pool on a hot day
- walking through dry leaves in the fall
- feeling the warm sunshine
- biting into a crunchy apple
- walking in snow drifts
- smelling freshly baked cookies
- hearing a bird singing

The wonders of nature.   Children can be helped to become attuned to the wonders of nature. One passes over things every day that can be quite beautiful. The *nature walk* is an activity to help children become aware of the wonder in the world. The children can be taken out of doors and asked to be very quiet as they walk to find *one* object that causes them to wonder. The object could be a leaf, or a rock, or a twig. The group can share what they find. Children can explain what they see of wonder in their object.

Summary

Human behavior is often divided into the cognitive domain and the affective domain. Cognitive behavior refers to the intellectual and thinking skills. The affective domain refers to the psychosocial skills—social perception, emotional status, values, and attitudes.

Handicapped children often have psychosocial problems in addition to their other handicaps. This aspect of their problem may be the most debilitating.

Handicapped children are likely to be rejected by parents, peers, and teachers, and disliked and ignored by others. Moreover, they are poor in perceiving social cues.

Among the characteristics of psychosocial problems are lack of schematic or organizational judgment, difficulty in perceiving the affective status of others, problems in socializing and making friends, problems in establishing family relationships, and poor self-concept. These difficulties tend to reinforce one another and impact all areas of learning.

The theory of psychosocial development offered by Erik Erikson provides the basis for many preschool programs. The personality of the individual develops through a series of interrelated stages, each of which is a critical period of development. Each period must be resolved in a positive way if future conflicts are also to be resolved. The early childhood stages include trust vs. mistrust (birth to one year), autonomy vs. shame and doubt (two to three years of age), and initiative vs. guilt (four to five years of age). Behavior modification techniques are important for teaching handicapped preschool children. The techniques include reinforcement, modeling, shaping behavior, and recording and monitoring behavior.

Play activity serves an important role in child development. It is a means through which children learn motor, cognitive, language, sensory, and social skills. The nonhandicapped child learns many of these skills through spontaneous play. Handicapped children, however, may need carefully planned and directed activities to learn how to play. Play for the handicapped child functions to facilitate growth of desired behaviors, to reinforce instructional activity, to inhibit inappropriate behavior, and to provide pleasure. The kinds of play include exploratory play, toy play, social play, and game play. A wide variety of activities can be used by the teacher to help the child develop psychosocial skills.

Review Questions

TERMS TO KNOW

a. *Erik Erikson*

b. *behavior modification*

c. *reinforcement*

d. *modeling*

e. *shaping behavior*

f. *spontaneous play*

g. *directed play*

h. *values clarification*

1. Describe four psychosocial problems a preschool child might have.
2. Some children have multiple problems. Describe three clusters of such problem behavior.
3. What are the implications of Erikson's theory of psychosocial development for the preschool child?
4. What is the theory underlying behavior modification?
5. Give an example of *reinforcement, modeling,* and *shaping behavior.*

6. What is the difference between *spontaneous play* and *directed play?*
7. What can the handicapped child learn through play?

References

ALLEN, K. *Mainstreaming in Early Childhood Education.* Albany, N.Y.: Delmar, 1980.

ALMY, M. Spontaneous Play: An Avenue for Intellectual Development. *Young Children,* 1967, 8.

BRYAN, T. Peer Popularity in Learning Disabled Children. *Journal of Learning Disabilities,* 1976, 5, 307–311.

BRYAN, T., AND J. BRYAN. *Understanding Learning Disabilities.* Sherman Oaks, Calif.: Alfred, 1978.

BRYAN, T., AND OTHERS. "Come On Dummy": An Observational Study of Children's Communications. *Journal of Learning Disabilities,* 1978, 9, 661–669.

COOKE, R., AND T. APOLLONI. Developing Positive Emotional Behaviors: A Study in Training and Generalization Effects. *Journal of Applied Behavior Analysis,* 1976, 9, 67–78.

DSM–III DIAGNOSTIC AND STATISTICAL MANUAL. *American Psychiatric Association,* 1980.

ERIKSON, E. *Childhood and Society.* 2nd ed. New York: W. W. Norton and Co., Inc., 1963.

GURALNICK, M. Social Interactions Among Preschool Children. *Exceptional Children,* 1980, 46(4), 248–253.

HARLAN, J., AND Y. LEYSER. Head Start Teachers' Use of Verbal Encouragement. *Exceptional Children,* 1980, 46(4), 290–291.

HARTLEY, R. Play—The Essential Ingredient. *Childhood Education,* 1971, 48(2).

KRATHWOHL, D., B. BLOOM, AND B. MASIA. *Taxonomy of Educational Objectives. Handbook II. Affective Domain.* New York: D. McKay, 1964.

KRASNER, L., AND L. ULLMAN, eds. *Research in Behavior Modification.* New York: Holt Rinehart & Winston, 1965.

KRONICK, D. An Examination of Psychosocial Aspects of Learning Disabled Adolescents. *Learning Disabilities Quarterly,* Fall 1978, 84–86.

MOORE, S. Social Cognition: About Others. *Young Children,* March 1979, 54–61.

O'LEARY, K., AND S. O'LEARY. *Classroom Management: The Successful Use of Behavior Modification.* 2nd ed. New York: Pergamon, 1977.

SIMON, S., AND OTHERS. *Values Clarification: A Handbook of Practical Strategies for Teachers and Students.* New York: Hart, 1972.

SIMON, S., AND R. O'ROURKE. *Developing Values with Exceptional Children.* Englewood Cliffs, N.J.: Prentice-Hall, Inc. 1977.

STRAIN, P., R. GABLE, AND J. HENDRICKSON. Peer Mediated Social Initiation: A Procedure for Promoting Social Behavior with Mainstreamed Children. *Journal of Special Education Technology,* 1978, 4, 33–38.

WEHMAN, P. Play Skill Development, in *Young Children with Special Needs,* eds. M. Fallen and J. McGovern. Columbus, Ohio: Chas. E. Merrill, 1978.

YARROW, L. Emotional Development. *American Psychologist,* 1979, 34, 951–957.

The Environment

Part **Three**

The Parent-Professional Partnership

PARENT INVOLVEMENT

SERVICES TO FAMILIES

PARENT RIGHTS

SUMMARY

Chapter **Nine**

Part III discusses the largest of the expanding systems, the environment. Some of the factors that affect the young child's life and development are outside of the child himself or herself and are beyond the elements of the school curriculum. The environment affecting the child's learning includes parents, the community, various agencies, as well as federal and state laws. All of these have an impact on decisions that are made and the way problems are handled. In this chapter, the discussion revolves around the parents, their responses to having an atypical child, and the ways they can manage their child and work with professionals. Chapter 10 deals with the services that schools can provide for preschool exceptional children, and the chapter also reviews highlights of legislation that promote this special service. Chapter 11 provides two case studies of preschool handicapped children, along with the individualized education program (IEP) developed for each child.

Parent Involvement

The involvement of parents in the education of their children is desirable for all children at any age. The involvement of parents who have preschool children with special needs is especially crucial for the following reasons (Stiles and others 1979):

> *Parents are in strategic positions;* they know their children better than anyone else and spend more time with them over an extended period.
> *Parents can compensate* for shortages of one-to-one services.
> *Parents can reduce cost* of instruction and other services.
> *Parents can solve time and distance problems,* particularly in rural areas.

In fact, Bronfenbrenner (1974) states that replicated results from two or more well-designed studies indicate that the family is the most economical as well as the most effective system for fostering and sustaining the development of the child. Furthermore, the involvement of the child's family as active participants is critical to the success of any intervention program. Thus, effective early intervention programs generally have three components in common, one of them being that parents are included as full participants (Allen 1980; Hayden 1978). The other two components are that intervention is started at a very early age and that a multidisciplinary team is involved in meeting the needs of a particular child.

Involving parents of young children with special needs in their children's educational program is not as simple as it sounds. Recognizing that one's child has a disability, whether short-term or lifelong, is a staggering blow from which one adjusts slowly and seldom totally (Cansler, and others 1975). This recognition, in turn, will have a profound effect on the functioning of the total family unit (Dunlap 1979). Unfortunately, there is a tendency on the part of professionals to label parents as rejecting, overprotective, unrealistic, or unaccepting when parents are merely exhibiting normal reactions to stress. These reactions are useful, coping behaviors which give parents time to strengthen their inner reserves, re-establish balance, and look for alternative actions.

Stages of Adjustment

The process of adjustment, which is similar to mourning, generally has three broad stages (Cansler, and others 1975; Fallen and McGovern 1978). No timelines can be affixed to the process because each person reacts so differently. In fact, it is typical for the two parents of the same child to be at different stages at a given point in time, which causes even more problems in the home. It is vital that professionals are aware of the parental and familial adjustment process so that they may be accepting of the accompanying behaviors. The attitude of the professional, based on the recognition that this process cannot be hastened, needs to be one of tolerance, rather than endorsement or rejection. The three stages of the adjustment process are outlined in Table 9–1.

Since parents may be in any one of these stages of the adjustment process, and thus passive or resistive, it can be readily seen why one of the four major dimensions of parent programs is getting parents to participate in the program (Lillie and Trohanis 1976). The other three dimensions are supporting parents emotionally, exchanging information with parents, and improving parent-child interactions. Although there is considerable overlap, each of these dimensions will be discussed separately.

TABLE 9–1   The Adjustment for Families of Handicapped Children

Stage	Typical Behavior(s)
1. Denial	Shock
	Flatly disregards the diagnosis
	Pretends diagnosis never occurred
	Diagnostic "shopping" for cause or cure
	Continuous training of child to disprove diagnosis
2. Intellectual Awareness	Anger
	Guilt
	Depression (anger turned inward)
	Grief; sorrow
	Disappointment
	Bitterness and shame
	Blame
3. Intellectual and Emotional	Organizes time and energy constructively
Adjustment (Acceptance)	Demonstrates realistic expectations for the child
	Advocates child program
	Cooperates and interacts appropriately

Adapted from D. Cansler and others. *Working with Families.* Winston-Salem, N.C.: Kaplan Press, 1975, p. 11–13.

Developing Parent Participation

One of the most successful ways to develop a genuine partnership with parents so that they participate with total commitment is to design and implement a program that meets the needs of parents as well as the needs of their children. This can be achieved to some extent by recognizing that parenting is an aggregate of learned skills, not something one knows "naturally." To teach these skills is a very worthwhile endeavor, for research shows that skillful parenting is the most effective and economical means for fostering the optimum development of the child (Meier 1977). Three obstacles generally interfere with the development of optimal parenting skills (White 1975) and these become particularly overwhelming when parenting involves a young child with special needs:

1. *ignorance:* Most parents are unprepared for the responsibility of parenting, and there is little sound, legitimate information to share. Parents thus do not know how to do their job—how to deal with a baby's curiosity or social development; how to recognize developmental milestones and provide appropriate experiences. Parents need to learn the nature of their role in "caregiving."

2. *stress:* The 8- to 24-month period is one of the most dangerous periods in life due to the child's intense curiosity, poor control of the body, lack of awareness of common dangers and the value of objects, and

the child's ignorance about the rights of others. There is resentment between siblings, extra work from a toddler, and possible tension between the parents over the neatness of the house. Parents need to learn how to cope with this stress.

3. *lack of assistance:* Due to the small, nuclear family and the mobility of Americans, parents may have no nearby relatives or friends to offer physical and/or psychological relief. Parents need to learn how to overcome this obstacle within their financial constraints, such as cooperative baby-sitting arrangements.

These obstacles can be overcome in parent programs if parents are motivated, involved, and accept their responsibility regarding the development of their child (Tjossem 1976). However, there are many factors which can interfere with parent participation, no matter how well a program is designed to meet the general needs of parents. Some of these factors are

> The child is living in a single parent household.
> The child is living in a multigenerational family under one roof.
> The child is living with working parent(s).
> The child has transferred from a different preschool program which had other goals and/or procedures.

These and other factors require modifications in the content and timing of parental participation. In addition, Dunlap (1979) suggests that families need relief from physical and time demands, and assistance, such as baby sitting, daycare, and homemaker services, particularly in low socio-economic areas. Young handicapped children in the family demand more time and care and create more money problems than their normal siblings do.

Supporting Parents Emotionally

Besides the stress that all parents experience in providing care to young children, parents of exceptional children experience additional feelings of guilt and inadequacy. Teachers of young handicapped children need to be alert to these feelings yet recognize that they are not therapists. The most important role here is being a good listener. Parents should be encouraged to express feelings and attitudes in the process of adjusting. They may need the professional simply as a "sounding board." Parents may need help in feeling content with daily interactions. The teacher may also be able to provide a feeling of personal worth for the parent; this is necessary for a stimulating home environment. Finally, parents can often provide each other with emotional support when given the opportunity to interact with each other, thus solving mutual problems and concerns.

Exchanging Information with Parents

Although parents need to know the ways that young children learn and their own role in this process, there are also many things that parents can tell professionals. The child's developmental history, the family's social history, and how the child acts and interacts on a daily basis are just the beginnings of two-way communication. As the needs of the child and the parent(s) change within the program, these changes should be incorporated into an ongoing evaluation so that when new objectives are formulated, parent input becomes an integral part of the process. This exchange of information can take place informally through parents' verbal comments or more formally through a needs-assessment questionnaire and a parent advisory council.

Improving Parent-Child Interactions

Parents should be encouraged to grow in their caregiving role through new ways of behaving in daily child management. One way of doing so is by having parents observe the teacher manage their child in a particular situation which also carries over to the home. Another technique is watching another parent or trying the new procedure with another child. When parents know that their attitude towards their child is more significant for encouraging later development than the minor problem at hand, they may relax and enjoy their own lives more.

Other Guidelines for Parent Involvement

As professionals working with parents, there are other guidelines that should be kept in mind. While professionals need to be objective, neutral, and somewhat detached, withdrawing behind a cool facade and becoming totally intellectualized does a disservice to families. On the other hand, allowing emotions to control or intrude upon activities may also be unconstructive, causing the professional to become overinvolved or overprotective (Seminar for the Development of Infants and Parents 1978).

Parents will become involved in educational programs for their children, whether home-based or center-based, if they are appropriately approached and appropriately involved (Karnes 1973). Constructive, cooperative parent-professional relationships, thus, are founded on the following suggestions (Fallen and McGovern 1978).

> Parents should participate fully as members of the educational team rather than play a subordinate or supplementary role.
>
> Professionals need to accept parents where they are in the adjustment process and learn to listen. Communicating with parents begins with listening.
>
> All relevant information should be shared with parents.
>
> Parents should have the principle responsibility for selecting goals and objectives; professionals should have the principle responsibility for selecting methodology and technology.
>
> Professional jargon should be eliminated or at least minimized.
>
> Support and encouragement should be given to parents as they struggle to cope with the frustrations and problems of raising a handicapped child on a day-to-day basis.

Services to Families

If the multidisciplinary team and family are seen as a cooperative team with common goals, it may be necessary to determine the particular expectations for each child-family unit and then provide the appropriate services. Possible services to families may include any or all of the following (Cansler and others, 1975):

1. Training in teaching methods
2. Interpretation of test scores
3. Counseling for family problems (group and/or individual therapy)
4. Coordination of other community resources
5. Help with behavior management
6. Transportation
7. Suggestions for home activities
8. Suggestions for inexpensive or home-made materials
9. Training for siblings
10. Meetings and workshops for parents and family groups

As parents participate in an intervention program, two adjustments become necessary: Parents assume the role of the learner as they are taught how to teach their child by presenting tasks in a clear, understandable manner and at a level geared to the child's ability; their relationship with their child is modified by their involvement in the educational process. Although curricula in parent intervention programs for young handicapped children show considerable diversity (Levitt and Cohen 1976), two areas frequently emphasized are *self-help skills* and *language*.

For instance, Weiss and Lillywhite (1976) list "101 ways to help the child learn to talk" which can be implemented by parents. Hatten and Hatten (1975) give parents of language-delayed children a precise, step-by-step guide of how to teach their children. Karnes (1977) has developed a kit of lesson cards, *Learning Language at Home,* to be utilized by parents. Some early childhood curriculum materials for language development, as well as other areas, are commercially available and thus accessible to parents (Mears 1975). Other outstanding materials for parents of preschoolers with special needs have been developed by the Saturday School in Ferguson, Missouri (no date).

One exemplary program, which involves parent(s) at a very high level is the *Portage Project* (Shearer and Shearer 1976). It covers five developmental areas: language, cognition, self-help, motor, and socialization. The rationale for this program includes the following:

- Learning occurs in the child's natural environment (the home).
- Skills generalize when taught by parent(s).
- Parents determine what and how the child will be taught.
- The entire family is more likely to be involved when program is at home.
- Self-help skills are more accessible in a home program than in a classroom.
- Instructional goals are individualized in a home program.

There are also economic advantages for this program, such as no need for a center or to transport children. Through the use of the *Portage Guide to Early Education* (Bluma and others 1976), parents are taught how to teach 580 sequential behaviors, what to reinforce, and how to observe and record behavior.

Whereas the Portage Project is a home-based parent-training model, there is also a center-based parent-training model, a home-center-based parent-training model which combines aspects of the first two models, and finally the parent-implemented preschool program where parents are responsible for delivery of services and evaluation, rather than professionals (Lillie and Trohanis 1976).

Another service to parents is supplying them with names of books and publications. Each of the following are appropriate for parents of preschool children.

Get a Wibble On, Move It
Ingham Intermediate School District, Division of Special Education, 2630 W. Howell Rd., Mason, Michigan 48854 ($2.00 each)—An enjoyable guide book for parents of a vision-handicapped child; gives suggestions for making home activities more stimulating and educational for the child.

Handling the Young Cerebral Palsied Child at Home
Nancie Finnie, E. P. Dutton & Co., Inc., 201 Park Ave., So., New York, New York 10003 ($3.50)—An extensive resource book for parents on activities, positioning and feeding tips, teaching ideas.

Let's Play to Grow: A Program of Play, Fitness and Fun
Joseph P. Kennedy, Jr. Foundation, 1701 K St. N. W., Washington, D.C. 20006 ($2.50)—An idea kit for the whole family with sport activities for all ages; includes an "I am a Winner" chart.

New Directions for Parents of Persons Who Are Retarded
Robert Perske, Abbington Press, 201 8th Ave., So., Nashville, TN, 37202 ($1.95)—A short book for parents on the different kinds of feelings they may be experiencing and ways of coping.

Parents Speak Out: Views from the Other Side of the Two Way Mirror
Ann P. Turnbull, H. Rutherford Turnbull, III, Charles E. Merrill Publishing Company, Columbus, Ohio 43216.

The Exceptional Parent
A magazine for parents; also has a book division with discount prices. Exceptional Parent, Dept. C, P. O. Box 4944, Manchester, New Hampshire 03108 ($10.00 a year).

Still another service is providing parents with names of national organizations which may provide information or other forms of assistance. In addition, many of these national organizations have state and local chapters. Table 9–2 lists some of the national organizations of special interest to parents.

The success of many intervention programs for young handicapped children hinges on the parent-professional partnership; the parents' ability to avoid a feeling of inadequacy; the professional's ability to avoid a feeling of threat and loss of control; overdependence by parents on the professional; and competition for the child's love and attention (Levitt and Cohen 1976). These issues need to be recognized and overcome as they occur. The keys to success seem to be flexibility and openness to parents' participation (Cansler and others 1975).

Parent Rights

Parents are usually very aware of their responsibilities to their exceptional child, but they are rarely aware of their rights as parents of an exceptional child or of their rights as people per se. According to PL 94–142, parents of children with exceptional needs have the following rights (Division for Exceptional Children, 1979):

Public schools must *inform parents* that their child is entitled to specific services.

TABLE 9-2 National Organizations of Special Interest to Parents

Name	Address	Service
Alexander Graham Bell Association for the Deaf	3417 Volta Pl., N.W. Washington, DC 20007 202/337-5220	National organization for parents and teachers interested in hearing impaired children; provides information on home training, amplification, and has a large library on deafness.
Allergy Foundation of America	801 Second Ave. New York, NY 10017 212/876-8875	Provides a listing of allergy clinics available across the country as well as informational pamphlets describing different allergies (pamphlets cost 50¢ each).
Amer. Assoc. for the Severely-Profoundly Handicapped	1600 W. Armory Way Seattle, WA 98119 206/543-4011	A new national organization, publishes a monthly newsletter for parents and professionals concerned with children having great needs for special assistance.
American Foundation for the Blind	15 West 11th St. New York, NY 10011 212/924-0420	Private agency that provides information and referral services for the public.
American Speech and Hearing Association	1801 Rockville Pike Rockville, MD 20852 301/897-5700	An educational and professional organization for speech, language, and audiology. Provides clinical referral services for those seeking clinical services. Free public information literature is available on request from the association.
Association for Children and Adults with Learning Disabilities (ACLD)	4156 Library Rd. Pittsburgh, PA 15234 412/881-1191	National organization within every state; provides information on advocacy, publications, and new developments related to children with learning disabilities.
Closer Look	Box 1942 Washington, DC 20013 202/833-4160	National information center to help parents find out about rights, how to get services, and locate a local group. Publishes a free newsletter, The Closer Report, with much helpful information.
Down's Syndrome Congress	Ms. Betty Buczynski 16470 Ronnies Drive Misawaka, IN 46544	National information service for and by parents of Down Syndrome retarded children; publishes a monthly newsletter on new information of special interest ($5 a year).
Epilepsy Foundation of America	1828 L St., N.W. Washington, DC 20036 202/293-2930	A national agency for people with epilepsy. Provides free information on epilepsy and its consequences and educational materials to individuals and groups dealing with seizures disorders. Provides referral service, monitors related legislative activity, and is a strong advocate to help obtain needed services and rights for those with epilepsy.

TABLE 9-2   (continued)

Name	Address	Service
Mental Health Association, National Headquarters	1800 North Kent St. Arlington, VA 22209 703/524-3352 703/524-4230	Provides referral services for parents as well as delivering workshops and seminars on the various aspects of mental health. Makes available to the public a large collection of free literature.
National Assoc. for Retarded Citizens	2709 Ave. E. East P.O. Box 6109 Arlington, TX 76011 817/261-4961	Has over 1900 state and local chapters; promotes programs for retarded children and their families.
National Assoc. for Visually Handicapped	305 East 24th St. New York, NY 10010 212/889-3141	Provides free learning materials for parents to help their children, including large print books and a monthly newsletter to keep families informed on the new techniques used with visually handicapped.
National Easter Seal Society for Crippled Children and Adults	2023 West Ogden Ave. Chicago, IL 60612 312/243-8400	National organization to provide rehabilitation services to persons with physical handicaps. Local societies are throughout the country.
National Hemophelia Foundation	25 West 39th St. New York, NY 10018 212/869-9740	Provides free literature on Hemophelia and the handicapping conditions which can result from this disease. Provides referral services and was directly responsible for the establishment of 23 diagnostic centers for Hemophelia across the country which provide training and rehabilitation.
National Multiple Sclerosis Society	205 East 42nd St. New York, NY 10017 212/986-3240	A voluntary health agency. Provides literature, counseling, training, referral, group recreational activities, loans of special equipment and financial support of Multiple Sclerosis Clinics in local hospital. Local chapters can be found throughout the country.
National Society for Autistic Children	169 Tampa Ave. Albany, NY 12208 518/489-7375	National organization with information on the education and welfare of children with severe needs in communication and behavior.
Spina Bifida Assoc. of America	343 S. Dearborn Chicago, IL 60604 312/662-1562	National association to distribute information to parents and professionals; has local chapters throughout the country.
United Cerebral Palsy Assoc., Inc.	66 East 34th St. New York, NY 10016 212/481-6300	National association for information and service needs to families with a child with cerebral palsy.

From Division for Exceptional Children. *Hand in Hand: Parents and Educators Planning Special Education for the Child.* Raleigh, N.C.: State Department of Public Instruction, 1979.

Public schools must *ask parents to participate* in making decisions and developing the educational program for their child.

Public schools must provide education to special needs children at *no cost to parents.*

Parents may request a due process hearing if they feel their child's current educational needs are not being met by the public school.

Thus, parents participate in three ways in their child's education according to law:

1. They give permission for assessment and for beginning or changing any special education for their child.

2. They attend and participate in meetings which develop the special education and learning goals for their child.

3. They agree to the written special education program and annual learning goals for their child.

In addition, parents of exceptional children should realize that they have the following rights (Gordon 1975):

- Freedom to feel that they have done the best they could.
- Freedom to enjoy life as intensely as possible, even though they have an exceptional child.
- Freedom to let their handicapped child have his or her own privacy.
- Freedom to have hostile thoughts once in a while without feeling guilty.
- Freedom to enjoy being alone at times.
- Freedom to tell people about their child's progress and achievements with a real sense of pride.
- Freedom to have their own hobbies and interests.
- Freedom to tell teachers and other professionals what they really feel about the job the professionals are doing and demand that their opinions be respected.
- Freedom to devote as much time as they want to the handicap cause and to get away from it for a while and return if they want.
- Freedom to tell their child if he or she displeases them even though their child has a handicap.
- Freedom to refrain from praising their child gratuitously, even though they have been told to offer much praise.
- Freedom to lie once in a while and say everything is fine; not to feel compelled to tell the truth to everyone who asks.
- Freedom to say at times that they do not want to talk about their problems or their handicapped child.
- Freedom to have an annual vacation without the children; have dates, celebrations, weekends away, time together to enhance their marriage.
- Freedom to spend a little extra money on themselves, even though they feel they can't afford it.

Gordon warns that parents who do not enjoy almost all these freedoms are in trouble because martyred parents are seldom appreciated by anybody, least of all by their exceptional child.

Summary

Involving parents in their child's educational program is critical for the improvement of the child and the success of the program. However, the foundation of the parent-professional partnership must be based on mutual trust and respect. Professionals must recognize each parent as a unique individual, with a past, present, and future unlike any other. Parents are simply people—not a category called "parents of exceptional children" who have stereotyped reactions to having a child with special needs. Yet there is little question that parents of exceptional children experience stages of adjustment: denial, intellectual awareness, and finally, intellectual and emotional adjustment.

Most parents' programs have four major but overlapping dimensions: developing parent participation, supporting parents emotionally, exchanging information with parents, and improving parent-child interactions.

Services to families include parent intervention programs, available publications, and national organizations of special interest to parents. Most parent intervention programs stress the language and self-help areas of development.

Finally, the rights of parents, both legally and personally, should be considered and respected by parents and professionals alike.

Review Questions

TERMS TO KNOW

a. *parenting*
b. *denial*
c. *diagnostic "shopping"*
d. *depression*
e. *acceptance*

1. Describe the three ages of adjustment which parents of handicapped children generally go through, along with typical behavior in each stage.
2. What obstacles interfere in the parenting of most children?
3. The four major dimensions of parents' programs are developing parent

participation, supporting parents emotionally, exchanging information with parents, and improving parent-child interactions. List one appropriate activity for each dimension.

4. Discuss in depth three different services which can be provided for families of handicapped preschoolers.

5. Parent training programs generally follow one of four models; name each.

6. What is Closer Look?

7. Complete the following chart:

Rights of a Handicapped Child's Parents

Personal	*Legal*
1.	1.
2.	2.
3.	3.
4.	4.

References

ALLEN, K. E. *Mainstreaming in Early Childhood Education.* Albany, N.Y.: Delmar, 1980.

BLUMA, S., AND OTHERS. *Portage Guide to Early Education.* (Rev. Ed.) Portage, Wis.: Cooperative Educational Service Agency, No. 12, 1976.

BRONFENBRENNER, U. *A Report on Longitudinal Evaluations of Preschool Programs, Volume II: Is Early Intervention Effective?* Washington, D.C.: U. S. Department of Health, Education, and Welfare, 1974.

CANSLER, D., G. MARTIN, AND M. VALAND. *Working with Families.* Winston-Salem, N.C.: Kaplan Press, 1975.

DIVISION FOR EXCEPTIONAL CHILDREN. *Hand in Hand: Parents and Educators Planning Special Education for the Child.* Raleigh, N.C.: State Department of Public Instruction, 1979.

DUNLAP, W. How Do Parents of Handicapped Children View Their Needs? *Journal of the Division of Early Childhood,* 1979, 1(1), 1–10.

FALLEN, N., AND J. McGOVERN. *Young Children with Special Needs.* Columbus, Ohio: Chas. E. Merrill, 1978.

GORDON, S. *Living Fully: A Guide for Young People with a Handicap, Their Parents, Their Teachers, and Professionals.* New York: John Day, 1975.

HATTEN, J., AND P. HATTEN. *Natural Language: A Clinician-Guided Program for Parents of Language-Delayed Children.* rev. ed., Tucson, Ariz.: Communication Skills Builders, 1975.

HAYDEN, A. Early Childhood Education, in *Early Intervention—A Team Approach,* eds. K. E. Allen and others. Baltimore, Md.: University Park Press, 1978.

KARNES, M. *Payoff of Early Intervention.* Chicago, Ill.: Council for Children with Learning Disabilities, 1973.

Karnes, M. *Learning Language at Home.* Reston, Va.: Council for Exceptional Children, 1977.

Levitt, E., and S. Cohen. Educating Parents of Children with Special Needs: Approaches and Issues. *Young Children,* 1976, 5.

Lillie, D., and P. Trohanis, eds. *Teaching Parents to Teach.* New York: Walker, 1976.

Mears, C., ed. *Early Childhood Curriculum Materials: An Annotated Bibliography.* Chapel Hill, N.C.: Technical Assistance Development System, University of North Carolina, 1975.

Meier, J. *The Long Range Results of Early Identification and Intervention and Some Salient Ethical/Social/Political Considerations.* Invited Address, Annual Conference of Council for Exceptional Children, Atlanta, Ga., 1977.

Saturday School. *Parent's Home Activity Guides.* Ferguson, Mo.: Parent-Child Early Education Program, no date.

Seminar for the Development of Infants and Parents. Parent-Professional Communication: Practical Suggestions. *The Exceptional Parent,* 1978, 8, 2.

Shearer, D., and M. Shearer. The Portage Project: A Model for Early Childhood Intervention, in *Intervention Strategies for High Risk Infants and Young Children,* ed. T. Tjossem. Baltimore, Md.: University Park Press, 1976.

Stiles, S., J. Cole, and A. Garner. Maximizing Parental Involvement in Programs for Exceptional Children. *Journal of the Division for Early Childhood,* 1979, 1(1), 68–82.

Tjossem, R., ed. *Intervention Strategies for High Risk Infants and Young Children.* Baltimore, Md.: University Park Press, 1976.

Weiss, C., and H. Lillywhite. *Communication Disorders: A Handbook for Prevention and Early Intervention.* St. Louis, Mo.: C. V. Mosby, 1976.

White, B. *The First Three Years of Life.* Englewood Cliffs, N.J.: Prentice-Hall, Inc., 1975.

Providing
Educational Services

EDUCATIONAL PROGRAM ALTERNATIVES

LEGISLATION AND THE YOUNG HANDICAPPED CHILD

THE TEAM APPROACH TO COMPREHENSIVE SERVICES

SUMMARY

Chapter **Ten**

The field of early childhood special education is still a new field of endeavor, and schools and other agencies are still groping to develop ways to deliver appropriate educational services to young children with special needs. This chapter discusses some of those efforts. Specifically, the chapter examines (1) placement options, (2) the provisions of Public Law 94–142, and other legislation for the young handicapped child, and (3) the team approach to comprehensive services for early childhood special education programs.

Educational Program Alternatives

Placement Options

An array of service alternatives and placement facilities is necessary to meet the requirements of all young children with special needs. Appropriate placement depends upon a number of factors: the severity of the disability, the age of the child, the nature of the handicapping condition, and the facilities offered by the school and the community. Both public and nonpublic educational services may be necessary to provide flexible arrangements for a child's diverse and changing needs.

Decisions related to the specific placement of an individual child must be based upon the recommendations which result from an individual comprehensive case study evaluation, the needs of the family, and a staff conference. The evaluation and staff conference for handicapped children under the law (PL 94–142) takes the format of an *individualized education program* (IEP). The nature and requirements of the IEP are discussed later in this chapter.

Several placement possibilities were discussed in Chapter 4;

Regular class and individual therapy. Placement is in a regular preschool setting for nonhandicapped children for part of the day plus individual therapy with special education or related personnel for part of the day. This might be an appropriate placement for a mildly handicapped child.

Noncategorical special class for diagnostic assessment and observation. Placement is with a small group of children with a variety of handicaps who have been identified through screening as needing additional assessment and observation. This group of handicapped children could meet on a daily basis and receive instruction as well as additional assessment.

Categorical special class placement. Placement is in a group of preschool children with a specific type of exceptionality. If early highly specialized and intensive therapy is needed (as with deaf children), this may be the placement of choice.

Home management training. Placement is in the home with provision of training for the family in home management skills. This might be the most appropriate for a severely handicapped very young child.

Combination programs. Combinations of the above programs can be used. In addition to the school, other agencies may be used in placement, such as mental health agencies, private agencies, Head Start programs, and hospital programs. Each community has different facilities available. Teachers should learn about these agencies and develop a cooperative relationship with them.

Special Considerations in Placement

Least restrictive environment. Public Law 94–142 requires that placement take into consideration the concept of the *least restrictive environment*. This means that to the extent appropriate, handicapped children are to be placed with nonhandicapped children. In terms of the law, the more the placement includes nonhandicapped children, the less restrictive that environment is considered to be. Conversely, the fewer the nonhandicapped children in a setting, the more restrictive that environment is considered. However, in practice it has been pointed out that for many children the "least restrictive environment" under the law may be the *most* restrictive for a particular child who cannot function in an environment with regular children. The concept of *least restrictive environment* is often interpreted as a mandate for *mainstreaming*, which it is not. Children are to be placed in a regular classroom only if such a placement is appropriate for them.

Continuum of alternative placements. The *least restrictive environment* feature of the law should be interpreted in conjunction with another feature of the PL 94–142 known as the *continuum of alternative placements*.

The law requires the school to have an array of services to meet the many needs of handicapped children. The following is a listing of possible placements, ranked from the least restrictive to the most restrictive:

- Regular classroom with no basic change in teaching procedures
- Regular class with indirect services within the regular class
- Regular class with direct services and instruction within the regular class
- Regular class with resource room services
- Self-contained special classroom with part-time instruction within the regular class
- Self-contained special class, full-time on a regular school campus
- Self-contained special class in a private day school facility
- Public residential school facility
- Private residential school facility
- Hospital program
- Home-bound instruction.

Figure 10–1 illustrates the concept of the continuum of educational program alternatives. The top point of the triangle is the most restrictive environment, while the base shows the least restrictive environment.

Alternative placements were designed for the elementary and secondary school student. Special adaptations and considerations must be made for the young child. One important consideration is that typically nonhandicapped preschool children are not yet in public school. This means that placing a handicapped child in the least restrictive environment presents particular problems with the young child. There is still an inadequate amount of research and experience to provide a structure of continuum alternative placements for the young child with special needs.

Categorical and noncategorical placements. Another consideration in placement is whether the child should be placed with children with the same category of exceptionality or whether the child should be in a setting with children with several areas of exceptionality (noncategorical). With young children, this problem is particularly pressing because educators are reluctant to stigmatize the young child by labeling the child with a handicapping condition. Further, it is difficult to differentiate the specific category of the problem with the young child, such as learning disabilities, language disabilities, mental retardation, emotional disturbance, or developmental lag. Therefore, such a differential diagnosis is often delayed and the child is placed in a noncategorical or cross-categorical setting. Children with a variety of handicaps, as well as nonhandicapped children, may be placed together. This setting also permits further observation and evaluation to take place. Such settings

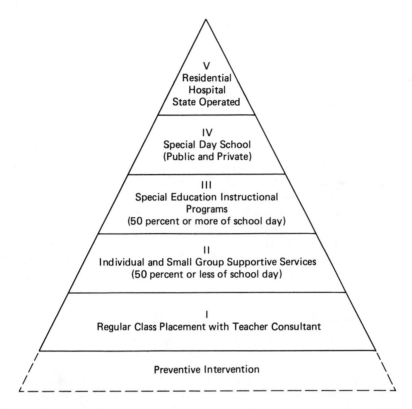

Figure 10–1 Continuum of Educational Program Alternatives *From Illinois Office of Education, Learning Disabilities Manual: Recommended Procedures and Practices.* Springfield, Ill.: State Board of Education, May 1978, p. 2.

may simply be designated as *developmental classes,* or *early childhood services.*

Even though a child may be placed in a noncategorical setting, it is necessary under PL 94–142 to specify the child's primary exceptionality during the evaluation process. This requirement exists because schools and states are reimbursed under the law by the number of children in each category.

Mainstreaming. The term *mainstreaming* refers to a method of providing educational services for exceptional children. The traditional approach had been to separate handicapped children and group them by category of exceptionality for educational purposes. Thus, there were separate classes for the blind, the deaf, the mentally retarded, and so on. Mainstreaming is a way of providing educational services to the exceptional children by integrating them in tne regular classroom. The blind child, crippled child, and learning-disabled child will be placed in the regular classroom with nonhandicapped children under a mainstream delivery system.

As mentioned earlier, this is erroneously thought of as implementation of the feature of PL 94–142 known as the *least restrictive environment*. Mainstreaming is but one type of delivery system, and it may not be appropriate for all handicapped children. Nevertheless, this method of serving handicapped children is growing at a rapid pace. Mainstreaming requires that regular teachers as well as special education teachers know about special education and handicapped children.

The problem that confronts the field of special education is that the concept of mainstreaming could be abused by failing to provide sufficient special education classes and personnel. There is danger that a poorly initiated mainstreaming movement can mean a backlash from teachers, parents, and the lay public. Several points should be kept in mind: (Zigler and Muenchow 1979).

1. Appropriate training for teachers and other personnel who work with handicapped children is needed. In the case of preschool children this includes volunteers, teachers, and related personnel.

2. Without adequate support personnel to assist regular class teachers with the handicapped, mainstreaming is doomed to failure. This means that preschool teachers, daycare teachers, Head Start teachers, and so on need supportive help from special educators for handicapped children in their charge.

3. Mainstreaming should not be viewed as a way to save money. Properly conducted, a mainstream program will cost as much as the self-contained special education classes.

4. Mainstreaming and its evaluation does not take place in a social vacuum. The point here is that for some children, "normalization" placement in a nonhandicapped setting is the wrong type of placement.

Some possible approaches to be considered for providing a mainstreaming setting for three- to five-year-old handicapped children are suggested by the Illinois State Board of Education (1979).

1. Have the special education program for three to five year olds located within the regular elementary building and allow them to partake in certain kindergarten activities during designated periods of the day or week. Coordinate activities between early childhood and preschool bilingual classes located in the same building by scheduling group activities together, such as field trips, music, art, snacks, physical education, language, lessons and the like.

2. Have special education programs for the special preschool children located in separate facilities but coordinated with local kindergartens in the public school by programming for the special preschool children to be with the kindergarten class for specified periods during the week.

3. Integrate more severely and profoundly handicapped preschoolers with less severely involved children. In essence, this endorses the concept of meeting least restrictive environment requirements through coordination internally with special education programs. For the more severely handicapped children, this setting may constitute a least restrictive alternative.

4. Utilize schools which have been abandoned because of declining enrollment as a setting for early childhood special education programs and institute additional programs within the building, such as Head Start, a kindergarten class, youth groups, and other child developmental programs.

5. Open early childhood special education programs in junior and community colleges or high schools where there are established child development programs for the students, and coordinate programs and activities between the two groups.

6. Coordinate early childhood special education programs (either school facilities or separate facilities) with existing community resources for preschoolers. Dually enroll exceptional preschoolers with local Head Start programs for specified days or weeks.

Handicapped Children—Birth to Three Years of Age

Although the provision of educational services for young handicapped children ages three to five is indeed complex, it is even more so for the infant population, birth to three years of age. To add to the complexity, no single agency has mandated responsibility for provision of services to this group of children. Programs must be individualized for the child and the child's family needs.

Services for the birth-to-three group occurs most frequently in one of three settings (Illinois State Board of Education 1979).

1. *Home-based approach.* Service is given to the child and family in the home. A staff person goes to the home to assist in the child's development and to assist parents in becoming the primary educator of the child.

2. *Center-based approach.* In this approach the parent brings the child to a central facility where there is a complete interdisciplinary staff for assisting the child.

3. *Combined home-based and center-based approach.* In this approach the child is brought to the center for a designated number of sessions per week, and there are also visits in the home and training for the parents.

Sample successful programs for birth-to-three populations include the Infant Stimulation-Mother Training Project (Badger 1977), the Florida Parent Education Infant and Toddler Program (Gordon and others 1977), and the Mother-Child Home Program (Levenstein 1977).

The following recommendations are made for programs for birth-to-three-year-old children (Illinois State Board of Education 1979):

1. Services for birth-to-three year olds once initiated should be comprehensive and systematic;

2. A transdisciplinary team should be responsible for birth-to-three programs with a parent-infant educator as the team coordinator;

3. Interagency services contract agreements should be worked out in the best interests of the child;

4. Parents should be involved in every aspect of service delivery;

5. All children should be reassessed at two years-six months of age, or before entering a program for children aged three-to-five;

6. Within any birth-to-three-year-olds program, an attempt should be made to meet the emotional, community, and legal needs of the parents as well as the educational and related service needs of the infant.

In general, there exists a lack of services for the handicapped child in the birth-to-three population. Indeed some physicians and other health personnel are reluctant to tell parents about their child's needs when they know that there are no services available in the home communities (Hayden 1979).

Public Law 94–142 does not include the birth-to-three population. However, as of 1977, ten states had legislation covering children from birth onward. The Developmental Disabilities network discussed later in this chapter is now servicing children in the birth-to-two age population.

Beyond the Preschool Years

Decisions about placement must also be made at the completion of the early childhood special education program. By this time, however, teachers and other related personnel have had the opportunity to observe the child over a long period of time and to assess the child's placement needs. Among the placement options at the completion of early childhood programs are the following: (1) the child could be placed in a regular kindergarten or first grade classroom, (2) the placement could be in a transitional class which would continue the special education and observation for a period of time, (3) the placement could be in a resource room in which case the child would be both in a regular classroom for part of the day and a small special education setting for a portion of the day, (4) the placement could be in a self-contained special education class either in the school or in the special education district which would permit a more intensive special education curriculum, (5) the placement could be in a public or private residential facility.

Whatever placement is recommended, it is important to take steps to assure a smooth transition to the continuing placement. Receiving teachers (be they kindergarten, first grade or special education teachers), should have a chance to observe the child, talk with parents, attend the annual review, and be familiar with the child's individualized education program (IEP). The early childhood special education teacher should spend some time on-site with the receiving teacher at the beginning of the new placement to acquaint the receiving teacher with the child's special needs.

Legislation and the Young Handicapped Child

The rights of all handicapped individuals have been protected in recent years with the passage of federal and state laws. The impact of this legislation affects the early childhood years as well. This section describes a number of laws that have particular pertinence for the young handicapped child and educational practices supported by the law. Teachers and other school personnel must be familiar with recent legislation concerning young handicapped children because the law affects so many aspects of the child's education.

Public Law 94–142

Special education took a major leap forward with the passage in 1975 of landmark legislation entitled *The Education for All Handicapped Children Act,* more frequently referred to as Public Law 94–142 (USOE August, 1977). Under this law, every handicapped child has a right to a *free appropriate public education.* Each state, in turn, must develop a state plan that is in compliance with the federal law. As a result, schools in every part of the nation are feeling the impact of this legislation. Although many states had previously, to one degree or another, instituted such practices as a team approach, written individualized plans, and had developed procedural safeguards, PL 94–142 specifically outlined a comprehensive system of special education practices. By enacting this permanent federal legislation mandate, Congress established a minimum standard for the education of handicapped children throughout the country (Lerner, Dawson, and Horvath 1980).

Section 504 of the Vocational Rehabilitation Act of 1973 is often discussed along with PL 94–142. Section 504 is a civil rights law, mandating equal program *accessability* for handicapped individuals. One subpart of Section 504 addresses public education and essentially repeats the same mandate of free appropriate public education for all handicapped children as is contained in PL 94–142. It is this portion of the law that requires public buildings, including schools, to accommodate handicapped individuals. For example, ramps are to be provided for those handicapped individuals who use wheelchairs.

Early childhood provisions under the law. The age range specified in PL 94–142 is three through twenty-one. However, there are definite exceptions in the law in regard to the three-to-five-year-old population. PL 94–142 states that the legislation does not apply to a state with respect to handicapped children ages three, four, and five years of age if that requirement is not consistent with state law. That is, if the particular state does not mandate special education for three to five year olds, then federal law could not override the state law. Twenty-seven states now have mandated legislation for early childhood handicapped children. Some states have permissive early childhood special education; that is the schools may provide services. Ten states have legislation for children starting at birth (Hayden 1979).

The individualized education program (IEP). One of the major provisions of Public Law 94–142 is the development of an *Individualized Education Program,* often referred to by the initials *IEP,* for each child identified as handicapped for federal funding purposes. The IEP is a written statement for a handicapped child that is developed and implemented in accordance with the act. It decribes the educational objectives for and the services to be provided to each handicapped child. The law also mandates the development of a team approach for the evaluation and writing of the IEP.

PARTICIPANTS AT THE IEP MEETING. The following participants are to be included in the IEP meeting:

1. A representative of the public agency (the school), who is qualified to provide or supervise special education;
2. The child's teacher;
3. One or both of the child's parents;
4. The child, where appropriate;
5. Other individuals, at the discretion of the parents or the school.

CONTENT OF THE IEP. The individualized education program for each child must include

1. A statement of the child's present levels of educational performance;
2. A statement of annual goals, including short-term instructional objectives;
3. A statement of the specific special education and related services in which the child will be able to participate in the regular education program.
4. The projected dates for initiation of services and the anticipated duration of the services; and
5. Appropriate objective criteria and evaluation procedures and schedules for determining, on at least an annual basis, whether the short-term instructional objectives are being achieved.

Procedural safeguards. There are several features built into the regulations for PL 94–142 designed to protect the rights of handicapped children. These mechanisms are known as *procedural safeguards* and include least restrictive environment (discussed in the previous section), protection in evaluation, due process, and confidentiality (Lerner, Dawson, and Horvath 1980).

PROTECTION IN EVALUATION. The law states that the child should be protected during the evaluation process. First evaluation materials must be administered in the child's native language or other mode of communication unless it is clearly not feasible to do so. Then, materials of evaluation should be validated for the specific purposes for which they are used, and evaluators are to be trained in giving the test. No single criterion may be used to make the evaluation. Finally, the team must be multidisciplinary and include at least one teacher or other specialist in the area of suspected disability.

DUE PROCESS. Due process means those legal procedures and protections for assuring that the child, the parents, and the school are afforded their rights under the law. Parents have the right to see all of their child's education records. Further, parents must be notified of any evaluation or placement plans, and this notice must be made understandable to the parents and provided in the parent's native language and/or communication mode. Parents must give their consent before any evaluation occurs and also before initial placement of a child into any special education program.

If there is any disagreement about identification, evaluation, or placement, the parents or the school can request an impartial hearing. If either the parent or the school is dissatisfied with the decision made at the hearing, a state-level hearing can be requested. The next legal step would be a civil action law suit.

CONFIDENTIALITY. PL 94–142, as well as other federal laws, specify confidentiality and procedural safeguards for all children. These rules concern storage, disclosure to third parties, retention, and destruction of personally identifiable information.

Special provisions for learning disabilities. A separate set of regulations was issued for PL 94–142, which apply to the procedures to be used to evaluate children with specific learning disabilities (USOE, December 29, 1977). These regulations are in addition to those that apply to other areas of handicapping conditions.

ADDITIONAL TEAM MEMBERS TO EVALUATE SPECIFIC LEARNING DISABILITIES. In addition to the regular team requirements listed in the law, the following members must be included on a team to evaluate specific learning disabilities:

> 1. The child's regular teacher. If the child does not have a regular teacher, a regular classroom teacher qualified to teach a child of his or her age should be consulted. For a child of less than school age, an individual qualified by the state educational agency to teach a child of his or her age should participate.
> 2. At least one person qualified to conduct individual diagnostic examinations of children, such as a school psychologist, a speech-language pathologist, or remedial reading teacher.

A clarification of the evaluation team requirements for learning-disabled children was issued by the Bureau of Education for the Handicapped. This statement specified that when evaluating children suspected of having specific learning disabilities, where an appropriate licensed, certified, or approved learning disability teacher is available, that person should serve on the multidisciplinary evaluation team (Bureau of Education for the Handicapped, April 19, 1978).

WRITTEN REPORT FOR SPECIFIC LEARNING DISABILITIES. The regulations require that the team prepare a written report of the evaluation which must include a statement of

> 1. Whether the child has a specific learning disability;
> 2. The basis for making the determination;
> 3. The relevant behavior noted during the observation of the child;
> 4. The relationship of that behavior to the child's academic functioning;
> 5. The educationally relevant medical findings, if any;
> 6. Whether there is a severe discrepancy between achievement and ability which is not correctable without special education and related services;

7. The determination of the team concerning the effects of environmental, cultural, or economic disadvantage.

Team members shall certify in writing whether the report reflects their conclusion. If not, the team member must submit a separate statement.

Incentive grants.   Two sources of funds are available for handicapped preschool education under PL 94–142. One source, through state entitlement money, depends upon the number of handicapped children counted by the state in its child-find activities. The other source is called *incentive grants,* which are available to states with approved state plans that offer services to three-to-five-year-old handicapped children. The incentive grant plan was devised to heighten the importance and cost-effectiveness of early intervention with handicapped children.

Developmental Disabilities

Another law which affects young handicapped children is the Developmental Disabilities Act (PL 95–602, 1978). According to this law, the term *developmental disability* means a severe chronic disability of a person which

1. is attributable to a mental or physical impairment or combination of mental and physical impairments;
2. is manifested before the person attains age twenty-two;
3. is likely to continue indefinitely;
4. results in substantial functional limitations in three or more of the following areas of major life activity:

self-care
receptive and expressive language
learning
mobility
self-direction
capacity for independent living, and
economic self-sufficiency; and

5. reflect the person's need for a combination and sequence of special, interdisciplinary, or generic care, treatment, or other services which are individually planned and coordinated.

Children not covered under PL 94–142 below the age of three might be covered by the Developmental Disabilities Act.

The First Chance Network is a collection of preschool handicapped projects located throughout the country. Originally called the Handicapped Children Early Education Program (HCEEP), they have been funded since 1968 by the agency now called the Office of Special Education (OSE) in the Department of Education. (This agency was formerly called the Bureau of Education for the Handicapped.) The purpose of the First Chance Network is to stimulate exemplary programs developed for young handicapped children. The impact has been the development of innovative methods and the dissemination of these ideas to others interested in the problems and potentialities of young handicapped children.

Head Start

The *Head Start* movement is well known in the United States and has been referred to several times in this book. As noted earlier, Head Start began in 1964 as part of the War on Poverty, funded by the Office of Economic Opportunity. The goal of this program was to offer preschool children from economically deprived homes a comprehensive program that would compensate for their deprivation. It was hoped that these opportunities would give such children a Head Start in life. The program involved aspects of medical and dental care, nutrition, parents' involvement, and socialization as well as educational intervention. The curricular strategies varied in these programs and the results of research regarding these curricula are discussed in Chapter 6.

In 1972, Head Start legislation was revised. The revised legislation required all Head Start programs to include a minimum of 10 per cent of their enrollment be identified as handicapped.

The Team Approach to Comprehensive Service

The kinds of problems affecting young handicapped children include physical, language, social, emotional, family, health, and cognitive factors. To provide comprehensive service for children with several problems, a team of professionals who can contribute expertise in a number of areas is needed. In addition to the teacher of the handicapped preschool child, other specialists provide assessment or therapy. Team members could include physicians, nurses, psychologists, social workers, physical therapists, occupational therapists, speech clinicians, audiologists, recreation workers, nutritionists, volunteers, parents, and others. The teacher, although not an expert in any of these specialties, should understand enough of each specialty to communicate intelligently and integrate the findings of each specialist in working with the child.

All of the specialists concerned with a particular child are considered the *child development team*. The teams can be *multidisciplinary, interdisciplinary* or *transdisciplinary*. On the *multidisciplinary* team the specialists work side-by-side, each performing the assigned responsibility. On the *interdisciplinary* team the specialists have developed common perceptions, and they learn to share responsibilities. Specialists are willing to cross the borders of their disciplines and assimilate knowledge from other areas. They may even at times substitute for each other in a particular activity. In short, they have learned to work together as a cohesive unit.

Getting a group of specialists to function as an interdisciplinary team is a difficult and challenging goal. Each specialist comes onto the team with a different set of skills and a different perspective of the child. These differences can constitute the strength of the team, or they can be a potential for role conflict. For example, if a feeding problem confronts a child, the nutritionist, nurse, physical therapist, speech pathologist, dentist, and physician could each provide helpful information. They could also disagree about the cause of the problem or the appropriate method of treatment. The way to help the child is to get the team to work together as an interdisciplinary unit (Holm 1978).

The term *transdisciplinary team* is sometimes used to highlight the interdisciplinary nature of the team. What is emphasized is the integration of therapy services and the avoidance of duplication of services by specialists. Often a multidisciplinary team approach results in the removal of a young child for separate therapy sessions with each designated specialist. The transdisciplinary approach, however, attempts to jointly plan goals and objectives which will integrate, rather than splinter, therapies.

It is at the staffing (or case conference) that the various specialists are asked to pool their findings. Holm (1978) has some specific suggestions for a team leader to hold a successful team staffing:

1. Be sure that all participants know each other and are aware of each person's professional affiliation.

2. Provide basic information in written form.

3. Have an outline or organized plan for the discussion.

4. Encourage all staff members to participate. They should both listen and talk.

5. Stimulate responses and exchange among members.

6. Summarize the discussion and state the decisions that are made at the appropriate point of the meeting.

Summary

There are several placement options for the young handicapped child: regular class with individual therapy; noncategorical special class for further assessment and observation; categorical special class; home management placement; and combination placements. The least restrictive environment means that handicapped children are to be placed with nonhandicapped children to the greatest extent possible. The continuum of alternative placements refers to the array of placements that a school district offers. Mainstreaming is a way of providing education services by placing handicapped children in regular classes.

The population of birth to three years of age constitutes a special group of handicapped children. They require very special kinds of assessment and services. Teachers must also consider decisions about placement after completion of preschool programs.

Public Law 94–142 is extremely important federal legislation for handicapped children. It assures free appropriate public education for every handicapped child. Whether three-to-five year olds are included in this legislation depends upon state law. The individualized education program (IEP) is the staff meeting under Public Law 94–142 at which decisions about placement and services are made. Procedural safeguards protect the rights of the handicapped child. They include protection in evaluation, due process, and confidentiality. There are some special procedures for evaluating children with specific learning disabilities under Public Law 94–142. Incentive grants are given to encourage programs in early childhood special education.

There is other federal legislation which affects the young handicapped child. A special federal law was recently passed for children with developmental disabilities. This law could provide services for the birth-to two-years-old population. The First Chance Network is designed to provide model demonstration projects in early childhood special education. Moreover, recent legislation on Head Start programs, first begun in 1964 under the Office of Economic Opportunity, requires that at least 10 percent of Head Start children be identified as handicapped.

The team approach to comprehensive services is needed to integrate the services of all the specialists working with the child.

Review Questions

TERMS TO KNOW

a. *least restrictive environment*
b. *continuum of alternative placements*
c. *categorical*
d. *noncategorical*
e. *mainstreaming*

f. *Public Law 94–142*
g. *IEP*
h. *procedural safeguards*
i. *Head Start*
j. *interdisciplinary team*

1. Name four placement options for the preschool handicapped child.
2. Define the *least restrictive environment*. Give an example of a least restrictive and most restrictive environment.
3. What is meant by *continuum of alternative placements*?
4. Give some advantages and disadvantages of *mainstreaming*.
5. Why is PL 94–142 so important?
6. What happens at an IEP meeting?
7. Find out what your state laws are concerning young handicapped children.

References

BADGER, E. The Infant Stimulation/Mother Training Project, in *Infant Education: A Guide for Helping Handicapped Children in the First Three Years*, eds. B. Caldwell and D. Stedman. New York: Walker, 1977.

BUREAU OF EDUCATION FOR THE HANDICAPPED. *DAS Bulletin No. 9*. Clarification of the Learning Disabilities Children. Informal Letter to Chief State School Officers, State Directors of Special Education, State Coordinators of Part B of EHA and State Coordinators of ESEA, Title I, Handicapped Program. Washington, D. C.: Government Printing Office, April 19, 1978.

GORDON, I., B. GRUNBAGH, AND R. JESTER. The Florida Parent Education Infant and Toddler Program, in *The Preschool in Action, Exploring Early Childhood Programs*, eds. M. Day and R. Parker. Boston: Allyn & Bacon, 1977, pp. 97–127.

HAYDEN, A. Handicapped Children, Birth to Age Three. *Exceptional Children*, 1979, 45, 510–517.

HOLM, V. Interdisciplinary Child Development Team, in *Early Intervention: A Team Approach*, eds. K. Allen, V. Holm, and R. Schiefelbusch. Baltimore, Md.: University Park Press, 1978, pp. 99–122.

ILLINOIS STATE BOARD OF EDUCATION. *Early Childhood Education for the Handicapped: Recommending Procedures and Practices*. Springfield, Ill.: Department of Specialized Services, 1979.

LERNER, J., D. DAWSON, and L. HORVATH, *Cases in Learning and Behavior Problems.* Boston: Houghton Mifflin, 1980.

LEVENSTEIN, P. The Mother-Child Home Program, in *The Preschool in Action: Exploring Early Childhood Programs,* eds. M. Day and R. Parker. Boston: Allyn & Bacon, 1977, pp. 28–49.

PL 95–602. *Rehabilitative Comprehensive Services and Developmental Disabilities Amendments of 1978.*

U.S. OFFICE OF EDUCATION. *Education of Handicapped Children. Federal Register, Part II.* Washington, D. C.: Department of HEW, August 23, 1977.

U.S. OFFICE OF EDUCATION. *Assistance to States for Education of the Handicapped: Procedures for Evaluating Specific Learning Disabilities. Federal Register, Part III.* Washington, D. C.: Department of HEW, December 29, 1977.

ZIGLER, E., AND S. MUENSCHOW. Mainstreaming: The Proof Is in the Implementation. *American Psychologist,* 1979, 34, 993–996.

Case Studies of Exceptional Preschool Children

Chapter **Eleven**

This chapter presents cases of preschool children who were identified as handicapped during the school screening and diagnostic process. These reports are exceptionally comprehensive. The children were referred for further diagnosis to a number of specialists and other institutions. Because of their comprehensiveness, they give the reader some conception of an interdisciplinary evaluation and the kind of information that is gathered. The chapter contains the *individualized education program* (IEP) that was developed for each child. The cases illustrate the interdisciplinary approach to the screening and diagnostic process and the development of an IEP. Case I is a child with multiple problems, and Case II is a child with primary speech and language problems.

In each case, the names and other identifiable information have been changed to protect the confidentiality and rights of the child and family. The reader may disagree with procedures that were listed and the specific objectives that were chosen, but the cases are presented as prepared by each of the professional teams.

Providing Individualized Programs

The Individualized Educational Program (IEP)

The IEP (which is discussed in Chapter 10) is intended to be a comprehensive effort. Beginning with screening and continuing with a referral, a child's competencies and lags are assessed so that if special education services are needed, the individualized program can be developed to meet that need. Figure 11–1 is a flowchart of the IEP process (Illinois Office of Education 1979). As can be seen, there are many levels to the process and several professionals who may become involved.

In actual fact, the child participates in a screening to identify potential problems and if difficulties are found, a complete case study is then recommended. The case study may be requested by parents,

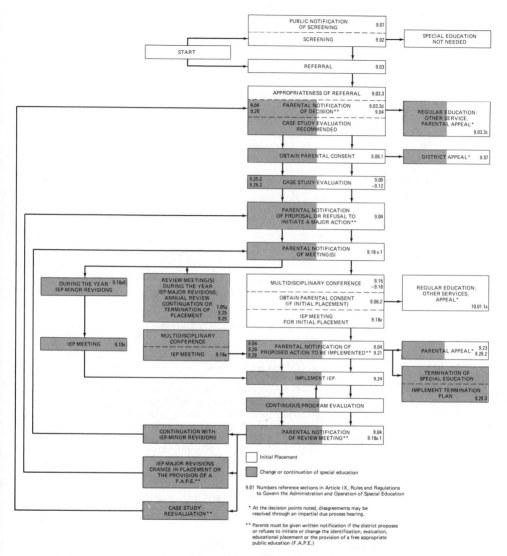

Figure 11–1   Individualized Education Program (IEP) Process   *From Illinois Office of Education. The Illinois Primer on Individualized Education Programs.* Springfield, Ill.: Department of Specialized Educational Services and Illinois Regional Resource Center, June, 1979, p. 2.

legal guardians, community agencies, school district personnel, or others having knowledge of the child's problem. The parent must be notified in writing that the referral has been made and must give written permission for the completion of the evaluations. Figure 11–2 is an example of the form used to request parental permission for the intent to conduct a multidisciplinary evaluation.

```
┌─────────────────────────────────────────────────────────────────────┐
│                              (Date) _____          │
│   Dear _____ ,                        │
│                     (Parent or Guardian)                              │
│   _____ has been referred by _____  │
│   to our _____ for an individual evaluation. The │
│   reasons for this referral are as follows:                           │
│                                                                       │
│   _____   │
│                                                                       │
│   _____   │
│   The therapist has studied the referral and gathered the following pre-evaluative data: │
│                                                                       │
│              Process                              Result              │
│                                                                       │
│   1. _____      _____    │
│                                                                       │
│   2. _____      _____    │
│   Based on the results of these measures, we feel this referral is warranted and that an │
│   evaluation would be necessary in assisting us in developing a more appropriate │
│   educational experience.                                             │
│                                                                       │
│   The evaluation procedures and their associated instruments that we will employ in │
│   the evaluation are as follows:                                      │
│                                                                       │
│   _____   │
│                                                                       │
│   _____   │
│   We estimate that these evaluative activities will be completed by _____ . │
│   Soon after their completion you will be invited to attend a multi-disciplinary staff │
│   conference at which the results of the evaluation will be reviewed and an │
│   educational plan will be developed for your child. Please be assured that no change in │
│   the educational placement of your child will be made without your knowledge. │
│                                                                       │
│   It is very important that you are aware of and understand your right to: │
│                                                                       │
│   1.   Review all records pertaining to your child and make copies thereof │
│   2.   Know the results of the evaluation                             │
│   3.   Object to this proposed evaluation                             │
│                                                                       │
│   We plan to begin the evaluation as soon as you sign and return the enclosed │
│   permission form. If you have any further questions, please do not hesitate to call. │
│                                                                       │
│                        Sincerely,                                     │
│                                                                       │
│              _____         │
│                        Signature                         Date         │
│                                                                       │
│              _____         │
│                        Title                             Phone        │
└─────────────────────────────────────────────────────────────────────┘
```

Figure 11–2   Notice of Intent to Conduct an Individual Evaluation

After the multidisciplinary evaluation has been completed, a written notice is sent to the parent specifying the date and time for a multidisciplinary meeting to develop, review, or revise an IEP (Figure 11–3). At the IEP meetings, the parent's written consent is again required for initial placement into a special education program. If the parent does not agree with the recommendation for placement, due process for appeal and hearing to determine further action can be requested. An IEP meeting must be held within thirty calendar days of a decision that the child needs special education services (Illinois Office of Education 1979).

Development of the Written IEP

As shown in Figure 11–2 and discussed in Chapter 10, the development of a written IEP is accomplished by (1) recording present levels of educational performance, (2) determining the child's needs and eligibility for special education, (3) deciding appropriate annual goals, (4) ascertaining specific education and related services and the extent to which participation is possible within regular education, (5) specifying transportation responsibilities and schedules, (6) developing short-term objectives for each goal that list evaluation procedures and schedules for noting accomplishment of each objective, (7) scheduling a date for the annual review meeting (Figure 11–4).

Staffing Notification   Date _____

Child's Name _____   Birthdate _____

Parents' Name _____

Address _____   District _____

Telephone No. _____

          Conference Date _____

                Time _____

              Place _____

Invited to Attend:

Figure 11–3 Staffing Notification

DEVELOPMENT OF A WRITTEN IEP

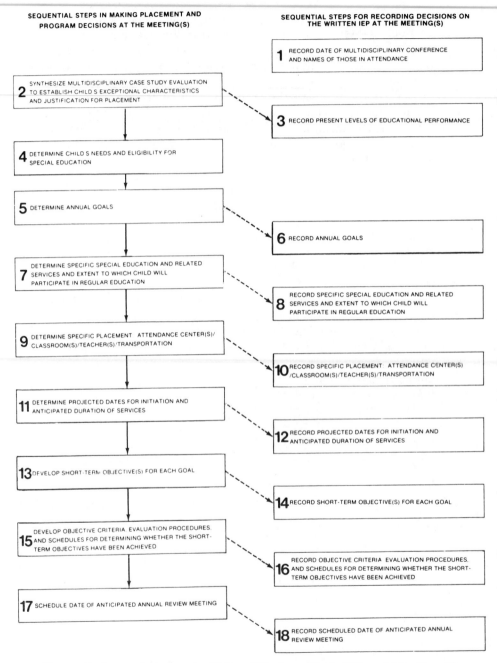

Figure 11–4 Development of a Written IEP *From Illinois Office of Education. The Illinois Primer on Individualized Education Programs.* Springfield, Ill.: Department of Specialized Education Services and Illinois Regional Resource Center, June, 1979, p. 24.

Case Study I: Alan

Case study I was conducted in the early childhood program known as Project Child Check. This program operates in St. Louis County, Missouri, and participates in child find operations.

Setting: Project Child Check, A County Project

Federal funds (PL 94–142) were approved for a St. Louis countywide program for three- and four-year-old children with special needs. The program, proposed and developed by several local educational agencies in St. Louis County, provides a broad spectrum of free educational services for three- and four-year-old handicapped children. Among the many services provided are developmental screenings, diagnoses, programming, educational in-service programs for early childhood specialists, and most importantly, services for parents.

Project Child Check is a countywide screening program for three- and four-year-old children in St. Louis County. Developmental screening services, coordinated by a coalition of twenty-four school districts, are free for all county residents. Children are eligible on their third birthday. While several screening instruments are used throughout the county, the instrument used for the child in this case was the *Developmental Indicators for the Assessment of Learning* (DIAL). All children are screened in the developmental areas of fine motor, gross motor, concepts, and communications. In addition, VASC (Verbal Auditory Screening) audiometers are used to screen auditory acuity, and Good-Lite vision screeners with symbol charts are used to screen vision.

If potential handicaps are identified as a result of the screening, complete diagnostic services are available from the local education agency or the Special School District of St. Louis County. Diagnosis may include the areas of cognition, fine motor, gross motor, speech and language, hearing, self-help skills, social skills, and perceptual-motor abilities. These are provided by a multidisciplinary team of specialists including a family service consultant, speech-language pathologist, psychologist, audiologist, occupational therapist, and physical therapist. Following diagnosis, the team of specialists meets with the parents to share and interpret their results and observations.

Several outcomes are possible: the child may be found to be non-handicapped; mildly to moderately handicapped; or severely and multiply handicapped. Mildly to moderately handicapped children are referred to the local education agency or the Regional Center for Developmental Disabilities.

Intervention services are available through the Special School District of St. Louis County for severely/moderately handicapped children. The Early Childhood Special Education Program in the Special School District of St. Louis County is a multifaceted program designed to meet the special needs and maximize the capabilities of the severely/multiply handicapped child whose problems require intervention beyond that available in the home or regular preschool setting. It includes both a home-based and a center-based component.

The purpose of the center-based component is to provide an educational environment appropriate to the individual needs of the child. Educational services are also delivered in a classroom with a certified early childhood special education teacher and teacher assistants. Children may receive any combination of home- and center-based services.

Each teacher is certified by the Missouri State Department of Education in early childhood special education. Many teachers have specialized training in another area of special education. The early childhood special education training includes background in preacademic and cognitive development, speech and language development, behavior management, gross and fine motor development, skills related to working with parents, design and implementation of Individual Education Programs, and intervention strategies for early childhood special education.

An ancillary staff composed of a family service consultant, psychological examiner, speech and language pathologist, physical therapist, and occupational therapist is available to provide

1. specialized consultation to teaching staff and parents
2. demonstration of techniques to teaching staff and parents
3. individual and/or group intervention in or out of the classroom environment as appropriate

When a child has been diagnosed as severely/multiply handicapped, an Individualized Educational Program (IEP) is developed outlining general goals and objectives for the first thirty days, including a placement of two program days in the center per week and parent training programs, as needed. Within those thirty calendar days, the Individual Education Program is revised to detail goals and objectives in deficit areas. This plan is written by the professional staff and the parent. While the IEP addresses the specific needs of the child, the total classroom program includes activities in all developmental areas.

The child attends for half-day. Afternoons are reserved for the home-based component of the program.

As designated in the IEP, a child may attend the in-center program two, three, or four days per week. The determination of the number of days assigned is based on individual needs, type and extent of services required, and the child's patterns.

The philosophy of this program encourages the development and generalization of individual skills through classroom implementation. Therefore, ancillary staff is available to assist the classroom teacher in designing goals, objectives, and intervention strategies to meet the needs of the child in all developmental areas. They may then provide whatever support is needed for the teacher to implement these goals and objectives on a daily basis. The ancillary staff is encouraged to provide direct service only when unusual problems exist which call for specialized skills in continuous monitoring of effects of intervention, or where the needed intervention requires highly specialized training. All services are provided free of charge to parents, including transportation of the child to the center on assigned days.

Children are not in attendance on Fridays. This time is reserved for staff development, case studies and reviews, coordination of services, and general planning.

This service delivery model provides for great flexibility in providing special education services to preschool children. For example, one child, a severe hemophiliac who needed physical and occupational therapy, was served in the home because it was medically unsafe to transport him on a bus. In another case, a child was diagnosed as having a severe articulation disorder which made his speech unintelligible. Concerns were expressed by the staff relative to the need of exposure and intervention with normal peers and good models. The staff assisted the parent in selecting an appropriate preschool setting and saw the child twice weekly for intensive speech services both in the classroom and in direct therapy.

The Case of Alan

The following case is that of Alan, a child of three years and three months. The first section presents reports made by the multidisciplinary evaluation team which includes the social worker, psychologist, pediatrician, speech and language pathologist, occupational therapist, physical therapist, and the special education coordinator of the Child Check program. Next the IEP that was developed for Alan is presented.

Summary of multidisciplinary evaluation reports.

REPORT OF CHILD CHECK EVALUATION CLINIC

Date of Evaluation:	*Name:* **Alan**
Student ID Number:	*Chronological Age:* **3 years**
	3 months
Home School District:	*Parents:* **Mort and Dot**
School Attending:	*Address:*
Grade: **Preschool**	
Referred by: **United Cerebral**	*Telephone:*
Palsy Association	
	Emergency:
Present at Staffing: **Mother, Early Childhood Special**	
Education Teacher, Occupa-	
tional therapist, Speech-Language	
therapist, Psychologist	

BACKGROUND AND SOCIAL HISTORY INFORMATION:
Alan (Social history information was provided by mother)
Conducted by social worker.

Alan is the younger of two children. His older sister, Susan, is six years of age. Alan was born three weeks prematurely and weighed 6 lb, 4 oz, at birth. The cord was wrapped around his neck at birth, cutting off oxygen. Alan remained in the hospital for seventeen days after birth because of problems with his respiratory system.

Developmentally, Alan was able to sit unsupported at nine to eleven months. He started taking steps at two years, and has been walking totally independently for the past nine months. Alan still falls often, and he tends to walk on his toes. He attained bowel and bladder control between two and a half and three years of age. His speech development appears to be within the normal range for his age. He can partially dress himself and can completely feed himself.

Medically, Alan had roseola at fifteen months and chicken pox at two and a half years. He has had two seizures, one of which related to the roseola. Following the second seizure, Alan was hospitalized for a complete workup at General Hospital. Tests indicate that he does have a proneness for seizures, and he was placed on a low dosage of phenobarbital.

Alan also has a hearing loss. Although he does not have a history of ear infections, he has always had fluid in his middle ears. A myringotomy was done at age two.

Alan has had no preschool experience. Socially and emotionally, Alan is described as a happy and curious child. He is somewhat attached to his family and does not always cooperate voluntarily with new acquaintances, but will after a period of adjustment. He likes to ride in a car and likes to play with trucks and trains. Alan plays fairly well with children, although he is still primarily playing along side other children, rather than with them. He does play *with* his sister.

PSYCHOLOGICAL EXAMINATION
(conducted by the psychologist)

Previous Test Data:

Children's Hospital. *Stanford-Binet Intelligence Scale*: CA 2–11, MA 2–8
    IQ 78
Peabody Picture Vocabulary Test (B): CA 2–11, MA 2–6
Vineland Social Maturity Scale: CA 2–11, MA 2–6
Verbal Language Development Test: CA 2–11, MA 2–5

Behavioral Observations:

Rapport was easily established with this child. Alan was initially shy but had no difficulty in separating from his mother. He came willingly with this examiner and was basically cooperative. Alan demonstrated behaviors that were withdrawn, but he was friendly and seemed to enjoy the individualized attention.

He could not be conditioned to perform all tasks presented and displayed a poor ability to comprehend and follow instructions. His task focus was inadequate for test purposes in that he was somewhat distracted by the toys in the room and noise in the hall. Alan worked with persistence in spite of his short attention span. Alan was slow to respond to test items and seemed to need time to organize his thinking before answering. He needed structure from this examiner before he could work productively. It was necessary to repeat the stimulus many times before Alan could respond appropriately.

Alan's expressive language skills were inadequate for test purposes. He made some spontaneous verbalizations, but his utterances were mostly unintelligible sounds. This affected his test performance negatively.

Tests Administered:

Stanford-Binet, (Form LM) (1972 Norms): CA 3–2, MA 2–10

Alan measures as functioning within the borderline range of intelligence. His test performance was penalized by his lack of attention and inadequate expressive language skills. His scores do compare favorably with those scores reported by the Children's Hospital.

Summary:

In summary, Alan appears to be functioning at a depressed level cognitively, and his expressive language skills are inadequate for his age level. However shy, inhibited behaviors did contribute negatively to his test performance, and this may be a minimal estimate of his abilities.

HEARING, SPEECH, AND LANGUAGE REPORT
(conducted by the Speech-Language pathologist)

Previous Testing:

Verbal Language Development Scale: CA 2–11, MA 2–5. (Children's Hospital)

Hearing:

Alan has a history of middle ear fluid and presently has tubes in his ear. Alan should be seen for further audiometric testing.

Speech:

The following are behaviors related to speech and language performance that were observed during the assessment procedures.

Normal control of the head and neck was observed. Breathing patterns were considered normal. The quality of vocalizations were rated as normal. An oral peripheral examination revealed a high vaulted palate. The soft palate could not be observed.

Hypersensitivity of the lips and tongue was noted. Lip posture was habitually open. Alan was unable to perform the following actions: smile, close and open lips a number of times, and round lips for (oo). Posture of the tongue was habitually held anteriorly. Alan was unable to perform the following actions: protrude beyond lip margin, protrude and point tip up and down, and lick lips. Alan was not able to imitate sounds presented from the articulation section of the *Preschool Language Scale.*

Informally assessed, Alan's speech was intelligible within context; in running contextual speech, intelligibility decreased. In general, his articulation skills appear to be within expectancy according to his chronological age, when speech-sound developmental scales are taken into consideration.

Language:

The *Preschool Language Scale* was administered and yielded the following results:

A. *Auditory Comprehension*
  1. *Basal at 2 years, 6 months*
  2. *Ceiling at 3 years, 6 months*
  3. *Auditory comprehension age 2 years, 7.5 months*
B. *Verbal Ability*
  1. *Basal at 2 years, 0 months*
  2. *Ceiling at 3 years, 6 months*
  3. *Verbal ability age 2 years, 1.5 months*

Performance on auditory comprehension tasks was below expectancy for Alan's chronological age. Analysis of his performance revealed difficulty in the areas of identifying action words, comprehending functions, comprehending prepositions, recognizing time concepts, matching sets, and grouping objects. Performance on verbal ability tasks was below expectancy for Alan's chronological age. Analysis of his performance revealed difficulty in the areas of repeating sentences and digits, responding to interrogatives, providing biographical information, and conversing in sentences. In addition, echolalic and preseverative responses were noted.

Alan demonstrated an inadequate attention span during the testing situation. He refused several test items, and he was easily distracted by environmental stimuli.

PHYSICAL ASSESSMENT
(conducted by the pediatrician)

Growth and Development:

His height was 38 inches (50 percentile). His head circumference was 20½ inches (50 percentile). Visual acuity could not be determined because of an inappropriate chart.

Coordination (Gross Motor Skills):

His gait appeared awkward. Gross motor skill appeared to be fair.

Coordination (Fine Motor Skills):

He was able to reach for objects (five months). He transfers objects from hand to hand (eight months). He has an adequate pincer grasp (nine months). He was able to retrieve a dropped object (one year). Buttoning medium size buttons—this task was not accomplished at all (four years). His estraocular muscle functions were good. (Age in parentheses indicates normal age for performance of the task.)

Physical Examination:

The physical exam revealed no significant physical findings except for an undescended right testicle at the time of this exam.

Current Medication:

Phenobarbital—15 mg in the morning, 30 mg in the evening. Immunizations are complete. He had chicken pox in February of 1978.

Summary:

Alan appears to be in good health at the time of this assessment. On examination today, his right testicle was not palpable, but mother states that it is descended. His gross motor skills appeared fair. He was unable to play catch with a ball. He was able to run. He was able to jump in place and balance on one foot for one second, but these tasks were performed awkwardly. When pulling to a standing position from a supine position, Alan had to roll laterally and get to a kneeling position before he stood up. His fine motor skills were fair but inconsistent. He was unable to string large beads or zip a zipper. However, he was able to build a five-block tower and put three pegs into a pegboard. He seemed to enjoy motion on the Merry Molehill. His muscle tone was hypotonic. He showed no tactile defensiveness but was somewhat adverse to any oral stimulation. Generally, he was quite cooperative and friendly. An occupational therapy evaluation is recommended.

OVERALL DIAGNOSIS
(written by the supervisor of Child Check)

This child appears to be severely/multiply handicapped.

Approved by:

ADDENDUM TO REPORT

FURTHER PSYCHOLOGICAL TESTING
(conducted by the psychologist)

Previous Test Data:

See file.

Present Test Data:

Stanford-Binet Intelligence Scale (Form LM) (Revised 1972 Norms)

Limit Testing

Developmental Test of Visual Motor Integration: CA 3–2, VMI 2–9

Limited testing on the *Stanford-Binet* was utilized to determine a more accurate estimate of Alan's cognitive potential. In that he was able to correctly perform three more items at the III–0 level, it would appear that he does have more normal intellectual skills than were previously revealed.

Alan had difficulty copying the designs presented on the *Developmental Test of Visual Motor Integration* but was able to draw a circle and a vertical line in imitation after this examiner modeled the motor pattern for him. This suggests a lag in graphomotor skills as well as in his ability to plan motor activities. He needs the exact structure to model before he can work productively.

Summary:

In summary, Alan can learn through imitation in a structured situation. He does have poor motor planning that will need remediation, but he does have more cognitive ability to bring to the learning situation.

FURTHER SPEECH AND LANGUAGE REPORT
(conducted by the speech and language pathologist)

On the *Vocabulary Comprehension Scale*, Alan earned the following scores for the individual subtests:

Subtest	Raw Score
1. Pronouns	3/17 (3 out of 17 correct)
2. Quality	4/6
3. Position	7/26
4. Size	3/6
5. Quantity	1/6

In terms of age expectancy for vocabulary comprehension, Alan did not demonstrate adequate comprehension for pronouns (I, mine, your, her, he, his, you and they), concepts of position (on, under, together, away from, up, top, apart, around, and in front of), and concepts of quality and quantity (same, and, all).

An expressive language sample was obtained utilizing a picture stimulus. Alan generally utilized one word to describe each picture, which consisted primarily of nouns. Alan also produced echolalic and perservative responses as previously noted.

FURTHER OCCUPATIONAL THERAPY REPORT
(conducted by the occupational therapist)

Physical Assessment:

Range of motion, strength, and muscle tone are within normal limits. Reflex development is abnormal. The asymmetrical tonic neck reflex and the symmetrical tonic neck reflex are present. In each position, a mild muscle tone change is present. Protective extension is delayed along with equilibrium reactions in standing. Hypermobility was noted in the hips.

Gross Motor Skills:

In preambulatory skills, Alan could do all activities asked of him, except log roll. He would roll segmentally, which is developmentally lower. In ambulatory skills, he could do most skills by imitation, developmentally within age limits.

If Alan was asked to perform a skill with no previous modeling of that skill, he would be unable to perform. Alan was noted as having motor planning problems. He was also noted as having a mild midline problem.

Fine Motor Skilis:

Fine motor skills are delayed. Alan uses a three-jaw chuck (grasp with three fingers) for small objects. His grasp strength comes from the ulnar side of his hand, rather than the radial. His reach is extremely open handed and deliberate. He could stack an eight-block tower. He had trouble stringing beads.

Perceptual Motor Skills:

Alan appeared to have poor perceptual motor skills. This could have been seen because of his low attention span in activities. Alan had trouble stringing beads and placing pegs. The deliberate reach and release could also be a factor here.

Conceptual Skills:

No size or shape constancy skills were observed.

PHYSICAL THERAPY REPORT
(conducted by the physical therapist)

Physical Assessment:

Range of motion is within normal limits, except hypermobility is noted in the hips and shoulders. Muscle atrophy is noted in the shoulder, girdle, trunk, and pelvic region.

Reflex Development:

No abnormal reflexes noted. Parachute response is present in the prone position. Equilibrium reactions are present in all positions on static and movable surfaces, except in standing, where it is fair.

Gross Motor Development:

A. *Preambulatory Skills:*

Alan is able to stand unassisted. Standing posture is characterized by a marked lordosis in the lumbar region. He creeps reciprocally.

B. *Ambulatory Skills:*

Alan is independent in ambulation and exhibits a normal gait pattern, with the exception of occasional knee recurvation during stance phase. Alan is able to climb upstairs and downstairs, alternating feet, holding on to a rail. Alan can come to a tip toe position independently, but he is unable to walk on his tip toes on command.

Summary:

Gross motor skills are at the 24- to 30-month level of development.

The IEP for Alan.   The written report for Alan developed at the IEP meeting is shown on the following pages.

TASK 1: PRESENT LEVEL OF EDUCATIONAL PERFORMANCE

Alan can stack blocks in imitation; he can point to body parts and to named objects, and he can name familiar objects and pictures (using one word). Alan can point to big and little. Alan uses many two-word utterances but does not combine noun-verb phrases appropriately. Alan can imitate sounds and can produce some animal sounds upon request or visual cue. He can go up and down stairs without assistance; he can climb up to the second level of the jungle gym but will not come down. Alan can feed himself with a spoon unassisted and drinks from a cup using both hands. There is much more spontaneous language at home than at school. Alan can name body parts (except nose and ears).

Task 2: Annual Goals and Short-Term Objectives

Goal I. Alan will be able to demonstrate, with objects, the prepositions *in, on,* and *under.*

Objective Ia Alan will put objects in positions using prepositions in imitation when presented with a verbal cue with 80 percent accuracy.

Objective Ib When asked a yes-no question using *in, on,* and *under,* Alan will respond appropriately 80 percent of the time.

Objective Ic Alan will put objects in positions using above prepositions when presented with a verbal cue 80 percent of the time.

Goal II. Alan will receptively identify pictures of five objects by their function.

Objective IIa In imitation, Alan will demonstrate the action associated with an object 90 percent of the time.

Objective IIb On verbal cue, Alan will demonstrate the action associated with an object 90 percent of the time.

Objective IIc Alan will select an object by its function from a group of two objects with 80 percent accuracy.

Objective IId Alan will select a picture by its function from a group of two pictures 80 percent of the time.

Goal III. Alan will identify fifteen action pictures using a two-word phrase: noun and verb.

Objective IIIa Alan will perform actions depicted in pictures following a verbal cue 80 percent of the time.

Objective IIIb Alan will select the appropriate action picture from a group of two when given a verbal direction with 80 percent accuracy.

Objective IIIc Alan will identify action pictures using a two-word phrase: noun and verb with 80 percent accuracy.

Goal IV. Alan will match an object when given three smaller choices.

Objective IVa Alan will match an object when given two dissimilar objects 80 percent of the time.

Objective IVb Alan will match an object when given three dissimilar objects 80 percent of the time.

Objective IVc Alan will match an object when given three similar objects 80 percent of the time.

Goal V. Alan will remain dry all day, when reminded by an adult.

Objective Va When on a 45-minute schedule, Alan will eliminate in the toilet when necessary and remain dry 80 percent of the time.

Objective Vb When on a 1½ hour schedule, Alan will eliminate when necessary and remain dry 80 percent of the time.

Objective Vc   Alan will remain dry 100 percent of the time while awake and eliminate in the toilet when necessary after being reminded by an adult.

Goal VI.   Alan will perform a motor task on verbal cue.

Objective VIa   Alan will perform a motor task by parallel imitation, with verbal cue, 80 percent of the time.

Objective VIb   Alan will perform a motor task by copying a model with verbal cue, 80 percent of the time.

Objective VIc   Alan will perform a motor task when given a verbal cue 80 percent of the time.

Goal VII.   Alan will respond appropriately to direct questioning with a yes or no when given the choice.

Objective VIIa   In the presence of visual, graphic, and auditory cues, Alan will respond to direct questions with a yes or no response with 80 percent accuracy.

Objective VIIb   In the presence of graphic and auditory cues, Alan will respond to direct questions with a yes or no response with 80 percent accuracy.

Objective VIIc   In the presence of graphic cues, Alan will respond to direct questions with a yes or no response with 80 percent accuracy.

Case Study II: Judy

The Setting: A Special Education Cooperative

There are a number of administrative arrangements for providing special services to preschool handicapped children. Case I illustrated a county special education arrangement. Case II is an example of a special education cooperative. In addition, services can be provided through an intermediate unit or by the individual school district. Each has different legal ramifications.

In a special education cooperative, several communities contribute funds to a central body and use this group as a resource to provide for children that have low-incidence types of handicap or for unusual programs that require greater resources than are available to individual districts. The joint agreement is a cooperative venture for the purposes of providing better services by grouping larger numbers of interested parties. The cooperative then hires staff and rents facilities to shelter both administrative and programming services.

Each cooperative elects a board of control. establishes articles of agreement, and determines the way in which the districts will interact with the cooperative. The cooperative directing the program described in Case II is one in which all of the diagnostics are completed at the district level. The referral to the cooperative begins after the district finds that it cannot service the child. If the local district has the population to justify a particular service, then the district is the unit best suited for administration of that program. Usually smaller districts are unable to provide exemplary programs due to the population limitations.

The cooperative for Case II serves eight school districts. It has administration offices and a full staff of professional teachers, supervisors, therapists, and office personnel.

Historically, special education cooperatives take care of programs for the more severely impaired child. In this case, the early childhood special education program offered through the cooperative serves children aged three to seven on a noncategorical basis. The program consists of half-day pre-primary classes or full-day primary classes. Screening and comprehensive study are directed by each district special education coordinator. Because it houses children with extraordinary service needs, there are also included on the early childhood special education staff, full-time speech therapists, child therapists, occupational therapists, physical therapists, and early childhood classroom teachers.

The primary classes are located in a regular K–6th grade building which gives the program flexibility for mainstreaming as the children are ready. The pre-primary classes are located in an independent structure which once housed a regular nursery school. Children are bused to the early childhood center and the day begins at 8:45 A.M. To maintain a ratio of five to one, each teacher has an aide in the classroom.

Therapists set up schedules for individual therapy as the services are recorded on the IEPs. Any changes in program must be reviewed with the parent and the teacher. The aides and professional staff try to keep the day running smoothly and are quite concerned that children are not removed from the class without justification. It becomes quite difficult to maintain a lesson unit with young children if they are coming and going on an irregular basis. Therapists and teachers make great effort to keep the schedules integrated.

The Case of Judy

The following case is that of Judy, a child three years and six months of age who has primary speech and language problems along with developmental lags. The first section presents multidisciplinary team evaluation reports by the social worker, speech and language pathologist, psychologist, and occupational therapist. This is followed by the IEP which highlights the speech area by demonstrating a hierarchy of receptive and expressive language skills which are needed for improving Judy's communication abilities.

Multidisciplinary evaluation reports.

SOCIAL HISTORY
(conducted by the social worker)

I. Identifying information:
  Child's name: Judy
  Chronological age: 3 years, 6 months
  Parents' names: Carol and Bob
  Address:
  Telephone:
  Date of report:

II. Reason for referral:

Judy was referred to the special education cooperative for a complete case study evaluation after the school district's regular pre-school screening.

III. Family background:

Judy is the fifth of six children born to the mother and the only girl. Three children were born during the mother's first marriage of nine years. The mother has had a tubal ligation as she feels she has enough to care for her six children.

The mother reported that she herself had pneumonia as a newborn infant and had to stay in the hospital for six weeks. Since that time, she has had a tendency to be anemic. The mother does not take iron pills because of the cost and because her "husband and children come first." She has tried to get food stamps but was turned down. She works long hours and is tired much of the time. She has many concerns about her children who are experiencing many struggles as they grow up. The mother appears to be very depressed and only rarely was seen smiling. The mother not only has had the physical and financial pressures of raising a large family, but she has had the loss of each of her own parents when she was only six and eight years old. After a year with her grandmother, she was then placed at an orphanage until she graduated from high school.

The mother and father and their family presently live above a bakery where they have lived for three years. The building has recently been sold, and they express concern that they could be asked to move. In addition to the six children, they have six cats and two dogs. The cats are strays their children have brought home and kittens born to the cats. The dogs belonged to the people who ran the bakery and were taken in by the parents when the bakery closed. The building appears to have been allowed to run down over the years, and the apartment was gloomy. Since people from the neighboring apartment came in to use the bathroom, it appears either that the bathroom is shared, or that their own bathroom was not in working order. The mother has a friend babysit when she goes to work about 3:30 in the afternoon. The friend brings her four children (the oldest, age eight) along and then spends the night since the mother does not get home until about 2:00 A.M. During the home visit there was a chaotic atmosphere.

The mother works irregular hours as a bartender but generally more than fifty hours per week. In addition to this, she also sells Avon products. The father is employed making window shades. During the home visit, the father was heard yelling and swearing several times.

IV. Description of child:

The mother described the pregnancy, delivery, and developmental milestones as normal. Because of the position Judy was in during the pregnancy, her feet now turn in. She should wear special orthopedic shoes, but the mother does not have the financial means for them. Judy is said to be in good health and was only taken to the emergency ward on one occasion when she had an ear infection. Judy walked at eleven months and generally has been faster than the other children, except in the area of toilet training. She is described as having been a poor eater—"even when she was on baby food."

Judy is described as being very jealous—pushing her brothers off her mother's lap when she sees them. (The eight and eleven year old still tend to sit on their mother's lap fairly frequently. The mother feels it makes them feel more secure.) The mother says she doesn't know why Judy is jealous. She says she has only been working for one year, "but perhaps that is the reason why." Judy is said to be extremely resentful of the baby sitter's five-year-old daughter. During the visit, Judy was observed hitting the girl for no apparent reason. The mother said Judy's tantrums are worse than any of the boys' were. "She will scream, 'It's mine,' or 'that's my mommy's' even when it isn't; she will scratch or hit with her hand or with an object. She has a very short temper and will throw fits if she doesn't have her own way. She also gets into things like the Avon lipstick samples—making quite a mess!"

Judy has been attending classes at the local Head Start program. The nurse came to the home and expressed surprise and pleasure in the fact that Judy was talking because she has been nonverbal and shy in spite of several months' attendance. Her speech was clear as she told me about a boy who hurt his eye at the park, and she was also heard singing. Most of the visit, however, she remained on her mother's lap. The mother said usually she doesn't sit down unless she's watching television. The mother also commented that Judy is a Mommy's girl, "but I don't know why."

The eighteen-month-old baby was described as "overactive." The mother says the baby "tears the house apart" and is breaking the crib. With that she said she wished she had the energy the kids have.

V. Summary and recommendations:

Judy's delays and inappropriate behaviors seem to stem from a needy home environment. Efforts should be made to obtain orthopedic shoes for Judy through family services at little or no cost to the family. Enrollment in the Early Childhood Education class along with enroll-ment in the Head Start program, if possible, will provide her with additional stimulation and a consistent, accepting environment. The mother says she would rather know now if Judy has a problem, so that help can be provided while she is still young. Though the mother has had a difficult life and appears to be depressed, it is obvious that she is concerned about her children and is doing the best she can under the difficult circumstances. The recommendation was made that she contact Family Services for support for herself in that she recognizes that she is depressed.

SPEECH AND LANGUAGE EVALUATION
(conducted by the speech and language pathologist)

Case History

Judy is the youngest of the six children of Mr. and Mrs. __. The mother reported pregnancy and birth history as having been normal.

Medical history is reported as nonsignificant with the exception of an ear infection at age two and a half.

Motor milestones were reportedly obtained within normal limits. The mother reported that Judy's speech and language development appeared delayed in comparison to her other children. Judy began to use single words at one year and phrases at one and one-half years. However, continued development has been delayed. The mother reported that she frequently has difficulty understanding Judy.

Judy was enrolled in a Head Start program. The mother reported that Judy was not generally verbal in that program. However, in the home environment she described Judy as highly verbal.

Evaluation

Administration of formalized measures was limited due to Judy's attending behaviors.

Inner Language

Judy's inner language skills appeared intact as demonstrated by appropriate manipulation of common items.

Receptive Language

Judy demonstrated receptive knowledge of body parts. Limited receptive knowledge was noted in the following vocabulary classes: *clothing, food, furniture, toys,* and *concepts.* Judy demonstrated a lack of receptive knowledge of *colors, shapes, prepositions,* with the exception of *in* and *on,* and the interrogatives *where, why,* and *when.* Judy was able to follow basic single-stage commands.

Judy achieved a single word vocabulary recognition age of 2–2, (CA 3–6), on the *Peabody Picture Vocabulary Test* (Form B). On the *Preschool Language Scale,* Judy achieved a receptive language age of two years six months. Judy passed 50 percent of the items at the three-year level. Judy demonstrated a delay in receptive knowledge of actor-agent relationships. Judy's receptive delay appears related to her attention span and a need for structured environmental stimulation.

Expressive Language

Judy displayed limited usage of expressive language. Utterances were characterized by basic sentences ("I can't get it," "I got it") and phrase structures ("Where my mom go?" "Someone break a doggie."). Utterances reflected primary usage of lower-level structures with emerging usage of higher-level constructs. Judy demonstrated appropriate usage of the interrogatives *where* and *what*, noun and verb, the pronouns, *I*, *me*, and *my*, the negations of *not* and *can't*, and usage of articles. However, analysis revealed lack of expressive usage of the copula *is*, verb-tense transformations, plurals, possessives, modifiers, the pronouns *he* and *she*, subject-verb agreement, interrogatives other than *what* and *where*, and interrogative reversals. However, it should be noted that this analysis was performed on a limited number of utterances. Expressive language skills are an area for further assessment.

Judy achieved an expressive language age of two years on the *Preschool Language Scale*. Judy passed 50 percent of the items at two and one-half years. It should be noted that utterances were frequently unrelated and/or disorganized.

Speech

Administration of the *Fisher-Logemann Test of Articulation Competence* revealed phonemic errors to be developmental in nature. However, in connected speech, Judy presents unpatterned consonant omissions. These omissions, accompanied by a limited vocal intensity, inappropriate inflectional patterns (at times, Judy "sang" versus speaking), and a labored rate frequently caused speech to become unintelligible. Judy was stimulable for improved patterns of production.

Oral Motor

Structure of the speech mechanism appears normal with the exception of a slight overbite which is attributed to thumb sucking.

Function of the speech mechanism appeared to indicate a delay in strength, precision, and rate of movement. Diadochokinetic rate appeared below norms for Judy's chronological age level. An extensive oral-motor assessment appears indicated to determine the functional level of prespeech skills. While Judy has adequate motor control for vegetative acts, she is described as a "picky eater."

Assessment was limited due to Judy's unresponsiveness to an intra-oral evaluation.

Auditory Memory

Judy consistently repeated three digits indicating an auditory memory span age equivalency of three years.

Auditory Acuity

Judy could not be conditioned for audiometric assessment. Based on Judy's language delay and speech patterns, a complete audiological assessment is recommended.

Behavioral Observations

Judy separated easily from her mother. She presented a limited attention span accompanied by inconsistent eye contact and inappropriate laughter. While Judy appeared related to the environment, her behavior patterns appeared immature.

Judy's limited verbalizations and immature behaviors indicate the need for a psychosocial evaluation.

Summary

Judy presents a moderate to severe receptive and expressive language delay accompanied by immature speech patterns. Judy presents a limited attention span which appears to be affecting increased cognitive growth.

Recommendations

1. Judy should be enrolled in individual diagnostic speech and language therapy sessions four times per week for thirty minutes each. Therapy should develop a home carry-over program.
2. Judy should be placed in the early childhood program.
3. Judy should receive a psychosocial evaluation.
4. Judy should be referred to the regional cooperative for an audiological evaluation.

PSYCHOLOGICAL REPORT
(conducted by the psychologist)

Reason for Referral

Judy was identified by the district screening program as a potential student for the Early Childhood Special Education program.

Background

Judy is the fifth of six children born to Mrs. ____. (See also social work report.) Judy has attended a Head Start program.

Test Administered

Stanford-Binet Intelligence Scale

Test Behavior

Judy showed the potential to be a pretty girl with blond hair and blue eyes. However, she displayed several immaturities during the testing session. Thumb-to-mouth, fingers entwined in her blouse, and nervous tapping of feet all interferred with optimal test rapport.

Her emotional dependence on her mother was a noticeable feature of her performance.

Test Results

On the *Stanford-Binet*, Judy successfully passed all items at the two-year-old level and obtained credits for success through age four. A corrected Mental Age of two years and ten months was obtained with an IQ of 78 determined. Her uneven performance pattern was noted at several age levels and suggests the possibility of a higher level of learning potential than the obtained scores. Questions requiring verbal responses, such as comprehension and opposite analogies, were refused and quickly brought a loss of attention.

Recommendations

Given Judy's social history, current emotional insecurity, and uneven level of intellectual performance, it is recommended that she be enrolled in the three-to-five-year-old early childhood program. Long-term goals should focus on rectifying these deficit areas. Furthermore, a psychosocial evaluation and ongoing supportive parent services are in order.

OCCUPATIONAL THERAPY ASSESSMENT
(conducted by the occupational therapist)

General Information

Judy was seen for an occupational therapy assessment during two sessions. Mrs. __ brought Judy for both sessions but did not accompany her during testing. Mother felt that Judy might perform better if she were not present. Reportedly, Judy attained motor milestones within normal limits.

Information obtained from the mother indicated that Judy objects to being touched at times. However, she does not seem irritable when held. She dislikes having her hair washed. She did not object to being tossed in the air or seem fearful of playground activities. The mother describes Judy as getting into many things at home and having a great amount of energy.

Testing Behaviors

When initially entering the testing situation, Judy seemed quiet and shy, speaking only to her mother. But when her mother left the room, Judy warmed up and began talking to the therapist. She assembled four preschool puzzles and then put them away in a self-organized manner. Judy attempted to cooperate with all the therapist's requests, yet at times she had difficulty following directions, possibly due to a lack of understanding of the verbal statements. During the initial session, she accepted minimal physical contact from the occupational therapist.

During the second assessment session, Judy seemed much more comfortable about physical contact initiated by the therapist. She appeared relaxed during play types of activities and hesitant to perform motor tasks on testing items. During this session, she initiated appropriate conversation with the therapist.

Results of Assessment

The adaptive behavior, gross motor and fine motor sections of the *Gesell Developmental Schedules*, were administered to Judy with the following results:

Adaptive behavior—functional level 35 months

Massed cubes:	builds bridge from model
Drawing:	names own drawing
Drawing:	copies circle
Colorforms:	places 3
Digits:	repeats 2

Gross motor—functional level 30 months

Rides:	tricycle using pedals
Jumps:	both feet
Large ball:	kicks without demonstration
Walks:	runs well
Stairs:	alternates feet going up

Fine motor—functional level 34 months

Massed cubes:	tower of ten
Pellets:	ten in bottle in thirty seconds
Drawing:	holds crayon by fingers

Personal-social skills reported by mother included feeding self, little spilling, putting on own shoes, washing face and hands, brushing teeth, carrying breakable objects, and helping to put things away. These skills appear to indicate a personal-social functional level of approximately three years.

On the *Developmental Test of Visual-Motor Integration,* Judy was not able to reproduce any of the geometric designs. She circled each of the designs presented in the student test booklet. The designs were then presented on separate pieces of paper to increase the visual organization and decrease distracting stimuli. With this adaption, Judy was generously credited with copying the circle. She was not able to copy the vertical or horizontal lines. However, when demonstrated, she was able to imitate the lines. Judy drew three lines for a cross. With the credit for copying the circle, Judy received a visual motor integration age equivalent to two years, ten months. During writing tasks, Judy consistently utilized her right hand to hold the writing tool. Her prehension pattern fluctuated between a radial-digital three-jaw chuck and a mature-digital grasp, with the thumb and index finger and the pencil resting on the middle finger. Her forearm was positioned on the table with the primary movements for writing centering in the wrist and elbow. She was not observed to cross her midline during writing and on other fine motor tasks, hand preference was not evident.

Clinical observations indicated questionable responses to tactile stimuli. Muscle tone in her upper extremities appeared adequate; contraction was not assessed. Eye pursuits across the midline appeared irregular. Judy had difficulty performing smooth, graded motor activities, including pronation-supination diadochokinetic movements. She demonstrated slight postural insecurity. Equilibrium and protective extension responses were delayed. When prone lying on a scooter board, Judy had a great deal of difficulty maneuvering. She was able to obtain a supine flexion position and maintain this position momentarily. Judy demonstrated a segmental rolling pattern. Head-righting reactions were not present when tipped laterally. When in a quadruped position, joint flexion was not noted with passive head rotation when assessing the tonic neck reflexes. However, a tight extension position of the elbows was suspected.

During play activities, Judy was able to imitate only simple upper extremity movement patterns. She correctly identified the following body parts: eyes, ear, nose, mouth, neck, shoulders, arms, hands, knees, feet, and stomach. When playing with sand, Judy was initially very hesistant to use both hands freely in the sand. With encouragement from the therapist, she used both hands and seemed to enjoy the sand play.

Summary

Judy was initially shy during the assessment. She was cooperative, yet appeared to have difficulty following some of the therapist's directions. On the *Gesell Developmental Schedules,* she scored functional levels of 35 months, 30 months, 34 months and approximately 36 months on adaptive behavior, gross motor, fine motor, and personal-social skills respectively. Her visual-motor integration age equivalent was two years, ten months. Her tactile responses were questionable. Equilibrium and fine-controlled motor activities were delayed. Midline problems were apparent from Judy not crossing her body midline with her upper extremities and irregular eye pursuits at midline. Postural insecurity was also noted. Bilateral motor coordination and motoric proficiency are suspected to be delayed.

Recommendations

1. Occupational therapy services twice a week to promote bilateral motor coordination, increase postural security, promote crossing midline, and improve postural-balance responses.
2. Implementation of developmental motor program in connection with classroom placement.
3. Placement in preprimary early childhood classroom.

The IEP for Judy. The written report for Judy developed at the IEP conference (Figures 11–5, 11–6, and 11–7) is shown on the following pages.

The speech and language IEP. In this case the speech and language

Participants	Title	Name: Judy
_____	Parent	Address:
_____	O.T.	Parent/Guardian: Bob and Carol
_____	Psychologist	Birthdate: Chronological age 3 years, 7 months
_____	Social Worker	MDS - IEP Conference Date:
_____	Speech Therapist	Telephone:
_____	Coord. E.C. Program	

Education Performance (areas to include: processing, academic, self-help, vocational, psychomotor, social and behavioral)

Test Information

Name of Test	Results	Date	Examiner
Gesell Developmental Scale	Adaptive behavior - 35 months, gross motor - 30 months fine motor - 34 months	6-79	OT
DVMIT	2 years 10 months - not able to produce geometric designs	6-79	OT
Binet	MA 2 years 10 months	6-79	Psyc.
PPVT	2 years 2 months	6-79	S-LT
Fischer-Logemann	Revealed phonemic errors to be developmental in nature	6-79	S-LT
Zimmerman Preschool lang.	2 years	6-79	S-LT

Observational Information

	Observer
Judy's response to test items showed some anxiety, and immaturity. She passed items at the two year level with a MA 2 - 10 level. She had difficulty with verbal items. Emotional security and separation need to be goals for development.	Psyc.
Receptive language was 2 - 2 on the Peabody. Her attention span was limited. Expressively, Judy uses basic sentences. Expressively she was at 2 1/2 year level. Moderate to severe language delay.	Speech-Lang.
Adaptive behavior at three years; gross motor skills at 20 months, fine motor skills at 34 months level. She did not cross her midline. Postural insecurity was noted. Balance responses are delayed.	OT

Figure 11–5   Individualized Education Program

pathologist developed an intensive and detailed program plan based on the preceding IEP.

SPEECH AND LANGUAGE PROGRAM PLANNING

Therapist: Speech-language

Name: Judy   Sex: F   Chronological age: 3–9

Therapy schedule: Sessions per week: 3

Length of sessions: 120 minutes

Attendance:

Present levels of performance

Language: Moderate receptive and expressive language delay.

Speech: Errors developmental in nature—errors with th (voiced and unvoiced), l, r

Oral motor: Delay in rote, strength, and precision of movement.

Hearing:

IEP goals: 1) increase receptive language skills; 2) increase expressive language skills; 3) improve the character pattern of speech production

Short-term Objectives: Receptive Language

1. Child will match item to item.
2. Child will identify item by pointing.
3. Child will select target items from a group of dissimilar items.
4. Child will select target item from a group of similar items.
5. Child will select target item from the natural environment.
6. Child will appropriately demonstrate function of target item in structured setting.
7. Child will appropriately demonstrate function of target item in natural environment.

Education Instruction

Student _____

Year _____

Special Instruction Placement:	Implementor	Amount	Beginning Date	Duration
Early Childhood Preprimary p.m.	Staff	Half day	9 - 79	Continual
Special Support Services to be Provided: Occupational Therapy	Staff	60 min	9 - 79	Continual
Speech and Language Therapy	Staff	120 min	9 - 79	Continual
Psychosocial Evaluation	Staff		9 - 79	
Regular Education Participation: Head Start Program		9-12 noon M - Th		

Justification for Placement:

Displays general development delay

Figure 11–6   IEP (continued)

Student <u>Judy</u>

Year <u>1979 - 1980</u>

Annual Goals	Implementor	Progress Comment
1. To increase receptive language skills	Staff	
2. To increase expressive language skills	Staff	
3. To improve the characteristic patterns of speech production	S.T.	
4. To increase attention span	Teacher	
5. To promote bilateral motor coordination	O.T.	
6. To increase postural security	O.T.	
7. To promote crossing the midline	O.T.	
8. To improve postural balance responses	O.T.	
9. To improve visual motor skills	Teacher	
10. To develop emotional maturity	Teacher	
11. To increase independence	Teacher	
12. To increase socialization skills	Teacher	

Comments:

Transportation provided by district. Eligible for extraordinary services. A referral for DSCC needs to be made to pursue assistance to family for special needs.

Figure 11–7 IEP (continued)

Key for model: immediate model (IM), delayed model (DM), imbedded model or question (QM), spontaneous production (SP).

To develop receptive knowledge of animals.

cow	elephant
pig	tiger
sheep	monkey
mouse	bear

turkey	snake
turtle	giraffe
frog	seal
squirrel	

To develop receptive knowledge of food.

apple	fish
orange	potatoes
pie	grapes
doughnut	turkey
pudding	salad
pear	celery
pineapple	hamburger
radishes	peas

To develop receptive knowledge of verbs.

blow	climb
throw	find
catch	hide
pour	swim
sweep	lock
draw	follow
bounce	push
kick	pull

To develop receptive knowledge of adjectives.

dirty	light
clean	fat
old	thin
new	messy
soft	broken
hard	straight
loud	crooked

quiet	curly
heavy	

To develop receptive knowledge of prepositions.

in front of	to
behind	above
under	below
next to	down

Short-term Objective: Articulation

Target sound: th (unvoiced)

I. To increase auditory discrimination skills.
   A. To auditorially discriminate gross sound differences.
   B. To auditorially discriminate the target sound from other speech sounds.
   C. To auditorially discriminate the target sound from similar speech sounds.
   D. To correctly identify the target sound in several contexts.

II. To establish the production of the target sounds.
   A. To produce the target sound in isolation or in a syllable.
   B. To produce the target sound in the prevocalic position.
      1. In single words.
      2. In phrases and/or short sentences.
      3. In sentences.
      4. Spontaneously in structured sentences and activities.
   C. To produce the target sound in the postvocalic position.
      1. In single words.
      2. In phrases and/or short sentences.
      3. In sentences.
      4. Spontaneously in structured activities.
   D. To produce the target sound in the intervocalic position.
      1. In single words.
      2. In phrases and/or snort sentences.
      3. In sentences.
      4. Spontaneously in structured activities.

    E. To produce the target sound in all positions.
       1. In single words.
       2. In phrases and/or short sentences.
       3. In sentences.
       4. Spontaneously in structured activities.
III. To carry over the use of the target sounds.
    A. To produce the target sound correctly on carryover situations.
    B. To produce the target sound in free speech in the therapy room, therapist present.
    C. To produce the target sound out of the therapy room.

Summary

This chapter presented two cases of preschool children who were identified as exceptional children. The cases involved construction of individualized programs and charts of the IEP process listing the various levels and requirements for the construction of goals and objectives. An actual example of a young boy and girl approximately the same age demonstrate the development of a written IEP.

    Case study I was a male child identified through a county special education setting. Case study II was a female child screened through a district program and staffed into a cooperative early childhood program. The county program and cooperative program can be contrasted and studied as well as examples of each of the special education program IEP forms.

Review Questions

TERMS TO KNOW

a. *IEP*
b. *special education cooperative*
c. *speech and language pathologist*
d. *joint agreement*

e. *occupational therapist*
f. *annual goals*
g. *physical therapist*
h. *short-term objectives*

1. Looking at Case Study I, could you project a description of the child's functional communication skills? How would the child function in imitation of language with peers and adults? Construct one goal and three objectives for social and functional problem solving.

2. In the development of a written IEP form, what is the first step? What is the final item to be included?

3. Do you feel that the present level of educational performance is clearly presented in Case II? What was omitted? What would you like to see added?

4. Is the length of time included in service needs for Case I and Case II? What would you suggest?

5. What type of arrangement does your local school district have for early childhood special services? If it is within a joint agreement, how does it operate?

6. There is a trend in special education to remove categories. Do you believe that this is a good trend? Why or why not?

7. If you could have total control of your district's special education program for early childhood, what would you do? Design your own early childhood program. Define what types of children you would serve, how you would find them, and what your program would contain.

References

ILLINOIS OFFICE OF EDUCATION. *The Illinois Primer on Individualized Education Programs.* Springfield, Ill.: Department of Specialized Educational Services and Illinois Regional Resource Center, June, 1979.

Tests for Screening and Diagnosing Young Children

Appendix **A**

Appendix A lists the names and brief descriptive information of tests that are designed for young children. Appendix A is divided into two sections: Part I, Screening Tests, and Part II, Diagnostic Tests.

Part I: Screening Tests

NAME OF INSTRUMENT: The ABC Inventory
AUTHOR(S):   Adair, N., and G. Blesch
PUBLISHER: Research Concepts
COPYRIGHT DATE: 1965
ADMINISTRATION: Individual
ADMINISTRATOR: Professional (diagnostician)
AGE: 3–6 to 6–6
PURPOSE: Test is designed to identify children who are likely to fail in kindergarten or who are not ready for first grade. Test includes items which require drawing, copying, folding, counting, memory, general information, colors, size and time concepts.
TESTING TIME: 9 minutes
TYPE OF RESPONSE: Verbal, nonverbal.

NAME OF INSTRUMENT: Bankson Language Screening Test
AUTHOR(S):   Bankson, N. W.
PUBLISHER: University Park Press
COPYRIGHT DATE: 1977
ADMINISTRATION: Individual
ADMINISTRATOR: Professional (teacher, diagnostician)
AGE: 4–1 to 8–0
PURPOSE: Instrument used to identify children in need of further language assessment. Test covers the following areas: semantic knowl-

edge, morphological rules, syntactic rules, visual perception, and auditory perception.

TESTING TIME: 25 minutes

TYPE OF RESPONSE: Verbal, nonverbal

NAME OF INSTRUMENT: Basic Concept Inventory

AUTHOR(S): Engelmann, S. E.

PUBLISHER: Follett Publishing Company

COPYRIGHT DATE: 1967

ADMINISTRATION: Individual

ADMINISTRATOR: Professional (teacher)

AGE: 3–0 to 10–0

PURPOSE: Criterion-referenced checklist used to measure basic concepts necessary for children to perform successfully in new learning situations. Subtests include basic concepts, sentence repetition and comprehension, and pattern awareness.

TESTING TIME: 20 minutes

TYPE OF RESPONSE: Verbal, nonverbal

NAME OF INSTRUMENT: Basic School Skills Inventory

AUTHOR(S): Goodman, L. and D. Hammill

PUBLISHER: Follett Publishing Company

COPYRIGHT DATE: 1975

ADMINISTRATION: Individual

ADMINISTRATOR: Professional (teacher)

AGE: 4–0 to 7–0

PURPOSE: Test used to evaluate areas that will affect children's academic success. Performance areas include basic information, self-help, handwriting, oral communication, reading readiness, number readiness, and classroom behavior.

TESTING TIME: 20 minutes

TYPE OF RESPONSE: Verbal, nonverbal

NAME OF ISTRUMENT: Birth-Three Scale

AUTHOR(S): Bangs, T. E., and S. Garrett

PUBLISHER: Teaching Resources

COPYRIGHT DATE: 1977

ADMINISTRATION: Individual

ADMINISTRATOR: Nonprofessional (parent)

AGE: 1 mo. to 3–0

PURPOSE: Scale to assess a child's abilities and level of functioning in the areas of oral language (comprehension and expression), problem solving, social-personal and motor development. It is suggested that observation of child's behavior be used in conjunction with the scale.

TESTING TIME: Varied

TYPE OF RESPONSE: Verbal, nonverbal

NAME OF INSTRUMENT: Boehm Test of Basic Concepts

AUTHOR(S): Boehm, A. E.

PUBLISHER: Psychological Corporation

COPYRIGHT DATE: 1969

ADMINISTRATION: Individual or small groups

ADMINISTRATOR: Professional (teacher, diagnostician)

AGE: 4–0 to 8–0

PURPOSE: Test measures children's mastery of concepts considered necessary for achievement in the first years of school. Concepts tested include those of space (location, direction, orientation, and dimension), time and quantity (number).

TESTING TIME: 30 minutes (15–20 minutes for each of two booklets)

TYPE OF RESPONSE: Nonverbal

NAME OF INSTRUMENT: Bruininks-Oseretsky Test of Motor Proficiency

AUTHOR(S): Bruininks, R.

PUBLISHER: American Guidance Service

COPYRIGHT DATE: 1976

Administration: Individual

ADMINISTRATOR: Professional

AGE: 4–6 to 14–6

PURPOSE: Test provides a means for measuring a child's fine and gross motor proficiency. Eight key areas of motor performance are assessed: balance, bilateral coordination, strength, upperlimb coordination, running, speed and agility, response speed, visual-motor control, and upper limb speed and dexterity.

TESTING TIME: 25 minutes

TYPE OF RESPONSE: Nonverbal

NAME OF INSTRUMENT: California Preschool Social Competency Scale
AUTHOR(S):   Levine, S., F. Elzey, M. Lewis
PUBLISHER: Consulting Psychologists Press
COPYRIGHT DATE: 1969
ADMINISTRATION: Individual
ADMINISTRATOR: Professional
AGE: 2–6 to 5–6
PURPOSE: Test designed to measure the adequacy of the social and interpersonal behavior of the children and the degree to which they assume social responsibility.
TESTING TIME: Untimed
TYPE OF RESPONSE: Rater

NAME OF INSTRUMENT: Carolina Developmental Profile
AUTHOR(S):   Lillie, D. L., and G. L. Harbin
PUBLISHER: Kaplan School Supply
COPYRIGHT DATE: 1975
ADMINISTRATION: Individual
ADMINISTRATOR: Professional (teacher)
AGE: 2–0 to 5–0
PURPOSE: Criterion-referenced checklist to test children's skills in the areas of fine motor, gross motor, perceptual reasoning, receptive and expressive language. Teacher can plan instructional objectives for those areas in which the child is weakest.
TYPE OF RESPONSE: Verbal, nonverbal

NAME OF INSTRUMENT: Cognitive Skills Assessment Battery
AUTHOR(S):   Boehm, A. E., and B. R. Slater
PUBLISHER: Psychological Corporation
COPYRIGHT DATE: 1974
ADMINISTRATION: Individual
ADMINISTRATOR: Professional (teacher)
                 Nonprofessional (aide)
AGE: 3–0 to 6–0
PURPOSE: Criterion-referenced instrument designed to provide a profile of children's cognitive strengths and weaknesses. General areas assessed include orientation and familiarity with the environment, coordination, discrimination, memory, comprehension, and concept formation.

TESTING TIME: 25 minutes

TYPE OF RESPONSE: Verbal, nonverbal

NAME OF INSTRUMENT: Comprehensive Identification Process (CIP)

AUTHOR(S): Zehrbach, R. R.

PUBLISHER: Scholastic Testing Service

COPYRIGHT DATE: 1976

ADMINISTRATION: Individual

ADMINISTRATOR: Professional (teacher, diagnostician)
Nonprofessional (parent)

AGE: 2–6 to 5–6

PURPOSE: Screening test to identify children who may need special medical, psychological, or educational assistance before they enter school. Test assesses eight areas of development which include fine motor, gross motor, cognitive-verbal, speech-expressive language, hearing, vision, social-affective, and medical.

TESTING TIME: 30 minutes

TYPE OF RESPONSE: Verbal, nonverbal

NAME OF INSTRUMENT: Cooperative Preschool Inventory (CPI)

AUTHOR(S): Caldwell, B. M.

PUBLISHER: Addison-Wesley

COPYRIGHT DATE: 1970

ADMINISTRATION: Individual

ADMINISTRATOR: Professional (teacher)
Nonprofessional (parent)

AGE: 3–0 to 6–0

PURPOSE: Test provides an indicator of a child's level of development prior to formal instruction. Test measures basic skills and concepts regarded as necessary for school success. General areas evaluated include basic information and vocabulary; number concepts; concepts of size, motion, color and time; social function; object classification; visual-motor performance; following instructions; and independence and self-help. A Spanish edition is available.

TESTING TIME: 20 minutes

TYPE OF RESPONSE: Verbal, nonverbal

NAME OF INSTRUMENT: Del Rio Language Screening Test

AUTHOR(S): Toronto, A. S., D. Leverman, C. Hanna, P. Rosenzweig, and A. Maldonado

PUBLISHER: National Educational Laboratory Publishers

COPYRIGHT DATE: 1975

ADMINISTRATION: Individual

ADMINISTRATOR: Professional (teacher)

AGE: 3–0 to 6–11

PURPOSE: Test devised to identify children with deviant language performance in English and Spanish and who require further evaluation. Test is comprised of five subtests: receptive vocabulary, sentence repetition-length, sentence repetition-complexity, oral commands, and story comprehension.

TYPE OF RESPONSE: Verbal, nonverbal

NAME OF INSTRUMENT: Denver Developmental Screening Test (DDST)

AUTHOR(S): Frankenburg, W. K., J. B. Dodds, and A. Fandal

PUBLISHER: LADOCA Project and Publishing Foundation

COPYRIGHT DATE: 1970

ADMINISTRATION: Individual

ADMINISTRATOR: Professional (teacher, diagnostician)
Nonprofessional (training required)

AGE: 1 mo. to 6–0

PURPOSE: Screening test to identify children with delays in the areas of motor, social, and language development. Responses are scored as normal, questionable, or abnormal.

TESTING TIME: 20 minutes

TYPE OF RESPONSE: Verbal, nonverbal, rater

NAME OF INSTRUMENT: Denver Prescreening Developmental Questionnaire (PDQ)

AUTHOR(S): Frankenburg, W. K.

PUBLISHER: LADOCA Project and Publishing Foundation

COPYRIGHT DATE: 1975

ADMINISTRATION: Individual

ADMINISTRATOR: Nonprofessional (parent)

AGE: 3 mo. to 6–0

PURPOSE: A brief *prescreening* questionnaire to identify those individuals who should be more thoroughly screened with the Denver Developmental Screening Test. Questionnaire is completed by parents.

TESTING TIME: 10 minutes

TYPE OF RESPONSE: Rater

NAME OF INSTRUMENT: Developmental Indicators for the Assessment of Learning (DIAL)

AUTHOR(S): Mardell, C., and D. Goldenberg

PUBLISHER: Childcraft Education Corporation

COPYRIGHT DATE: 1972, 1975

ADMINISTRATION: Individual

ADMINISTRATOR: Professional (teacher, diagnostician)
Nonprofessional (training required)

AGE: 2–6 to 5–6

PURPOSE: A prekindergarten screening test for identifying children with potential learning problems. Areas measured include gross motor, fine motor, concepts, communication, and social-emotional development.

TESTING TIME: 25 minutes

TYPE OF RESPONSE: Verbal, nonverbal, rater

NAME OF INSTRUMENT: Developmental Profile

AUTHOR(S): Alpern, G. D., and T. J. Ball

PUBLISHER: Psychological Development Publications

COPYRIGHT DATE: 1972

ADMINISTRATION: Individual

ADMINISTRATOR: Professional (teacher, diagnostician)

AGE: 6 mo. to 12–0

PURPOSE: Test designed to use interview technique to quickly screen large populations and to clinically assess individual children's developmental competencies in the areas of physical, self-help, social, academic, and communication development. Test contains enough information to construct individual programs and to provide pre- and postevaluative information.

TESTING TIME: 30 minutes

TYPE OF RESPONSE: Rater

NAME OF INSTRUMENT: Developmental Screening Inventory (DSI)

AUTHOR(S): Knobloch, H., and B. Pasamanick

PUBLISHER: Psychological Corporation

COPYRIGHT DATE: 1966, 1974

ADMINISTRATION: Individual

ADMINISTRATOR: Nonprofessional (parent)

AGE: 1 mo. to 3–0

PURPOSE: Test developed by physicians for parents to use in serial observation of their children. Subtests measure the following areas: gross motor, fine motor, language, personal, social, and adaptive development.

TESTING TIME: 15 minutes

TYPE OF RESPONSE: Rater

NAME OF INSTRUMENT: Developmental Test of Visual Motor Integration (VMI)

AUTHOR(S): Beery, K., and N. Buktenica

PUBLISHER: Follett Publishing Company

COPYRIGHT DATE: 1967

ADMINISTRATION: Individual or group

ADMINISTRATOR: Professional (teacher)

AGE: 2–0 to 15–0

PURPOSE: Test to screen children who may have potential visual perceptual or motor behavior problems. Test requires that children reproduce various geometric figures which are arranged in order of increasing difficulty.

TESTING TIME: 10 minutes

TYPE OF RESPONSE: Nonverbal

NAME OF INSTRUMENT: Eliot-Pearson Screening Inventory

AUTHOR(S): Meisels, S. J., and M. S. Wiske

PUBLISHER: Eliot-Pearson

COPYRIGHT DATE: 1976 (Revised)

ADMINISTRATION: Individual

ADMINISTRATOR: Professional (teacher, diagnostician)
Nonprofessional (students of child development)

AGE: 4–0 to 6–0

PURPOSE: Screening test used to evaluate children's perceptual, cognitive, language, and motor development. Information from a health history, parent questionnaire, and vision and hearing screening is used in conjunction with results from the screening inventory.

TESTING TIME: 15 minutes

TYPE OF RESPONSE: Verbal, nonverbal, rater (rater for parent questionnaire)

NAME OF INSTRUMENT: Goldman-Fristoe-Woodcock Test of Auditory Discrimination

AUTHOR(S): Goldman, R., M. Fristoe, R. Woodcock
PUBLISHER: American Guidance Service
COPYRIGHT DATE: 1970
ADMINISTRATION: Individual
ADMINISTRATOR: Professional
AGE: 4–0 to adult
PURPOSE: Test designed to evaluate speech sound discrimination under both quiet and distracting noise conditions. A tape recorder is required for administration.
TESTING TIME: 15 minutes
TYPE OF RESPONSE: Nonverbal

NAME OF INSTRUMENT: Infant Behavior Inventory
AUTHOR(S): Scheafer, E., and M. Aaronson
PUBLISHER: National Institute of Mental Health
COPYRIGHT DATE: 1975 (not copyrighted)
ADMINISTRATION: Individual
ADMINISTRATOR: Professional (teacher)
AGE: 1–0 to 3–0
PURPOSE: Inventory consists of 115 descriptions of possible infant behaviors covering the areas of attentiveness, concentration, distractibility, fatigue, perseverance, verbal expressiveness, and so on.
TESTING TIME: 25 minutes
TYPE OF RESPONSE: Rater

NAME OF INSTRUMENT: Inventory for Language Abilities
AUTHOR(S): Minskoff, E. H., D. E. Wiseman, and J. G. Minskoff
PUBLISHER: Childcraft Education Corporation
COPYRIGHT DATE: 1972
ADMINISTRATION: Individual
ADMINISTRATOR: Professional (teacher)
AGE: 4–0 to 8–0
PURPOSE: Screening device used by the classroom teacher to identify children with possible language disabilities. Subtests include auditory reception, visual reception, auditory association, visual association, verbal expression, manual expression, auditory memory, visual memory, grammatic closure, visual closure, auditory closure, and sound blending.
TYPE OF RESPONSE: Rater

NAME OF INSTRUMENT: Learning Accomplishment Profile (LAP) and the Infant Lap
AUTHOR(S): Sanford, A.
PUBLISHER: Kaplan School Supply
COPYRIGHT DATE: 1974
ADMINISTRATION: Individual
ADMINISTRATOR: Nonprofessional (parent)
                Professional (teacher)
AGE: 0 to 6
PURPOSE: A developmental checklist for assessment and planning individual prescriptive programs in 6 areas of development: gross motor, fine motor, social skills, self-help skills, language and cognition.
TYPE OF RESPONSE: Verbal, nonverbal

NAME OF INSTRUMENT: Minnesota Child Development Inventory
AUTHOR(S): Ireton, H. R., and E. J. Thwing
PUBLISHER: Behavior Science Systems
COPYRIGHT DATE: 1972
ADMINISTRATION: Individual
ADMINISTRATOR: Nonprofessional (parent)
AGE: 1–0 to 6–0
PURPOSE: Instrument for using mother's observations to measure the development of her child on eight scales: general development, gross motor, fine motor, expressive language, comprehension-conceptual, situation comprehension, self-help, and personal-social development.
TESTING TIME: 45 minutes
TYPE OF RESPONSE: Rater

NAME OF INSTRUMENT: Motor Free Visual Perception Test
AUTHOR(S): Colarusso, R. P., and D. D. Hammill
PUBLISHER: Pro-ed
COPYRIGHT DATE: 1972
ADMINISTRATION: Individual
ADMINISTRATOR: Professional (teacher, diagnostician)
                Nonprofessional (parent)
AGE: 4–0 to 8–0
PURPOSE: Test to measure a child's visual-perceptual abilities without involving a motor component. Subtests include visual discrimination, figure-ground, spatial relations, visual closure, and visual memory.

TESTING TIME: 10 minutes

TYPE OF RESPONSE: Nonverbal

NAME OF INSTRUMENT: Motor Problems Inventory

AUTHOR(S):   Riley, G. D.

PUBLISHER: Western Psychological Services

COPYRIGHT DATE: 1972

ADMINISTRATION: Individual

ADMINISTRATOR: Professional (diagnostician)

AGE: 3–0 to 11–0

PURPOSE: Screening procedure used to identify children with possible neurological impairments. Test requires direct observation. Areas assessed include small muscle coordination, laterality, and gross motor coordination.

TESTING TIME: 10 minutes

TYPE OF RESPONSE: Nonverbal

NAME OF INSTRUMENT: Move-Grow-Learn (Movement Skills Survey)

AUTHOR(S):   Orpet, R. E., and L. L. Heustis

PUBLISHER: Follett Publishing Company

COPYRIGHT DATE: 1971

ADMINISTRATION: Individual

ADMINISTRATOR: Professional (teacher, diagnostician)

AGE: 3 to 9 years

PURPOSE: Survey to evaluate selected aspects of a child's motor development. Assessment is based upon examiner's observations of the child in classroom, playground, and gymnasium activities. Survey is intended for use with Frostig-Maslow Move-Grow-Learn program.

TYPE OF RESPONSE: Nonverbal

NAME OF INSTRUMENT: Northwestern Syntax Screening Test (NSST)

AUTHOR(S):   Lee, L.

PUBLISHER: Northwestern University Press

COPYRIGHT DATE: 1969

ADMINISTRATION: Individual

ADMINISTRATOR: Professional (diagnostician)

AGE: 3 to 8 years

PURPOSE: Screening device to quickly identify children who are delayed in syntactic development. Test measures both receptive and expressive use of syntactic forms.

TESTING TIME: 20 minutes

TYPE OF RESPONSE: Verbal, nonverbal

NAME OF INSTRUMENT: Peabody Picture Vocabulary Test (PPVT)

AUTHOR(S): Dunn, L.

PUBLISHER: American Guidance Service

COPYRIGHT DATE: 1965, 1980

ADMINISTRATION: Individual

ADMINISTRATOR: Professional

AGE: 2–5 to adult

PURPOSE: Designed to provide an estimate of a subject's verbal intelligence through measuring hearing vocabulary; measures receptive language.

TESTING TIME: 15 minutes

TYPE OF RESPONSE: Nonverbal

NAME OF INSTRUMENT: Photo Articulation Test (PAT)

AUTHOR(S): Pendergest, K., S. E. Dickey, J. W. Selmar, and A. L. Soder

PUBLISHER: Interstate Printers and Publishers

COPYRIGHT DATE: 1969

ADMINISTRATION: Individual

ADMINISTRATOR: Professional (diagnostician)

AGE: 3 to 12 years

PURPOSE: Test provides a total picture of child's articulation of all consonants, vowels, and common blends within the initial, medial, and final positions as well as in isolation. Test acts as a tool to enable decisions to be made concerning the necessity of speech therapy.

TESTING TIME: 5 minutes

TYPE OF RESPONSE: Verbal

NAME OF INSTRUMENT: Predictive Screening Test of Articulation

AUTHOR(S): Van Riper, C., and R. Erickson

PUBLISHER: Division of Continuing Education, Western Michigan University

COPYRIGHT DATE: 1968

ADMINISTRATION: Individual

ADMINISTRATOR: Professional (speech clinician)

AGE: 5 to 6 years

PURPOSE: Test to differentiate children who will master their misarticulation errors without speech therapy from those who may persist in their errors without therapy.

TESTING TIME: 8 minutes

TYPE OF RESPONSE: Verbal

NAME OF INSTRUMENT: Preschool Attainment Record (PAR)

AUTHOR(S): Doll, Edgar A.

PUBLISHER: American Guidance Service

COPYRIGHT DATE: 1967

ADMINISTRATION: Individual

ADMINISTRATOR: Professional (teacher)
Nonprofessional (parent)

AGE: 6 mo. to 7 years

PURPOSE: A rating scale and checklist used to measure a child's physical, social, and intellectual development. Any adult closely associated with the child can complete the form.

TESTING TIME: 30 minutes

TYPE OF RESPONSE: Rater

NAME OF INSTRUMENT: Preschool Language Scale

AUTHOR(S): Zimmerman, I. L., V. G. Steiner, and R. L. Evatt

PUBLISHER: Charles E. Merrill

COPYRIGHT DATE: 1969

ADMINISTRATION: Individual

ADMINISTRATOR: Professional (diagnostician)

AGE: 1–6 to 7–0

PURPOSE: Instrument used to measure children's language development. Scale consists of two main parts—auditory comprehension and verbal ability. A supplementary articulation section is also included.

TESTING TIME: 30 minutes

TYPE OF RESPONSE: Verbal, nonverbal

NAME OF INSTRUMENT: Preschool Screening System

AUTHOR(S): Hainsworth, P., and R. Hainsworth

PUBLISHER: Early Recognition Intervention System

COPYRIGHT DATE: 1974

ADMINISTRATION: Individual or group

ADMINISTRATOR: Professional
                                   Nonprofessional (parent)

AGE: 3–0 to 5–4

PURPOSE: Parent questionnaire and quick screening survey to provide information about a three- to five-year-old child's language, visual-motor, body awareness, and control skills.

TESTING TIME: 15 minutes

TYPE OF RESPONSE: Verbal, nonverbal, rater

NAME OF INSTRUMENT: Primary Self-Concept Inventory

AUTHOR(S):   Muller, D., and R. Leonetti

PUBLISHER: Teaching Resources

COPYRIGHT DATE: 1973

ADMINISTRATION: Individual or group

ADMINISTRATOR: Professional (teacher, diagnostician)

AGE: 4 to 10 years

PURPOSE: Test to evaluate areas of self-concept relevant to school success. Test measures three domains of self-concept: social-self, personal-self, and intellectual-self. Instructions can be given in either English or Spanish.

TESTING TIME: 15 minutes

TYPE OF RESPONSE: Nonverbal

NAME OF INSTRUMENT: Quick Neurological Screening Test

AUTHOR(S):   Sterling, H. M., M. Mutti, N. V. Spalding

PUBLISHER: Academic Therapy Publications

COPYRIGHT DATE: 1977

ADMINISTRATION: Individual or Group

ADMINISTRATOR: Professional (diagnostician)

AGE: 4 to 18 years

PURPOSE: Test used to detect neurological deficits in children. Test covers the following areas: emotional, intellectual, sensory-motor development, muscle coordination, readiness for number concepts, and auditory-visual perception.

TESTING TIME: 20 minutes

TYPE OF RESPONSE: Nonverbal, rater

NAME OF INSTRUMENT: Quick Screening Scale of Mental Development
AUTHOR(S):   Banham, K. M.
PUBLISHER: Psychometric Affiliates
COPYRIGHT DATE: 1963
ADMINISTRATION: Individual
ADMINISTRATOR: Professional (diagnostician)
AGE: 6 mo. to 10 years
PURPOSE: Test provides mental age ratings in the following areas: body coordination, manual performance, speech and language, listening, attention, number concepts, play interests, and general mental level.
TESTING TIME: 30 minutes
TYPE OF RESPONSE: Verbal, nonverbal

NAME OF INSTRUMENT: Receptive-Expressive Emergent Language Scale (REEL)
AUTHOR(S):   Bzoch, K. R., and R. League
PUBLISHER: Tree of Life Press
COPYRIGHT DATE: 1972
ADMINISTRATION: Individual
ADMINISTRATOR: Professional
AGE: 1 mo. to 3 years
PURPOSE: Test provides a means of measuring children's language development in the first three years of life. Test covers the areas of receptive, expressive, and inner language.
TESTING TIME: 25 minutes
TYPE OF RESPONSE: Rater

NAME OF INSTRUMENT: Riley Articulation and Language Test
AUTHOR(S):   Riley, C. M. D.
PUBLISHER: Western Psychological Services
COPYRIGHT DATE: 1971
ADMINISTRATION: Individual
ADMINISTRATOR: Professional (diagnostician)
AGE: 4 to 7 years
PURPOSE: One- to two-minute screening test used to identify children most in need of speech therapy. Test provides an objective articulation loss score, a standardized language loss score and a language function score.

TESTING TIME: 2 minutes
TYPE OF RESPONSE: Verbal

NAME OF INSTRUMENT: Riley Preschool Developmental Screening Inventory
AUTHOR(S): Riley, C. M. D.
PUBLISHER: Western Psychological Services
COPYRIGHT DATE: 1969
ADMINISTRATION: Individual
ADMINISTRATOR: Professional (teacher)
AGE: 3 to 6 years
PURPOSE: School readiness measure used to identify preschool children most likely to need special assistance in adjusting to normal school situation. Test requires that children copy designs and draw a person.
TESTING TIME: 10 minutes
TYPE OF RESPONSE: Nonverbal

NAME OF INSTRUMENT: Screening Test for Auditory Comprehension
AUTHOR(S): Carrow-Woolfolk, E.
PUBLISHER: Teaching Resources
COPYRIGHT DATE: 1973
ADMINISTRATION: Group
ADMINISTRATOR: Professional (diagnostician)
AGE: 3 to 6 years
PURPOSE: Screening test used to identify children with receptive language difficulties. Test consists of 25 items which were taken from the Test for Auditory Comprehension of Language. Test evaluates child's knowledge of vocabulary, morphology and syntax.
TESTING TIME: 10 to 15 minutes
TYPE OF RESPONSE: Nonverbal

NAME OF INSTRUMENT: Sequenced Inventory of Communication Development
AUTHOR(S): Hedrick, D. L., E. M. Prather, and A. R. Tobin
PUBLISHER: University of Washington Press
COPYRIGHT DATE: 1975
ADMINISTRATION: Individual
ADMINISTRATOR: Professional (diagnostician)
AGE: 4 mo. to 4 years

PURPOSE: Test used to screen children's abilities in the areas of expressive language (which includes imitation, initiating, and responding), length, grammatic and syntactic structures of verbal output, articulation and receptive language (which includes behavioral items that test sound and speech discrimination, awareness, and understanding).

TESTING TIME: 45 minutes

TYPE OF RESPONSE: Verbal, nonverbal, rater

NAME OF INSTRUMENT: Southern California Perceptual-Motor Tests

AUTHOR(S): Ayres, A. J.

PUBLISHER: Western Psychological Services

COPYRIGHT DATE: 1968

ADMINISTRATION: Individual

ADMINISTRATOR: Professional

AGE: 4 to 8 years

PURPOSE: Series of six tests used to evaluate children's perceptual-motor functioning. Subtests include imitation of postures, crossing midline of body, bilateral motor coordination, right-left discrimination, and standing balance (eyes open and eyes closed).

TESTING TIME: 20 minutes

TYPE OF RESPONSE: Verbal, nonverbal

NAME OF INSTRUMENT: Test of Auditory Comprehension of Language

AUTHOR(S): Carrow-Woolfolk, E.

PUBLISHER: Teaching Resources

COPYRIGHT DATE: 1973

ADMINISTRATION: Individual

ADMINISTRATOR: Professional

AGE: 3 to 6 years

PURPOSE: Test designed to measure a child's auditory comprehension of language structure in English or Spanish. It encompasses vocabulary, morphology, and syntax. A series of 101 three picture plates are used.

TESTING TIME: 25 minutes

TYPE OF RESPONSE: Nonverbal

NAME OF INSTRUMENT: Verbal Language Development Scale

AUTHOR(S): Mecham, M. J.

PUBLISHER: American Guidance Service

COPYRIGHT DATE: 1971

ADMINISTRATION: Individual

ADMINISTRATOR: Professional (teacher, diagnostician)

AGE: 1 mo. to 16 years

PURPOSE: Scale used to measure child's performance on verbal tasks. The test, which is an extension of the communication portion of the Vineland Social Maturity Scale, allows for interviews with the child's parent or teacher.

TESTING TIME: 30 minutes

TYPE OF RESPONSE: Rater

NAME OF INSTRUMENT: Wepman Auditory Discrimination Test (ADT)

AUTHOR(S): Wepman, J. M.

PUBLISHER: Language Research Associates

COPYRIGHT DATE: 1973

ADMINISTRATION: Individual

ADMINISTRATOR: Professional (diagnostician)

AGE: 5 to 8 years

PURPOSE: Screening test to evaluate children's auditory discrimination abilities. Test requires that children indicate whether matched words are the same or different.

TESTING TIME: 15 minutes

TYPE OF RESPONSE: Verbal, nonverbal

Part II: Diagnostic Tests

NAME OF INSTRUMENT: Adaptive Behavior Scales

AUTHOR(S): Nihira, N., R. Foster, M. Shellhas, and H. Leland

PUBLISHER: American Association on Mental Deficiency

COPYRIGHT DATE: 1975 (Revised)

ADMINISTRATION: Individual or group

ADMINISTRATOR: Professional (teacher)
                 Nonprofessional (parent)

AGE: 3 years to adult

PURPOSE: Behavior rating scale for school children, mentally retarded, and emotionally maladjusted individuals. Scale assesses how an individual copes with environmental demands as it taps different behavior domains.

TESTING TIME: 20 minutes

TYPE OF RESPONSE: Rater

NAME OF INSTRUMENT: Arizona Articulation Proficiency Scale: Revised

AUTHOR(S): Fudala, J. B.

PUBLISHER: Western Psychological Services

COPYRIGHT DATE: 1970

ADMINISTRATION: Individual

ADMINISTRATOR: Professional (teacher, diagnostician)
Nonprofessional (training required)

AGE: 3 years to adult

PURPOSE: Test used to determine a child's articulation proficiency. Scale assesses child's pronunciation of initial and final consonants as well as vowel sounds. Test identifies individuals who are in need of speech therapy.

TESTING TIME: 25 minutes

TYPE OF RESPONSE: Verbal

NAME OF INSTRUMENT: Bayley Scales of Infant Development (BSID)

AUTHOR(S): Bayley, N.

PUBLISHER: Psychological Corporation

COPYRIGHT DATE: 1969

ADMINISTRATION: Individual

ADMINISTRATOR: Professional (diagnostician)
(Test is to be given with the mother present)

AGE: 2 mo. to 2–6

PURPOSE: Mental and motor scale which provides an evaluation of infants' early mental and psychomotor development. Scale is to be used in conjunction with the Infant Behavior Record in order to obtain information regarding qualitative aspect of infant behavior.

TESTING TIME: 45 minutes

TYPE OF RESPONSE: Nonverbal

NAME OF INSTRUMENT: Bender Motor Gestalt Test

AUTHOR(S): Bender, L.

PUBLISHER: American Orthopsychiatric Association

COPYRIGHT DATE: 1946 (Revised 1964)

ADMINISTRATION: Individual or group

ADMINISTRATOR: Professional (diagnostician)

AGE: 4 to 12 years

PURPOSE: Nonverbal measurement used to detect visual-perceptual difficulties and the possible presence of brain damage. Test can also be used as a supplement to a personality evaluation.

TESTING TIME: 10 minutes

TYPE OF RESPONSE: Nonverbal

NAME OF INSTRUMENT: Brigance Diagnostic Inventory of Early Development

AUTHOR(S): Brigance, A.

PUBLISHER: Curriculum Associates

COPYRIGHT DATE: 1978

ADMINISTRATION: Individual

ADMINISTRATOR: Professional and paraprofessional

AGE: 1 mo. to 6 years

PURPOSE: Criterion-referenced test which integrates assessment-diagnosis with record keeping, objective setting, and instructional planning. Areas assessed include psychomotor skills, self-help, speech and language, general knowledge and comprehension, reading, printing, and math.

TESTING TIME: Untimed

TYPE OF RESPONSE: Nonverbal, verbal

NAME OF INSTRUMENT: Carrow Elicited Language Inventory

AUTHOR(S): Carrow, E.

PUBLISHER: Teaching Resources

COPYRIGHT DATE: 1974

ADMINISTRATION: Individual

ADMINISTRATOR: Professional (diagnostician)

AGE: 3–0 to 7–11

PURPOSE: Test to obtain performance data on the child's control of grammar. Inventory provides a means of identifying language problems by determining specific linguistic structures with which child has difficulty.

TESTING TIME: 45 minutes

TYPE OF RESPONSE: Verbal

NAME OF INSTRUMENT: Children's Apperception Test (CAT)

AUTHOR(S): Bellak, L., and S. Bellak

PUBLISHER: Western Psychological Services
COPYRIGHT DATE: 1965
ADMINISTRATION: Individual
ADMINISTRATOR: Professional
AGE: 3 to 10 years
PURPOSE: Pictures of animals in one set and pictures of humans in another are designed to evoke the fantasies relating to the problems of feeding, other oral activity, sibling rivalry, parent-child relations, aggression, toilet-training, and other childhood experiences.
TESTING TIME: 45 to 60 minutes
TYPE OF RESPONSE: Verbal

NAME OF INSTRUMENT: Circus
AUTHOR(S):   Scarvia, A., and others
PUBLISHER: Addison-Wesley
COPYRIGHT DATE: 1974
ADMINISTRATION: Group
ADMINISTRATOR: Professional (teacher)
AGE: 4 to 6 years
PURPOSE: Fourteen subtests designed to measure the instructional needs of individual children so classroom activities can be planned to meet each child's needs.
TYPE OF RESPONSE: Nonverbal

NAME OF INSTRUMENT: Columbia Mental Maturity Scale
AUTHOR(S):   Burgemeister, B., L. H. Blum, and I. Lorge
PUBLISHER: Psychological Corporation
COPYRIGHT DATE: 1972
ADMINISTRATION: Individual
ADMINISTRATOR: Professional (diagnostician)
AGE: 3–6 to 10–0
PURPOSE: Test originally developed for use with cerebral-palsied and deaf children. A pictorial classification test which requires subject to identify the drawing that does not belong.
TESTING TIME: 18 minutes
TYPE OF RESPONSE: Nonverbal

NAME OF INSTRUMENT: Detroit Test of Learning Aptitude (DTLA)
AUTHOR(S):   Baker, H., and B. Leland

PUBLISHER: Bobbs-Merrill
COPYRIGHT DATE: 1967
ADMINISTRATION: Individual
ADMINISTRATOR: Professional
AGE: 4 years to adult
PURPOSE: This is an individual test of mental functioning. There are nineteen subtests measuring various elements of mental processing.
TESTING TIME: 45 to 60 minutes
TYPE OF RESPONSE: Verbal, nonverbal

NAME OF INSTRUMENT: Developmental Articulation Test
AUTHOR(S): Hejna, R.
PUBLISHER: Speech Materials
COPYRIGHT DATE: 1959
ADMINISTRATION: Individual
ADMINISTRATOR: Professional
AGE: 3 to 8 years
PURPOSE: An articulation test designed to assess consonant sounds on a developmental scale. It provides useful information for comparing a child's functioning with that of the norm.
TESTING TIME: 30 minutes
TYPE OF RESPONSE: Verbal

NAME OF INSTRUMENT: Development Test of Visual Perception (DTVP)
AUTHOR(S): Frostig, M.
PUBLISHER: Consulting Psychologists Press
COPYRIGHT DATE: 1966 (revised)
ADMINISTRATION: Individual or group
ADMINISTRATOR: Professional (diagnostician)
AGE: 3 to 8 years
PURPOSE: Test to evaluate perceptual skills of young children in five different areas: eye motor coordination, figure ground, constancy of shape, position in space, and spatial relationships.
TESTING TIME: 45 minutes
TYPE OF RESPONSE: Nonverbal

NAME OF INSTRUMENT: Goldman-Fristoe-Woodcock Auditory Skills Test Battery
AUTHOR(S): Goldman, R., M. Fristoe, and R. Woodcock

PUBLISHER: American Guidance Service

COPYRIGHT DATE: 1969

ADMINISTRATION: Individual

ADMINISTRATOR: Professional (teacher)

AGE: 3–8 to adults

PURPOSE: Test to evaluate child's ability to discriminate speech and sounds under both quiet and distracting noise conditions. Subtests include auditory selective attention test, diagnostic auditory discrimination test, auditory memory test, and sound-symbol test.

TESTING TIME: 60 minutes

TYPE OF RESPONSE: Verbal

NAME OF INSTRUMENT: Goodenough-Harris Drawing Test

AUTHOR(S): Goodenough, S. L., and D. B. Harris

PUBLISHER: Psychological Corporation

COPYRIGHT DATE: 1963

ADMINISTRATION: Individual or group

ADMINISTRATOR: Professional (diagnostician)

AGE: 3 to 15 years

PURPOSE: Group or individual test to assess cognitive and intellectual maturity through a person's drawing. Value of test is its use as part of a battery of tests. Subtests include draw-a-man, draw-a-woman, draw-yourself.

TESTING TIME: 13 minutes

TYPE OF RESPONSE: Nonverbal

NAME OF INSTRUMENT: Hiskey-Nebraska Test of Learning Aptitude

AUTHOR(S): Hiskey, M.

PUBLISHER: Marshall Hiskey

COPYRIGHT DATE: 1966

ADMINISTRATION: Individual

ADMINISTRATOR: Professional

AGE: 3 to 16 years

PURPOSE: Intelligence test developed to meet the demand of testing the deaf. This test was standardized on deaf and hard of hearing children. An attempt was made to sample a wide variety of internal functions. All items were chosen with special reference to limitations of deaf children. There are twelve subtests.

TESTING TIME: 30 to 45 minutes

TYPE OF RESPONSE: Nonverbal

NAME OF INSTRUMENT: Illinois Test of Psycholinguistic Abilities (ITPA)
AUTHOR(S):   Kirk, S., J. McCarthy, and W. Kirk
PUBLISHER: University of Illinois Press
COPYRIGHT DATE: 1971
ADMINISTRATION: Individual
ADMINISTRATOR: Professional
AGE: 2–6 to 10–0
PURPOSE: Test based on a three-dimensional model of communication, stressing skills in auditory, visual, and motor areas. The purpose is to see the strengths and weaknesses of individual children compared to themselves in the twelve subtests.
TESTING TIME: 50 to 60 minutes
TYPE OF RESPONSE: Verbal, nonverbal

NAME OF INSTRUMENT: Infant Intelligence Scale
AUTHOR(S):   Cattell, P.
PUBLISHER: Psychological Corporation
COPYRIGHT DATE: 1960 (Revised)
ADMINISTRATION: Individual
ADMINISTRATOR: Professional (diagnostician)
AGE: 3 mo. to 2–6
PURPOSE: Test is a downward extension of the revised Stanford-Binet Scale. It provides a mental age for children 3 to 30 months of age.
TESTING TIME: 30 minutes
TYPE OF RESPONSE: Verbal, nonverbal

NAME OF INSTRUMENT: Language and Learning Disorders of the Pre-academic Child
AUTHOR(S):   Bangs, T. E.
PUBLISHER: Western Psychological Services
COPYRIGHT DATE: 1968
ADMINISTRATION: Individual
ADMINISTRATOR: Professional (diagnostician)
AGE: 1 mo. to 6 years
PURPOSE: Battery designed to provide a diagnosis, help identify the etiology, present essential information for treatment and training, and demonstrate gains as measured by reassessment of child's language and cognitive development.
TESTING TIME: 75 minutes
TYPE OF RESPONSE: Verbal

NAME OF INSTRUMENT: Laradon Articulation Scale

AUTHOR(S): Edmonston, W.

PUBLISHER: Western Psychological Services

COPYRIGHT DATE: 1960–1963

ADMINISTRATION: Individual

ADMINISTRATOR: Professional

AGE: 1–0 to 8–6

PURPOSE: Picture articulation test which is based on a model phonemic system. Test yields an articulation age score, a raw score, an intelligibility index and three potential programmatic scores.

TESTING TIME: 30 minutes

TYPE OF RESPONSE: Verbal

NAME OF INSTRUMENT: Learning Accomplishment Profile Diagnostic Assessment Kit (LAP-D)

AUTHOR(S): Sanford, A., and others

PUBLISHER: Kaplan School Supply

COPYRIGHT DATE: 1975

ADMINISTRATION: Individual

ADMINISTRATOR: Professional (teacher)

AGE: 0 to 6 years

PURPOSE: Criterion-referenced diagnostic assessment in five areas of development.

TESTING TIME: 60 minutes

TYPE OF RESPONSE: Verbal, nonverbal, rater (parent)

NAME OF INSTRUMENT: Leiter International Performance Scale

AUTHOR(S): Leiter, R.

PUBLISHER: Stoetling Co.

COPYRIGHT DATE: 1948, 1980

ADMINISTRATION: Individual

ADMINISTRATOR: Professional

AGE: 2 to 18 years

PURPOSE: This test was a response in effort to construct tests applicable across cultures. A distinctive feature of the test is the almost complete absence of instructions, either spoken or pantomine. It was designed to cover a wide range of functions, which is appropriate for many handicaps and nonbiased assessment.

TESTING TIME: Untimed (about 45 minutes)

TYPE OF RESPONSE: Nonverbal (performance)

NAME OF INSTRUMENT: Lexington Developmental Scale (Short Form)

AUTHOR(S):   Child Development Centers of United Cerebral Palsy of the Bluegrass

PUBLISHER: United Cerebral Palsy of the Bluegrass

COPYRIGHT DATE: 1975

ADMINISTRATION: Individual

ADMINISTRATOR: Professional (teacher)
                 Nonprofessional (parent)

AGE: 11 mo. to 6 years

PURPOSE: Instrument used to assess children's development in the following areas: motor, language, cognitive, emotional, and personal-social development. Scale can be used to assess children, to plan curricula, to evaluate progress, and to help parents understand their child.

TESTING TIME: 30 minutes

TYPE OF RESPONSE: Verbal, nonverbal

NAME OF INSTRUMENT: A Manual for the Assessment of a "Deaf-Blind" Multiple Handicapped Child—Revised Edition

AUTHOR(S):   Collins, M. T., and J. M. Rudolph

PUBLISHER: Midwest Regional Resource Center for Services to Deaf/Blind Children

COPYRIGHT DATE: 1978

ADMINISTRATION: Individual

ADMINISTRATOR: Professional (teacher)

PURPOSE: Comprehensive checklist used to obtain information about a child's development in the following areas: self-help skills, social, gross motor, fine motor, communication, and cognition.

TESTING TIME: 25 minutes

TYPE OF RESPONSE: Rater

NAME OF INSTRUMENT: McCarthy Scales of Children's Abilities

AUTHOR(S):   McCarthy, D.

PUBLISHER: Psychological Corporation

COPYRIGHT DATE: 1972

ADMINISTRATION: Individual

ADMINISTRATOR: Professional

AGE: 2–6 to 8–6

PURPOSE: It consists of eighteen tests grouped into six overlapping scales. It was designed to assess preschoolers' functioning at the time of testing. It avoids the term IQ because of misleading connotations. Assesses strengths and weaknesses in important areas, using materials suitable for both sexes and various racial, ethnic, and socioeconomic groups.

TESTING TIME: 50–75 minutes

TYPE OF RESPONSE: Verbal, nonverbal

NAME OF INSTRUMENT: Memphis Comprehensive Developmental Scale

AUTHOR(S): Quick, A.

PUBLISHER: Fearson Publishers

COPYRIGHT DATE: 1973

ADMINISTRATION: Individual

ADMINISTRATOR: Professional (teacher, diagnostician)
Nonprofessional (parent)

AGE: 3 mo. to 5 years

PURPOSE: Scale includes evaluation of children's personal-social, gross motor, fine motor, language and perceptual-cognitive development. Test is divided into intervals of three months.

TYPE OF RESPONSE: Rater

NAME OF INSTRUMENT: Neonatal Behavioral Assessment

AUTHOR(S): Brazelton, T. B.

PUBLISHER: J. B. Lippincott

COPYRIGHT DATE: 1976

ADMINISTRATION: Individual

ADMINISTRATOR: Professional (usually medical)

AGE: Birth to 1 mo.

PURPOSE: Neonatal scale is a psychological scale for the newborn infant. It allows for the assessment of the infant's capabilities along the dimension of adjusting to the environment and gaining mastery of physiological equipment.

TESTING TIME: 20 to 30 minutes

TYPE OF RESPONSE: Nonverbal

NAME OF INSTRUMENT: Psychoeducational Evaluation of the Preschool Child

AUTHOR(S): Jedrysek, E., L. Pope, Z. Klapper, J. Wortis

PUBLISHER: Grune and Stratton

COPYRIGHT DATE: 1972

ADMINISTRATION: Individual

ADMINISTRATOR: Professional

AGE: 3–0 to 6–6

PURPOSE: Test designed to assess the child's present functioning and level of achievement in various areas and identify deficits. Curriculum guides are provided. Areas covered include physical functioning, short-term retention, sensory status, perceptual functioning, competence in learning, language competence, and cognitive functioning.

TESTING TIME: Indefinite

TYPE OF RESPONSE: Verbal, nonverbal

NAME OF INSTRUMENT: Stanford-Binet Intelligence Scale

AUTHOR(S): Terman, L.

PUBLISHER: Houghton-Mifflin

COPYRIGHT DATE: 1972 (Revised)

ADMINISTRATION: Individual

ADMINISTRATOR: Professional

AGE: 2 years to adult

PURPOSE: A singular test which assesses the various levels of functioning that go into the "g" factor of global intelligence.

TESTING TIME: 60 to 90 minutes

TYPE OF RESPONSE: Verbal, nonverbal

NAME OF INSTRUMENT: Templin-Darley Tests of Articulation (revision of original Templin-Darley Screening and Diagnostic Tests of Articulation)

AUTHOR(S): Templin, M. C., and F. L. Darley

PUBLISHER: University of Iowa

COPYRIGHT DATE: 1969

ADMINISTRATION: Individual

ADMINISTRATOR: Professional (diagnostician)

AGE: 3 to 8 years

PURPOSE: Test used to evaluate articulation proficiency and to identify articulation errors. The diagnostic test consists of nine overlapping subtests including the screening test which is used to indicate a child's general articulation adequacy.

TESTING TIME: 10 minutes (screening)
               30 minutes (diagnostic)

TYPE OF RESPONSE: Verbal

NAME OF INSTRUMENT: Test of Basic Experiences (TOBE)

AUTHOR(S): Moss, M. H.

PUBLISHER: CTB-McGraw-Hill

COPYRIGHT DATE: 1970, 1975

ADMINISTRATION: Group (six children in a group)

ADMINISTRATOR: Professional (teacher, diagnostician)

AGE: 3 to 7 years

PURPOSE: Test measures concepts and experiences that are required for a child's effective participation in the early years of school. Subtests include language, mathematics, science, social studies, and general concepts. A Spanish edition is available.

TESTING TIME: 25 minutes (per section)

TYPE OF RESPONSE: Nonverbal

NAME OF INSTRUMENT: Utah Test of Language Development

AUTHOR(S): Mecham, M. J., J. L. Jex, and J. D. Jones

PUBLISHER: Communication Research Associates

COPYRIGHT DATE: 1967

ADMINISTRATION: Individual

ADMINISTRATOR: Professional (diagnostician)

AGE: 9 mo. to 16 years

PURPOSE: Test designed to measure expressive and receptive language skills in children ages 9 months to 16 years.

TESTING TIME: 35 minutes

TYPE OF RESPONSE: Verbal, nonverbal

NAME OF INSTRUMENT: Uzgiris-Hunt Ordinal Scales of Psychological Development

AUTHOR(S): Uzgiris, I., and J. McV. Hunt

PUBLISHER: University of Illinois Press

COPYRIGHT DATE: 1966

ADMINISTRATION: Individual

ADMINISTRATOR: Professional

AGE: 2 weeks to 2 years

PURPOSE: This test covers the equivalent of Piaget's sensorimotor phase. It was developed to assess the functioning within the various different parts of that phase. Originally, it was developed to measure the effects of specific environmental conditions on rate and course of development of infants.

TESTING TIME: no time limit

TYPE OF RESPONSE: Verbal, nonverbal

NAME OF INSTRUMENT: Vineland Social Maturity Scale

AUTHOR(S): Doll, E. A.

PUBLISHER: American Guidance Service

COPYRIGHT DATE: 1965

ADMINISTRATION: Individual

ADMINISTRATOR: Professional (teacher, diagnostician)
Nonprofessional (parent)

AGE: 1 mo. to adult

PURPOSE: Test used to assess individual's level of social maturity, competence, and independence. Items are designed to elicit factual descriptions of the examinee's behavior in the following areas: self-help, self-direction, occupation, communication, locomotion, and socialization.

TESTING TIME: 25 minutes

TYPE OF RESPONSE: Rater

NAME OF INSTRUMENT: Wechsler Preschool and Primary Scale of Intelligence (WPPSI)

AUTHOR(S): Wechsler, D.

PUBLISHER: Psychological Corporation

COPYRIGHT DATE: 1974 (Revised)

ADMINISTRATION: Individual

ADMINISTRATOR: Professional

AGE: 4–0 to 6–6

PURPOSE: Single test which attempts to assess all global levels of functioning. It has both performance and verbal items, and from its results both a performance and a verbal IQ can be computed. Besides use as a measure of general intelligence, it has been used as an aid in psychiatric diagnosis.

TESTING TIME: 60 to 90 minutes

TYPE OF RESPONSE: Verbal, nonverbal

Suggested Materials for Early Childhood Special Education

Appendix **B**

Appendix B provides brief descriptions of teaching materials suitable for young children. They are classified as: I. Perceptual-Motor; II. Concepts; III. Communications; IV. Social-Affective; and V. Comprehensive (covers two or more developmental areas).

I. Perceptual-Motor

Chambers, Irene. *Let's Look for Program: Project Me,* 1972

VENDOR: Bowmar

PURPOSE: *Let's Look for Program: Project Me* assists individual children in the development of visual and linguistic skills in preparation for formal learning experiences and helps them to become aware of relationships to people and objects in the environment.

DESCRIPTION: Filmstrip pictures are projected on a floor-based screen from the rear of the room, creating a total environment into which children project themselves and with which they interact.

Cheves, Ruth. *Ruth Cheves Program I: Visual-Motor Perception,* 1969.

VENDOR: Teaching Resources

PURPOSE: This visual-motor perception program is designed to foster the development of basic patterns of learning and an understanding of the concepts of spatial organization, sequences, geometric shapes, and associations. The program can be used with children in preschool through second grade.

DESCRIPTION: Consisting of form puzzles, geometric shapes and associations, phonic puzzles and games, and quantity-number relationships, this program allows the teacher to assess visual-motor abilities and provides tasks to stimulate the learning process.

Developmental Learning Materials. *Big Box: Visual Perception.* 1974.

VENDOR: Developmental Learning Materials

PURPOSE: This unit is designed to help children develop visual learning in six basic areas: (1) color, shape, size; (2) visual closure; (3) visual memory; (4) visual discrimination; (5) visual motor (fine); and (6) visual language concepts. The unit is intended to be a resource box of exercises and activities and is not meant to represent an entire program.

DESCRIPTION: The *Big Box* is a storage box for activity cards and curriculum materials for four separate methods of instruction.

Dubnoff, Belle and Irene Chambers. *Dubnoff School Program I: Perceptual-Motor Exercises.* 1968.

VENDOR: Teaching Resources

PURPOSE: The purpose of this program is to help children who have perceptual disabilities develop the skills necessary for reading and writing.

DESCRIPTION: This program consists of three levels of perceptual-motor exercises dealing with perceptual skills and prewriting abilities.

Fairbanks, Jean H. and Janet Robinson. *Fairbanks-Robinson Program.* Level I, 1969. Level II, 1968.

VENDOR: Teaching Resources

PURPOSE: This program is designed to help children develop skills in the following areas: form and size orientation; figure-ground discrimination; part-whole organization; left to right progression; sequencing; direction following; visual-spatial judgment; visual-motor integration; tactile discrimination; and manipulation and dexterity.

DESCRIPTION: Divided into two levels, this program is designed for use with no more than two students and includes activities such as tracing, coloring, copying, cutting, pattern copying, dot-to-dot designs, and puzzles.

Frostig; Marianne and Phyllis Maslow. *Frostig Move-Grow-Learn Program.* 1969.

VENDOR: Follett Publishing Company

PURPOSE: The *Move-Grow-Learn* Program (MGL) is a movement education program which is intended to enhance the total development of preschool and primary school children. In addition to promoting good health, a sense of physical well-being, and the development of sensory motor skills, MGL helps children develop self-awareness, the awareness of time and space, the ability to communicate, the ability to interact with others, the ability to perceive self in relation to the environment, the ability to solve problems, and the ability to learn.

DESCRIPTION: MGL are printed on 181 color-coded 4 × 6 cards; includes a 64-page *Teacher's Guide*; and includes activities in body awareness, coordination, agility, strength, flexibility, and balance.

Karnes, Merle and others. *Early Childhood Enrichment Series: Toys to Develop Perceptual Skills.* 1970.

VENDOR: Milton Bradley

PURPOSE: The curriculum materials in this unit are designed to help children, either individually or in small groups, develop skills in discrimination and perception.

DESCRIPTION: This program includes seven sets of materials and an instructor's guide which contains sixty lessons for using the materials.

II. Concepts

Hodgins, Audrey and Merle Karnes. *Early Childhood Enrichment Series: Development of Number Readiness,* 1970.

VENDOR: Milton Bradley

PURPOSE: The materials in this kit are designed to be included in small-group learning centers where preschool and kindergarten children practice and expand their number readiness skills.

DESCRIPTION: This kit includes a series of manipulative materials in four areas: matching-grouping; discerning-reproducing; one-to-one correspondence-grouping; and expressing number groups with manipulative materials.

Karnes, Merle, *Goal: Mathematical Concepts.* 1973.

VENDOR: Milton Bradley

PURPOSE: This program is designed to provide opportunities for children in small groups to develop initial mathematical concepts.

DESCRIPTION: This is a sequential program of 137 lessons in seven areas: geometric shapes; sets and one-to-one correspondence; whole numbers and rational counting; numerals; addition-subtraction; measurement; and patterning-progression.

Lavatelli, Celia S. *Early Childhood Curriculum: A Piaget Program.* 1973.

VENDOR: American Science and Engineering

PURPOSE: The *Early Childhood Curriculum* (ECC) is designed and organized to foster the development of mental operations and associated language in the areas of classification; number, measurement, and space; and seriation. The program is designed to lay a foundation for the emergence of concrete operations and move the child from Piaget's preoperational stage into the Piagetian stage of concrete operations.

DESCRIPTION: The core of this program is a short training system conducted by the teacher with three or four students several times a week during which they work with concrete materials to solve problems and develop language.

Resnick, Lauren, Renee Feingold, and Sally Litwak. *The Early Learning System.* 1971.

VENDOR: Educational Developmental Laboratories

PURPOSE: *The Early Learning System* (ELS) is designed to individualize teaching of basic skills and concepts; to help each child become more responsible; to diagnose, instruct, test, and reteach; and to involve the teacher, child, and parent in the learning process.

DESCRIPTION: This system focuses on 194 basic skills and concepts which are stated in 51 objectives and subdivided into seven units, each of which includes several lessons with a sequence of clearly stated objectives.

Springle, Herbert. *Inquisitive Games: Discovering How to Learn.* 1969.

VENDOR: Science Research Associates

PURPOSE: This program is designed to help children develop skills in classifying, analyzing, generalizing, and problem solving.

DESCRIPTION: The program is organized around a combination of small-group activities and games for up to four students which provide strategies for gathering, organizing, and processing information.

Springle, Herbert. *Inquisitive Games: Exploring Number and Space.* 1967.

VENDOR: Science Research Associates

PURPOSE: This program was designed to complement an existing math curriculum or to be used with informal mathematics teaching.

DESCRIPTION: This is a set of math-oriented games and activities for young children to enhance their understanding of basic mathematical concepts.

III. Communication

Dunn, Lloyd, James O. Smith, and Kathryn Horton. *Peabody Language Development Program: Level P.* 1968.

VENDOR: American Guidance Service

PURPOSE: This program is designed to help children develop skills in perception, conceptualization, and expansion of language through an activity approach. *Level P* uses a large number of materials and makes extensive use of the tactile and visual modes of stimulation. The program begins with "labeling language," then moves to an emphasis on the syntactical and grammatical structure of language, and finally to the stimulation of logical thinking. *Level P* can be used with disadvantaged kindergarten children, school-age trainable retardates, lower primary educable mentally retarded children, and normal three- and four-year-old prekindergarten children.

DESCRIPTION: The 180 daily lesson plans contained in this program make use of story posters, puppets, mannequins, plastic color chips, and cards.

Englemann, Siegfried, Jean Osborn, and Therese Englemann. *Distar Language I.* 1967.

VENDOR: Science Research Associates

PURPOSE: This program is designed to teach children the language of instruction by teaching basic language concepts. It is intended to be used with small groups of children.

DESCRIPTION: This system utilizes a structured approach to developing language skills to ensure that the child is able both to understand and to use the language concepts taught.

Karnes, Merle. *Game Oriented Activities for Learning (GOAL)—Language Development.* 1972.

VENDOR: Milton Bradley

PURPOSE: The program is designed for small groups (5–8), and the target population is primarily those learning disabled in language or older retarded children. The activities center on the five processes defined in the ITPA: reception, association, expression, memory, and closure.

DESCRIPTION: There are 337 lesson plan cards, divided into eleven language and processing areas (all the ITPA subtests except sound blending), each of which is linked to different games and materials provided in the kit.

Karnes, Merle. *Learning Language at Home.* 1977.

VENDOR: Council for Exceptional Children

PURPOSE: This kit includes two carefully sequenced programs to foster a well-developed language system. The program extends itself into the home by involving parents in varied learning activities.

DESCRIPTION: Utilizing materials readily available in the classroom or home, this system includes two programs, each of which contains 200 lessons sequenced according to difficulty in four areas of development: motor, auditory, visual, and verbal.

Minskoff, Esther, Douglas Wiseman, and Gerald Minskoff. *The MWM Program for Developing Language Abilities.* 1972.

VENDOR: Childcraft Education Corporation

PURPOSE: The MWM is based upon the ITPA. This is both a developmental and remedial program. The primary purpose is to screen and remediate language disabilities. A secondary purpose is developmental—when so used the program is organized around three language clusters: verbal, visual-motor, and readiness.

DESCRIPTION: Closely linked with the ITPA, the MWM provides separate manuals for different linguistic processes (reception, association, expression, memory, and closure); each area is subdivided, and several tasks or lessons are given for each subarea.

Spruegel, Catherine, Iva Nance, and Merle Karnes. *Early Childhood Enrichment Series: Learning to Develop Language Skills.* 1970.

VENDOR: Milton Bradley

PURPOSE: This unit, which emphasizes labeling skills, associative quantities, and categories, provides enrichment activities to help children develop language skills and improve their verbal expression. Attention is also focused on divergent as well as convergent responses, and special emphasis is given to the development of sequential, associative, and expressive language skills.

DESCRIPTION: This program contains twelve different components relating to the development of language skills.

IV. Social-Affective

Developmental Learning Materials. *Big Box: Body and Self-Awareness.* 1974.

VENDOR: Developmental Learning Materials

PURPOSE: The *Big Box* is designed to help the young child develop an awareness of his or her own body, discover how it relates to other living things that are encountered daily.

DESCRIPTION: *Big Box* includes a file box of approximately 180 activity cards broken into two categories: body awareness and self-awareness.

Linford, M., L. Hipster, and R. Silikovitz. *Self-Help Instruction.* Part III of Systematic Instruction for Retarded Children: The Illinois Program. 1972.

VENDOR: Interstate Printers and Publishers

PURPOSE: This material is designed to be used by teachers working with preschool children, especially those who show developmental delays.

DESCRIPTION: This curriculum consists of four sections: dressing, eating, toilet training, and grooming. The principles of behavioral analysis and management, task analysis, and errorless learning are used to teach the child to independently perform a variety of self-help skills.

V. Comprehensive (covers two or more developmental areas)

Bank Street College of Education. *Early Childhood Discovery Materials.* 1973.

VENDOR: Macmillan Company

PURPOSE: *Early Childhood Discovery Materials* were developed by the Bank Street College of Education in New York to encourage the development of the child's language skills, conceptual skills, perceptual skills, and motor skills. To achieve these goals, the materials were designed to help the child reach out to other people, express thoughts so that others can understand, develop cognitive processes, understand what others are saying, solve simple problems, and feel success and pride in emotional and intellectual growth.

DESCRIPTION: Materials in this program are divided into two groups which are based on specific themes and are designed to extend and reinforce specific skills.

Cemrel, Inc. *Language and Thinking Program.* 1973.

VENDOR: Macmillan Company

PURPOSE: The *Language and Thinking Program* is designed to help children, from three to seven years of age, develop language and cognitive skills. It emphasizes visual and auditory discrimination, vocabulary, and basic reasoning skills.

DESCRIPTION: This program consists of ten packages of multimedia material including cassettes, transparencies, picture cards, games, and manipulatives.

Dunn, Lloyd, Lillie Chun, Doris Crowell, Leota Dunn, Lynn Alevy, Elanor Yackel. *Peabody Early Experience Kit.*

VENDOR: American Guidance Service

PURPOSE: The *Peabody Early Experience Kit* is designed to enhance children's affective, cognitive, and linguistic abilities. The major emphasis is on the developmental, not the remedial, level. The program utilizes pictures, puppets, and a series of lessons sequenced in difficulty.

DESCRIPTION: Materials are organized in four distinct task areas for affective, cognitive, and linguistic development. There are 1000 activities.

Manolakes, George, Robert Weltman, Marie Jepson Scian, and Louis Waldo. *Try: Experiences for Young Children.* 1967.

VENDOR: Nobel and Nobel

PURPOSE: This program fosters the development of visual-motor skills and provides opportunities for oral language expression, individualized activities, and an organized sequence of learning experiences. It also involves active participation by the learner.

DESCRIPTION: The activities in this program are organized into tasks at three levels of difficulty—each task includes an *Activity Book* providing visual perception experiences and extended activities.

Nimnicht, Glen and Edna Brown. *The Toy Lending Library.* 1972.

VENDOR: Silver Burdett

PURPOSE: *The Toy Lending Library* is designed to develop a bond between parent and child culminating in a better self-image and increased confidence on the part of the child. The program, which is designed to prepare children for school, utilizes toys to foster the child's development of language-perception skills, healthy self-concepts, concept formation, and problem-solving ability.

DESCRIPTION: After attending an eight-week course to learn how to use the toys, parents are able to work with their children and enhance their development.

Rowland, Pleasant. *Beginning Readiness.* 1974.

VENDOR: J. B. Lippincott

PURPOSE: *Beginning Readiness* is a program for children who need more experience with basic readiness skills, have a short attention span, have difficulty following directions, and have difficulty expressing themselves.

DESCRIPTION: In this program skills and concepts are introduced, developed, and reinforced through the teacher's use of multimedia materials.

Model Programs
for Early Childhood
Special Education

Appendix **C**

The programs listed in Appendix C are model early childhood special education programs arranged in alphabetical order by states.

ALABAMA

Rural Infant Stimulation Environment
University of Alabama
P.O. Box 2592
University, AL 35486

ARIZONA

Outreach Program
University of Arizona
College of Education
Second and Vine Street
Tucson, AZ 85721

CALIFORNIA

Children's Service Center
Casa Colina Hospital
255 E. Bonita Avenue
Pomona, CA 91767

Early Childhood Institute
University of California at Los Angeles
Graduate School of Education
Moore Hall
Los Angeles, CA 90024

Early On Program
Department of Special Education
San Diego State University
San Diego, CA 92182

Reverse Mainstream
Outreach-Salvin School
1925 Budlong Avenue
Los Angeles, CA 90007

COLORADO

SEED Program
Sewall Rehabilitation Center
1360 Vine Street
Denver, CO 80206

University of Colorado
Department of Communication Disorders and Speech Science
934 Broadway
Boulder, CO 80309

DISTRICT OF COLUMBIA

Home Start
A home-based child development program
Office of Child Development
Office of Human Development
Department of Education
P.O. Box 1182
Washington, D.C. 20013

GEORGIA

Rutland Center
National Technical Assistance Office
698 N. Pope Street
Athens, GA 30601

ILLINOIS

Children's
Development Center
650 North Main
Rockford, IL 61103

United Cerebral Palsy
Northwestern Illinois and Peoria
  Association for Retarded
  Children
913 N. Western Avenue
Peoria, IL 61603

University of Illinois
403 East Healey
Champaign, IL 61820

Western Illinois
University
27 Horrabin Hall
Macomb, IL 61455

INDIANA

Institute for Child
Study
Indiana University
10th and Bypass 46
Bloomington, IN 47401

Preschool Outreach
Program
Ball State University
305 North McKinley Avenue
Muncie, IN 47306

KANSAS

Kansas Research
Institute for the Early
Childhood Education
of the Handicapped
University of Kansas
Summerfield Annex A
Lawrence, KS 66045

LOUISIANA

Early Childhood
Program Center
Arlington Street
Ruston, LA 71270

MAINE

Project Maine Stream
Outreach
P.O. Box 25
Cumberland Center, ME 04021

MARYLAND

Baltimore Public
Schools
Division for Exceptional
  Children
Education Annex 510
Calvert and 23rd Streets
Baltimore, MD 21218

MASSACHUSETTS

ERIN Inc. (Early
Recognition
Intervention Network)
376 Bridge Street
Dedham, MA 02026

LINC Outreach
Tufts University
28 Sawyer Avenue
Medford, MA 02155

Project Optimus
Outreach
Southshore Mental Health
  Center
77 Parkingway
Quincy, MA 02169

MICHIGAN

Alpena-Montmorency
Alcona Intermediate
School District
1691 M–32 West
Alpena, MI 49707

High Scope
Educational Research
Foundation
600 N. River Street
Ypsilanti, MI 48197

Project PAR—A
Program for Young
Children with
Learning Disabilities
Saginaw County Child
    Development Centers, Inc.
Kresge Child Development
    Training Center
1921 Annesley Street
Saginaw, MI 48605

MINNESOTA

St. Paul Public School
#625
1930 Como Avenue
St. Paul, MN 55108

MISSISSIPPI

Project Run
North Mississippi Retardation
    Center
P.O. Box 967
Oxford, MS 38655

MISSOURI

Parent-Infant
Program
Central Institute for the Deaf
818 South Euclid
St. Louis, MO 63110

Saturday School: A
School-Home
Learning Program for
Four Year Olds
Parent-Child Early Education
    Program
Ferguson-Florissant School
    District
655 January Avenue
Ferguson, MO 63135

NEW JERSEY

Institute for Study of
Exceptional Children
Educational Testing Service
Princeton, NJ 08541

NORTH CAROLINA

Access to Mainstream
Outreach Training
Project
P.O. Box 160
Powellsville, NC 27967

Chapel Hill Outreach
Project
Lincoln Center
Chapel Hill-Carrboro Schools
Chapel Hill, NC 27514

Frank Porter Graham
Child Development
Center
Highway 54 Bypass West 071–A
University of North Carolina at
    Chapel Hill
Chapel Hill, NC 27514

Technical Assistance
Development Systems
NCNB Plaza, Suite 500
Chapel Hill, NC 27514

NORTH DAKOTA

PACT—Parents and
Children Together
Southeast Mental Health and
    Retardation Center
700 First Avenue South
Fargo, ND 58102

STP - Stimulating to
Potential (Parents
and Children Working
Together)
Southeast Mental Health and
    Retardation Center
700 First Avenue South
Fargo, ND 58102

OHIO

First Chance Project
Outreach
252 Lowry Hall
Kent State University
Kent, OH 44242

OREGON

Beaverton School District 48
P.O. Box 200
Beaverton, OR 97005

Child Neurology Clinic
Good Samaritan Hospital and
   Medical Center
2222 N.W. Lovejory, Suite 361
Portland, OR 97210

Training Research Infant and Child Center
Todd Hall
Monmouth, OR 97361

PENNSYLVANIA

HICOMP Outreach Project
304 Cedar
University Park, PA 16802

Family Centered Resource Project
Berks County Intermediate Unit
   #14
2900 St. Lawrence Avenue
Reading, PA 19606

RHODE ISLAND

Educational Technology Center, Inc.
Box 64
Foster, RI 02825

TENNESSEE

Clinch-Powell Educational Cooperative
P.O. Box 279
Tazewell, TN 37879

PEACH - Program for Early Attention to Children with Handicaps
Division of Special Education
Department of Instruction
Memphis City Schools
2597 Avery Avenue
Memphis, TN 38112

The RIP Expansion Project
2400 White Avenue
Nashville, TN 37204

Urban Observatory
1101 17th Avenue South
Nashville, TN 37212

TEXAS

Dallas Independent School District
3700 Ross Avenue
Dallas, TX 75209

Lubbock Independent School District
1628 19th Street, C.O. Annex
Lubbock, TX 79401

UTAH

Utah State University
Exceptional Child Center
UMC 68
Logan, UT 84322

VIRGINIA

Child Study Center
Old Dominion University
Hampton Boulevard
Norfolk, VA 23508

Education for Multihandicapped Infants
University of Virginia Medical
   Center
P.O. Box 232
Charlottesville, VA 22908

Williamsburg Area
Child Resource Inc.
P.O. Box 299
Lightfood, VA 23090

WASHINGTON

Model Preschool
Center for
Handicapped
Children
Experimental Education Unit
WJ–10
Child Development & Mental
Retardation Center
University of Washington
Seattle, WA 98195

Western States
Technical Assistance
Resource (WESTAR)
University District Building.
JD–06
1107 N.E. 45th Street, Suite 215
Seattle, WA 98105

WISCONSIN

Curative Workshop of
Milwaukee
Demmer-Kiwanis Children's
Division
9001 W. Watertown Plank Road
Milwaukee, WI 53226

The Portage Project
412 E. Slifer Street
P.O. Box 564
Portage, WI 53901

Publishers of Early Childhood Special Education Tests and Materials

Appendix **D**

ABC School Equipment Company
437 Armour Circle Northeast
Atlanta, GA 30324

Academic Therapy Publications
1539 Fourth Street
San Rafael, CA 94901

Achievement Products, Inc.
P.O. Box 547
Mineola, NY 11501

Adapt Press, Inc.
808 West Avenue North
Sioux Falls, SD 27104

Adaptive Therapeutic Systems, Inc.
162 Ridge Road
Madison, CT 06443

Addison-Wesley Testing Service
South Street
Reading, MA 01867

Allied Education Council
P.O. Box 78
Galien, MI 49113

American Association on Mental Deficiency
5201 Connecticut Avenue Northwest
Washington, DC 20015

American Guidance Service
Publishers Building
Circle Pines, MN 55014

American Orthopsychiatric Association
49 Sheridan Avenue
Albany, NY 12210

American Science and Engineering, Inc.
20 Overland Street
Boston, MA 02215

American Speech and Hearing Assoc. (ASHA)
9030 Old Georgetown Rd Northwest
Washington, DC 20014

Ann Arbor Publishers
P.O. Box 1446
Ann Arbor, MI 48104

Behavior Science Systems, Inc.
P.O. Box 1108
Minneapolis, MN 55440

Bell & Howell, A-V Products Division
7100 McCormick Road
Chicago, IL 60645

BFA Education Media
Division of C.B.S.
2211 Michigan Avenue
Santa Monica, CA 90404

Bobbs-Merrill Company, Inc.
4300 West 62nd Street
Indianapolis, IN 46268

Bowmar
622 Rodier Drive
Glendale, CA 91201

Charles E. Merrill Publishing Company
1300 Alum Creek Drive
Columbus, OH 43216

Childcraft Education Corporation
20 Kilmer Road
Edison, NJ 08817

Cleo Learning Aids
3957 Mayfield Road
Cleveland, OH 44121

Cole Supply
103 East Bird Street
Pasedena, TX 77501

Communication Research Associates, Inc.
P.O. Box 11012
Salt Lake City, UT 84111

Communication Skill Builders, Inc.
817 E. Broadway
Tucson, AZ 85733

Community Playthings
Rifton, NY 12471

Consulting Psychologists Press, Inc.
577 College Avenue
Palo Alto, CA 94306

Council For Exceptional Children
Publication Sales
1920 Association Drive
Reston, VA 22091

Creative Playthings, Inc.
Princeton, NJ 08540

CTB-McGraw Hill
Del Norte Research Park
Monterey, CA 93940

Cuisenaire Company of America
12 Church Street
New Rochelle, NY 10905

Curriculum Associates, Inc.
5 Esquire Road
North Billerica, MA 01862

Delacorte Press
1 Dag Hammerskjold Plaza
245 E. 47th Street
New York, NY 10017

Developmental Learning Materials
7440 Natches Avenue
Niles, IL 60648

Dexter and Westbrook, Ltd.
11 South Center Avenue
Rockville Center, NY 11571

Didax
P.O. Box 2258
Peabody, MA 01960

Division of Continuing Education
Western Michigan University
Kalamazoo, MI 49008

Early Recognition Intervention System
P.O. Box 1635
Pawtucket, RI 02862

Edmark Associates
13241 Northrup Way
Bellevue, WA 98005

Educational Activities, Inc.
P.O. Box 392
Freeport, NY 11520

Educational Development Laboratories
McGraw-Hill Book Company
1221 Avenue of the Americas
New York, NY 10020

Educational Teaching Aids
159 W. Kinzie Street
Chicago, IL 60610

Eliot-Pearson
Department of Child Study
Tufts University
105 College Avenue
Medford, MA 02155

Fearon Publishers, Inc.
2165 Park Boulevard
Palo Alto, CA 94306

Filmstrip House, Inc.
432 Park Avenue South
New York, NY 10016

Follett Publishing Company
1010 West Washington Boulevard
Chicago, IL 60607

Fred Sammons, Inc.
Box 32
Brookfield, IL 60513

Functional Aids for the Multiply
    Handicapped
United Cerebral Palsy Association, Inc.
66 East 34th Street
New York, NY 10016

General Electric Company
Education Support Project
P.O. Box 43
Schnectady, NY 12301

General Learning Corporation
250 James Street
Morristown, NJ 07960

Grune & Stratton
111 Fifth Avenue
New York, NY 10003

Holt, Rinehart & Winston
School Department, Box 3323
Grand Central Station
New York, NY 10017

Houghton-Mifflin Company
1 Beacon Street
Boston, MA 02107

Ideal School Supply Company
11000 South Laverne Avenue
Oak Lawn, IL 60453

Information Resources
Stanford University
Stanford, CA 94035

Instructo Corporation
North Cedar Hollow Road
Paoli, PA 19301

Instructor Publications, Inc.
Dansville, NY 14437

Interstate Printers & Publishers
19–27 North Jackson Street
Danville, IL 61832

J. A. Preston Corporation
71 Fifth Avenue
New York, NY 10003

J. B. Lippincott Company
Educational Publishing Division
East Washington Square
Philadelphia, PA 19105

Kaplan School Supply Corporation
600 Jamestown Road
Winston-Salem, NC 27103

LADOCA Project & Publishing Foun.,
    Inc.
East 51st Avenue and Lincoln Street
Denver, CO 80216

Language Research Associates, Inc.
175 East Delaware Place
Chicago, IL 60611

Learn-X Corporation
1600–2400 Eighth Avenue
Lake City, MN 55041

Macmillan Company
Front and Brown Street
Riverside, NJ 08075

Mafax Association, Inc.
90 Cherry Street
Box 519
Johnstown, PA 15902

Markham Distributors, Inc.
507 Fifth Avenue
New York, NY 10017

McGraw-Hill, Webster Division
Manchester Road
Manchester, MO 63011

Marshall S. Hiskey
5640 Baldwin
Lincoln, NB 68507

Media Projects, Inc.
201 East 16th Street
New York, NY 10003

Midwest Regional Resource Center for
  Services to Deaf-Blind Children
P.O. Box 420
Lansing, MI 48902

Milton Bradley Company
443 Shaker Road
East Long Meadow, MA 01028

Modern Education Corporation
P.O. Box 721
Tulsa, OK 74101

Nasco
901 Janesville Avenue
Fort Atkinson, WI 53538

National Educational Laboratory
Publishers, Inc.
P.O. Box 1003
Austin, TX 78767

National Institute of Mental Health
5600 Fishers Lane
Rockville, MD 20857

New American Library
Educational Division
120 Woodbine Street
Bergenfield, NJ 07621

New Century, School Department
440 Park Avenue South
New York, NY 10016

Nobel & Nobel Publishers, Inc.
1 Dag Hammerskjold Plaza
New York, NY 10017

Northwestern University Press
1735 Benson Avenue
Evanston, IL 60201

Open Court Publishing Company
Box 599
LaSalle, IL 61301

Opportunities for Learning
5024 Landershim Boulevard
Dept. B7
North Hollywood, CA 91601

Playworld Systems
P.O. Box 227
New Berlin, PA 17855

Prentice-Hall International, Inc.
Englewood Cliffs, NJ 07632

Pro-ed
333 Perry Brooks Building
Austin. TX 78701

Psychological Corporation
304 East 45th Street
New York, NY 10017

Psychological Development Publica-
  tions
P.O. Box 3198
Aspen, CO 81611

Psychometric Affiliates
P.O. Box 3167
Munster, IN 46321

Research Concepts
1368 East Airport Road
Muskegon, MI 49444

Research Press
2612 North Mattis Avenue
Champaign, IL 61820

Scholastic Testing Services, Inc.
480 Meyer Road
Bensenville, IL 60106

Science Research Associates, Inc.
259 East Erie Street
Chicago, IL 60611

Silver Burdett Company
250 James Street
Morristown, NJ 07960

Simon & Schuster
Rockefeller Center
630 Fifth Avenue
New York, NY 10020

Speech Materials
P.O. Box 1713
Ann Arbor, MI 48106

St. Martin's Press
175 Fifth Avenue
New York, NY 10010

Stoetling Company
1350 South Kostner Avenue
Chicago, IL 60623

Teaching Resources Corporation
100 Boylston Street
Boston, MA 02116

Technical Assistance Development Systems (TADS)
803 Churchill
Chapel Hill, NC 27514

Toy Tinkers
A. G. Spaulding & Brothers
807 Greenwood Street
Evanston, IL 60201

Tree of Life Press
1329 Northeast Second Street
P.O. Box 447
Gainesville, FL 32601

Trend Enterprises, Inc.
Box 3073
St. Paul, MN 55165

United Cerebral Palsy of the Bluegrass, Inc.
P.O. Box 8003
465 Springhill Drive
Lexington, KY 40503

University of Illinois Press
Urbana, IL 61801

University of Iowa
Bureau of Educational Research & Service
Extension Division
C–20 East Hall
Iowa City, IA 52242

University of Washington Press
Seattle, WA 98105

University Park Press
Chamber of Commerce Building
Baltimore, MD 21202

Vort Corporation
P.O. Box 11133
Palo Alto, CA 84338

Western Psychological Services
12031 Wilshire Boulevard
Los Angeles, CA 90025

Glossary

ABBERATION: Any mental or physical disorder that causes a deviation.

ACCELERATION: Process by which a child with excellent ability can complete the work of school grades at a rate of more than one grade per year.

ACUITY: How well one is able to hear sounds and see visual images.

ADVOCACY FORCE OR ADVOCATE: To plead for or defend; in special education one who represents and upholds the child's interests in lieu of parents or guardians.

AFFECTIVE: Having to do with or relating to emotions and intrinsic feelings.

ATYPICAL: A trait that is in some way marked by a difference from others of a specific type, class, or category.

AUDIOLOGIST: A trained professional who measures hearing acuity, diagnoses hearing losses, and assists in fitting hearing aids.

AMELIORATION: The process of lessening pain or improving deficiencies.

AMPLIFICATION: The process of strengthening or enhancing sounds.

BASELINE: Period in applied behavioral analysis when data is collected and charted before implementing the intervention strategies.

BILATERAL: Pertains to both sides of the body.

BIOCHEMICAL TREATMENT: Intervention by groups of drugs such as amphetamines which have a stimulant effect on the central nervous system or barbiturates which depress the central nervous system.

CLEFT PALATE: A congenital fissure of the roof of the mouth.

CONGENITAL DEFECT: A deformity present at birth.

CORRELATION: The relationship between factors.

CUTANEUS: Of, relating to, or affecting the skin.

DEVIATION: (see atypical)

DIDACTIC MATERIALS: Educational tools designed specifically for the purpose of teaching a skill or group of skills.

DIFFERENTIAL DIAGNOSIS: The distinguishing of a disease or condition from others with similar symptoms.

ENDOCRINOLOGIST: A physician who specializes in the hormonal (glandular) system.

FUNCTIONAL BEHAVIORS: Behaviors already mastered by the individual or those necessary for survival in society.

INCIDENCE: Range of occurrence or influence of a condition or disease.

INTEGRATION: The process of teaching handicapped and nonhandicapped children in the same setting.

INTERVENTION: To apply external influences to modify the status quo; in applied behavioral analysis this refers to the systematic application of cues, prompts, reinforcers, and so on to alter behavior.

LOW BIRTH WEIGHT: Infant weighing less than five pounds, 2 ounces (2500 grams) at birth.

MODALITY: The pathways through which an individual receives information and thereby learns. The "modality concept" postulates that some individuals learn better through one modality than another; a child may be classified as a visual or an auditory learner.

NEUROLOGIST: A physician whose area is neurological problems, or problems of the central nervous system, such as epilepsy and cerebral palsy.

ORTHOPEDIC SPECIALIST: A physician concerned with the growth, repair, and care of muscles, tendons, joints, and bones.

OTOLOGIST: A physician who specializes in diagnosis and treatment of ear problems.

PARAPROFESSIONAL: A trained aide who assists a professional person; for example, a teacher's aide.

PINCER GRASP: Coordination of thumb and index finger.

PREVALENCE: The percentage of the population at large that is effected by a disease or handicap at a given time.

PROGNOSIS: A forecast of the probable course or outcome of a particular disease, illness, or condition.

PROSTHETIC INTERVENTION: The addition of an artificial part (arm, leg) to the human body or the addition of a supporting device which enables the body part to function more efficiently.

REBUS SYMBOLS: Representations of words or syllables which take the form of pictures of objects or symbols whose names resemble the intended words or syllables in sound.

RELIABILITY: The dependability of an individual item; in diagnosis the term refers to the consistency of results of a given test instrument.

RESIDUAL HEARING: Auditory ability of an individual after injury or impairment without amplification; usually only strong enough to distinguish sounds of high intensity.

RIGIDITY: Maintaining an attitude when such a set is no longer appropriate.

ROSEOLA: Children's disease commonly called "German Measles."

SEIZURE: An internal physical attack which results in mild, moderate, or severe physical dysfunctioning.

SPEECH PATHOLOGIST: A professional who is trained and certified to evaluate, diagnose, and treat speech and language problems.

STANDARD DEVIATION: A measure of dispersion of a frequency distribution which reveals the relationship of a given score to the mean.

STANDARDIZATION: The process of generalization; in educational measurement, this refers to the norming procedure whereby through testing a sample population, general evaluative criteria are established.

STEREOGNOSIS: Tactile discrimination; the ability to discern an object's physical traits through handling.

STEREOTYPIC BEHAVIOR: Repetitive, prolonged, and uncommon behavior associated especially with severely retarded or emotionally disturbed individuals.

STUTTERING: To speak with involuntary disruption or blocking of speech.

TARGET BEHAVIORS: Individual's actions which are selected for modification in an applied behavioral analysis and upon which the intervention focuses.

TRAUMA: A disordered psychic or behavioral state resulting from mental or emotional stress or physical injury.

VALIDITY: The degree to which something is appropriate to the end in view; when used in diagnosis, it refers to the extent with which a test or instrument measures what it is purported to measure.

Author Index

Wilt, M., 196
Wing, L., 188
Winkler, P., 65
Wolfensberger, W., 98
Wolff, P. H., 129
Wood, F., 97
Wooden, H., 32

Yarrow, L., 208
Ysseldyke, J., 99

Zausmer, E., 40
Zehrbach, R., 64, 66
Zeitlin, S., 71, 84, 85, 89, 90
Zigler, E., 250

Subject Index

Accommodation, 128, 160–61
Adaptive behavior, deficits in, 36
Adaptive supports, 145–46
Affective domain, 207. *See also* Emotional
 disorders; Social and affective
 problems; Social and affective skills
Aggressive, acting out behavior, 51
Amniocentesis, 44
Amniography, 44
Apgar Rating, 61
Aphasia, 190
Arizona Articulation Proficiency Scale, 81,
 320
Articulation, 184–85
 errors, 46, 194
Assessment, 61–100
 criterion-referenced, 78, 121
 norm-referenced, 78, 121
 overview, 61–63
 See also Diagnostic process; Locating
 process; Screening process
Assimilation, 128, 160–61
Asthma, 44
Ataxia, 41
Athetosis, 41
Attentional deficit disorders, 49
Atypical motor development, 135–37
 deficits in muscle control, 137
 deficits in muscle strength, 137
 deficits in muscle tone, 136–37
 kinds, 136
 motor deviations, 136–37
Auditory impairment, 32–36
 early identification, 34–35
 impact on the young child, 35–36
 measurement of severity, 33–34

screening, 34–35, 79–80
 symptoms, 34
 types, 32–33
Auditory perception, 184
Autism, 49, 191, 212
 autistic-like behavior, 51
 infantile, 51
Autonomy, 213
Ayres Southern California battery, 94,
 318

Babbling, 180, 185
Bayley Scales of Infant Development, 94,
 320
Behavioral disorders. *See* Emotional
 disorders
Behavioral model of assessment, 89
Behavior modification, 215–17
 baseline, 217
 modeling, 194, 216
 recording and monitoring behavior,
 216–17
 reinforcement, 162, 194, 215–16
 shaping behavior, 216
Bender-Gestalt Test, 320–21
 Koppitz scoring, 79
Birth defects, 39–45
Blindisms, 32
Blindness, definition, 28
Boehm Test of Basic Concepts, 81, 304
Braille, 28
Brain-injured, 47. *See also* Specific
 learning disabilities
Brazelton Neonatal Scale, 61, 328
Bruinicks-Oseretsky Test of Motor
 Proficiency, 94, 304